Preventing Things from Falling Further Apart

The Preservation of Cultural Identities in Postcolonial African, Indian, and Caribbean Literatures

To Dr. Dolan Hubbard:
Thank you for being an
academic father, a professional
mentor, and a colleague. A special
Thank you for letting our son
borrow your name!

Paul M. Mukundi 04/30/2010

Published by
Adonis & Abbey Publishers Ltd
P. O. Box 43418
London
SE11 4XZ
http://www.adonis-abbey.com
Email: editor@adonis-abbey.com

First Edition, April 2010.

Copyright 2010 © Paul Mukundi.

British Library Cataloguing-in-Publication Data.
A catalogue record for this book is available from the British Library.

ISBN: 978190704704 (HB)/ 9781906704711(PB)

The moral right of the author has been asserted.

Preventing Things from Falling Further Apart

The Preservation of Cultural Identities in Postcolonial African, Indian, and Caribbean Literatures

Paul M. Mukundi

For:

Hannah G. Mukundi,
Lucy W. Mukundi,
Dolan L. Mukundi,
Denton I. Mukundi.

TABLE OF CONTENTS

ACKNOWLEDGEMENTS

I wish to thank my professors at Morgan State University, especially Dr. Meena Khorana, for her expert advice. I am also indebted to Dr. Wendell Jackson and Dr. Dolan Hubbard who encouraged me during the writing of this book, and mentored me both during my graduate study at Morgan State University and during my early stages as a lecturer. In addition, I extend my appreciation to Dr. Rose Ure Mezu for providing compelling intellectual inspiration before and during the writing of this work. I am grateful to the librarians at Enoch Pratt Free Library, Loyola College, John Hopkins University, Towson University and Morgan State University Libraries for their help in tracing information vital to this project. Still further, I am grateful for the support provided by Mrs. Ella I. Stevens, Administrative Specialist, and Ms. Valerie Marine, Administrative Assistant, in the Department of English & language Arts at Morgan State University. Thanks are also due to many friends, and especially to leaders and parishioners of Faith & Grace Worship Center, Inc. for their encouragement. I owe special thanks to my wife, Mrs. Lucy W. Mukundi, and son, Dolan L. Mukundi, for their unwavering support during the period that I was absorbed in the writing of this book.

PREFACE

My interest in postcolonial studies was first aroused by tales of colonization that were told by my mother during my childhood days. These narrations were meant for my elder siblings and perhaps my mother - aware that I understood little about the challenges, struggles and courage the accounts signified - did not think I would be impacted by such abstruse stories. My mother, like most women in the colonial period, had not fought in the forest, but she was a supporter of the *mau mau* cause. The *mau mau* was an underground movement composed of warriors from the Gikuyu, Meru and Embu ethnic communities with the aim of overthrowing the colonial administration in Kenya. As such, my mother's stories centered on how she helped deliver food to the *mau mau* insurgents, how my late father was at one point arrested, and how she was always beaten by colonial officers and their African collaborators whenever they questioned her about my late father's role in the struggle for independence. Her moving stories were later authenticated by my grandparents, also *mau mau* supporters, who narrated their own versions.

Armed with the curiosity of how my parents, grandparents and many other Kenyans fought for the country's independence, I found the subject of colonization irresistible. More importantly, I wanted to find out how *my people* triumphed, in spite of such well-executed efforts to annihilate them. Thus, during my early school days at Kairichi Primary School, I developed a keen interest in the stories of such Kenyan legends as Dedan Kimathi, Waiyaki wa Hinga, Paul Ngei, Achieng' Oneko, Koitalel arap Samoei and Ronald Ngala. I discovered that Kenya's colonial situation was not significantly different from those of other African countries. I likened some of the Kenyan heroes to prominent African personalities such as Tanzania's Kinjeketile Ngwale, who led the maji maji uprising; and Samora Machel, the Mozambican revolutionary. It was also during these pre-high school years that I first read Chinua Achebe's *Things Fall Apart*, although, other than sympathizing with Ikemefuna, I grasped little from the novel.

Over the years, I have become interested in how Africans and other formerly colonized peoples have amalgamated aspects of both their precolonial and colonial pasts during a postcolonial era that offers both hopes and challenges. For instance, many formerly colonized peoples have embraced Western education, and made efforts to create Western-like institutions. They have also accepted English names as first names, while retaining indigenous names as middle and last names.

Similarly, they have adopted both traditional and Western mannerisms in their modes of dressing, socio-cultural activities, etc. Even during prominent ceremonies such as weddings, a fusion of both traditional and Western values is evident. In most African communities, for example, the dowry is still paid, wine-carrying ceremonies held, and cultural counseling provided - all before a church wedding ceremony is finally held.

It is with this background that I endeavored to conduct a study on how formerly colonized peoples continue to retain their cultures in an environment that is irreversibly impacted by Western influence. From the onset, I wish to acknoweledge that the topics explored by the writers of postcolonial Africa, India, and the Caribbean have been the subject of discussion for the last half century. However, I must state, the cultural damage caused in the three, main formerly colonized regions of the continent of Africa, the country of India, and the Caribbean region has rarely been the subject of a single comparative study. In addition, while beneficial research has been undertaken by the many critics who have viewed postcolonial creative works from these regions as protest against colonialism and neocolonism, it is necessary to re-examine works from these regions in an attempt to discover the degree to which indigenous protest goes hand-in-hand with efforts to preserve elements of the indigenous cultures.

One may wonder why novels from these specific countries have been singled out for evaluation. To begin with, I have preferred to examine selected fiction rather than other genres for two reasons: first, the novel, being long, provides adequate material for discussion; and second, the novel can realistically reflect a people's life and history. While some of the themes in these works may center on the annihilation of precolonial cultures, others deal with the injustices of the postcolonial era. These injustices of the postcolonial period may involve the marginalization of an entire community by the mainstream society, or the oppression of certain social classes by the elite. Even so, this investigation does not cover all works written by each author; instead, I have have selected works that seem best to describe complex cultural processes. Thus, although one can find disparate themes in the works of the selected writers, I have treated only those that relate to the preservation of culture.

Consequently, this study investigates how postcolonial fictional writers view the cultural experiences of the peoples of Africa, India, and the Caribbean during and after colonization. Specifically, it centers on the examination of the indigenous peoples' responses to the colonial effort to replace indigenous languages, education, religion, and social order with colonial ones. Because space allows for the analysis of only a few works written by selected authors, I will evaluate from the African region, Ngugi wa Thiong'o's *Petals of Blood* and Zakes Mda's *Ways of Dying*; from India, Mahasweta Devi's *Chotti Munda and His Arrow* and Arundhati Roy's *The God of Small Things*; and from the Caribbean, Jamaica Kincaid's *A Small Place* and Maryse Condé's *Segu*.

I have chosen only those geographical locations from which more prominent postcolonial fictional works are deemed to have been written. Moreover, this study focusses on territories of unrelated sizes not only because it would be practically impossible to choose regions of equal geographical size and population density, but also because it assumes that the themes evident in the selected works are more imperative than the geographical area from which each work derives. The sole factor considered in focusing on these regions, or their segments, is that they were once under colonial rule. These locations include Kenya and South Africa in Africa, India in Asia, and Antigua and Guadeloupe in the Caribbean. Kenya was chosen because of its strong anticolonial protest that was spearheaded by the *Mau Mau*, while South Africa was selected because of the diversity in its culture and population. India, the two selected African countries and Antigua suffered the colonial domination of the British, while Guadeloupe was colonized by the French. Although India is neither a continent such as Africa nor a transnational region such as the Caribbean, it deserves attention because of its relatively large size, which is approximately one-third the size of the United States. In addition, the country has a population of approximately 1.13 billion people.

This study was influenced mainly by three discrete approaches. First, the selected creative works provided crucial information regarding the struggle for the conservation of the local people's cultural identity. Second, works regarding cultural integration enabled me to view culture as a dynamic rather than static phenomenon. While acknowledging that colonialists eroded certain aspects of indigenous cultures and replaced them with their own, I found the principle of hybridity, which combines both foreign and indigenous cultures, to be helpful in explaining the process by which former colonies have retained some of the colonial institutions. Third, the writings of postcolonial theorists provided the framework within which the works under study were analyzed.

While this book cannot exhaust the wide and complex subject of cultural preservation in the postcolonial era, it is my hope that it will provide the reader with information on how some aspects of indigenous cultures have survived the onslaught of imperial influence, and how these cultural values continue to be the means by which formerly colonized peoples identify themselves as distinct from other societies.

January 2010

CHAPTER 1

POSTCOLONIALISM AND CULTURE: THE AMBIVALENT PAIR

Introduction

Whenever a people are dominated, the most obvious evidence of such domination is physical abuse. Indeed, even in the wars that are taking place across the globe today, tales of physical torture, unlawful arrests and extra-judicial killings attract more attention than any other forms of dehumanization. This trend appears to bolster the belief that physical denigration has more far-reaching effects than other types of oppression, or that little or no domination takes place if physical abuse is absent.

It must be pointed out, however, that, although physical violence may be deemed the most degrading form of oppression, this violence goes hand in hand with - and is sometimes preceded by - other equally devastating forms of denigration. It is for this reason that scholars, in their efforts to expose the effects of colonization, have focused on both physical and other types of suppression such as cultural, psychological, spiritual, etc. Among these forms, cultural oppression occupies a prominent position not only because it is societal rules that determine what is or is not oppression, but also because most forms of oppression target a people's culture.

Consequently, colonization and cultural domination are interwoven, and one may not delve into one at the exclusion of the other. Postcolonization, which stems from colonization, is likewise intertwined with culture, especially if it is considered as centering on the period during which formerly colonized peoples reassert themselves and reject the place assigned to them by erstwhile colonial powers. Unfortunately, the terms "postcolonialism" and "culture" have been variously defined, and it is imperative that I refer to some of these definitions before stating how I intend to treat these concepts in this book.

1.1 What is Postcolonialism?

Undoubtedly, the term "postcolonial" remains an ambivalent and blurry concept. Indeed, "postcolonial," when used to describe a very long and complex era in very diverse regions, nations and cultures is, to say the

1

least, seriously inadequate. Perhaps one of the reasons why postcolonialism remains an imprecise concept is because the formerly colonized peoples themselves had different precolonial, colonial, and even postcolonial experiences. One cannot say, for example, that those colonized by the French and those colonized by the British encountered the same forms of oppression. In addition, even different ethnic groups within one country did not undergo similar oppression, because colonial powers' strategies differed from one group to another. Thus, the different measures, forms and methods of oppression necessitated equally different means of anticolonization.

Some scholars have considered postcolonialism as encompassing life after imperial domination of the "other" by people of European descent. For instance, while admitting that "Postcolonialism is not a narrowly systematized and unitary theory" (7), Anshuman Prasad states that postcolonialism "is rooted in - and, in some ways, may even be seen as a logical outcome of - the historical processes of European/Western colonization and decolonization" (7). The problem with this view of postcolonialism is that it tends to place the experiences of minority groups in the West, such as African Americans, in the postcolonial canon. In fact, in "Beyond the Commonwealth: Postcolonialism and American Literature," Deborah L. Madsen advocates for the inclusion of writings by authors of marginalized American communities in the canon of postcolonial literature. She identifies these marginalized communities as including "Native Americans, Chicano/as, Afro-Hispanic and African-American peoples" (2). Given that the groups mentioned by Madsen were and continue to be dominated by Western imperialism, one may be tempted to deem their writings postcolonial.

However, as Leela Gandhi writes, the term "postcolonialism" implies more than just the period after colonization because,

> ... [t]he emergence of anti-colonial and 'independent' nation-states after colonialism is frequently accompanied by a desire to forget the colonial past. (4)

Gandhi's definition accentuates the fact that the formerly colonized nations have attained independence, although, as I will imply throughout this volume, this independence is only partial. The fact that the groups mentioned by Madsen did not gain political independence and emerge as political entities in the same way that nations in Africa, Asia, the Caribbean, etc, did indicates, at the simplest level, that these groups have faced different experiences from the latter ones. Indeed, the brand of domination that these American groups have undergone is significantly different from that of former colonies. Today's African American, for example, grows up hearing about and sometimes experiencing some form of racial discrimination. On the contrary, an African who resides in Africa rarely becomes a victim of racial discrimination, because, of course, Africans are the majority in his or her community. The African, instead, contends with neocolonialism, where fellow Africans employ colonial principles in political, economic and/or social transactions. Because space does not allow for a discussion of the highly complicated experiences of minorities in American, it will suffice to state that because of these communities' distinct circumstances, postcolonial concepts such as anticolonialism and neocolonialism may not apply to them, or may have dissimilar meanings. This notwithstanding, as Helen Gilbert and Joanne Tompkins concur, postcolonialism, even for the territories recognized as formerly colonized, may not merely refer to,

> ...a temporal concept meaning the time after colonisation has ceased, or the time following the politically determined Independence Day on which a country breaks away from its governance by another state ... [because] postcolonialism is, rather, an engagement with and contestation of colonialism's discourses, power structures and social hierarchies. (2)

Postcolonialism, then, must not be perceived as one monolithic, homogeneous body. Instead, despite the limitations implied in its ambiguity, postcolonialism must be considered as encompassing a series of actions pertaining to hegemonic and posthegemonic activities by and for both the colonizers and the colonized. Thus, as Elleke Boehmer states,

> [r]ather than simply being the writing which 'came after' empire, *postcolonial* literature is that which critically scrutinizes the colonial relationship. (3)

3

In line with Boehmer's argument, writings that expose or resist marginalization may be included in this canon.

Consequently, colonial effects on local culture during and after colonization will be included in this study, because, as Roderick McGillis points out, postcolonialism encompasses not only colonial, postcolonial, and neocolonial, but also multicultural, diasporic, and post-independence literatures (xxii). However, as Gandhi suggests, the notion of colonization is central to postcolonialism, because,

> ...[t]he mere repression of colonial memories is never, in itself, tantamount to a surpassing of or emancipation from the uncomfortable realities of the colonial encounter. (4)

Indeed, even if there were no neocolonization, the overarching damage done by colonization is enough to warrant attention. Several questions would, however, remain unanswered even if the meaning of the term postcolonialism were to be agreed upon. What period would this postcolonial era cover? What issues would be considered postcolonial? What types of literatures would/would not fit into this category? I wish to return briefly to the assertion that the postcolonial period comprises of several other mini-periods, including the colonial, anticolonial, postindependent, neocolonial, etc. What justifies the inclusion of works written during these stages in the postcolonial canon is because they contend with issues pertaining to past and/or present domination by the West. This notwithstanding, I wish to point out that the postcolonial issues that pervaded non-Western countries during the time that doyen of African literature, Chinua Achebe, wrote *Things Fall Apart* are not necessarily the same issues that I and my young family face today. Therefore, labeling postcolonial the entire period after colonization overlooks the many changes that have taken and continue to take place.

Indeed, even within just only a few years, there has occurred a great shift in the way the West interacts with the rest of the world. In the 1980s and 1990s, for instance, the West used to lecture African political leaders in a condescending and patronizing manner. In my own country, Kenya, I remember that former president, Daniel Moi, was constantly engaged in a war of words with the West, a West which tirelessly lambasted him in a manner that suggested that his brand of leadership was only possible in "backward Africa." Of course this was largely the practice of Western governments even in other former colonies. However, during the period of Kenya's postelection violence of 2008, I noticed the way Western powers, fearing the accusation that they were neocolonizing Africa, quickly urged the African Union to initiate a peace process. Diplomats of these countries issued veiled threats to the leaders if they failed to negotiate and arrive at a power-sharing deal, and at the same time promised goodies if the leaders agreed to the Kofi Annan-brokered peace deal. The fact is that this process, despite the fact that it was carried out by African leaders, was undertaken at the behest and prodding of Western powers. This is undoubtedly a new form of neocolonialism.

Furthermore, the notion of globalization, whose impacts on cultural identity I hope to evaluate in future, also adds to the complexities of postcolonialism. Globalization has obviously taken colonial overtones, because it involves the transfer of technological and other innovations from the West to other nations. Indeed, rarely has globalization referred to the transfer of knowledge or machinery from former colonies to the West. As expected, this one-sided transfer not only connotes an asymmetrical power structure, but provides room for imperialistic dependence, where poor nations are forced to adopt foreign social, political and economic policies.

It is therefore factual that the domination of non-Western cultures, countries and peoples has taken different forms from those used several years ago. Nowadays, it is even possible for any foreign powers and individuals to use such technological media as YouTube, Facebook or Twitter to influence millions of people who may be thousands of miles away. It is also possible for people to watch movie trailers or even full movies online. Besides, postmodernism, another Western principle, has impacted virtually all cultures across the globe. These new realities necessitate a review of the term postcolonialism as a means of describing today's state of affairs in the former colonies, because it is unconvincing that the term can be determinably used to refer to contemporary situation. For this reason, I prefer the term *neopostcolonialism* for this day's forms of Western influence. My preference for this term is informed by three factors. First, Western domination is not new - hence the term *new postcolonialism* is not suitable. Second, the term *neopostcolonialism* implies a continuation of the postcolonial, while at the same time highlighting a shift within this

5

period. Third, this term helps in delineating the periods as it underscores the fact that neopostcolonialism has been preceded by both colonial and postcolonial periods.

Despite my preference of the term neopostcolonialism for today's form of imperialism, I will refer to literatures under study in this volume as postcolonial. I will use this more amorphous term for several reasons. First, the above-mentioned features of neopostcolonialism, both regarding the use of technology and the shift in West's engagement with its former colonies, are not demonstrated in the works under scrutiny. Second, because the works discussed in this volume cover several regions and countries, each of which has its own unique characteristics, it would be improper to use a more specific term. Third, the works under study cover a wide period and may not fit such time-specific terms as post-independent or neopostcolonial. Besides, this study cuts across periods, because it evaluates the effects of colonization and postindependence on indigenous cultures.

1.2 What is Culture?

Terry Eagleton acknowledges that, "[c]ulture is said to be one of the two or three most complex words in the English language," (1) not only because of its ambivalent nature but also because of its multifacetedness. Fred Inglis also writes that the definition of culture presents a challenge, because,

> ...[i]t nowadays seems impossible to describe the most commonplace details of everyday life without using the word 'culture.' (1)

Despite their admission that a precise definition of culture is nearly impossible, these and other scholars attempt to underline the most compelling notions about the concept. Eagleton observes that culture, "inherits the imposing mantle of religious authority, but also has uneasy affinities with occupation and invasion" (2).

This observation attempts to connect culture with religious and political beliefs, and at the same time shows religious and political domination as tantamount to cultural assault. Eagleton also considers culture as, "the complex of values, customs, beliefs and practices which constitute the way of life of a specific group" (34).

Unfortunately, each of the elements mentioned by Eagleton is as inexact as culture itself. However, this definition suggests accurately that culture is part and parcel of a specific people's world view. The use of the terms "complex" and "way of life" underscore both the intricateness and multifacetedness of this concept. On his part, Inglis differentiates culture from politics by arguing that "politics is struggle and culture is harmony" (31). While Inglis's consideration of culture as "harmony" is credible because culture is what makes members of a community co-exist peacefully, it ignores the fact that lack of harmony does not necessarily mean that a people's culture is under siege. Ying-yi Hong defines culture as, "*networks of knowledge*, consisting of learned routines of thinking, feeling and interacting with other people, as well as a corpus of substantive assertions and ideas about aspects of the world" (4).

While this definition captures the fact that culture is best demonstrated in interactions with others, it appears to limit culture to mere interactions and assertions. It must be stated that even such daily activities as cooking and dressing are cultural in nature. On their part, Stephen Pfohl and Aimee Van Wagenen define culture as,

> …what gives human social life its meaning. Cultural practices delineate the real, imaginary, and symbolic boundaries between specific groups of human animals and the wide realm of energetic materiality in which we humans find ourselves. (1)

This definition is preferred because it depicts culture as a dynamic, rather than static, way of life that includes both a people's beliefs and their materials.

Given the complexity of the term "culture," the purpose of this volume is not to promote or discredit any definition of the subject. Instead, my intention is to trace some of the major components of culture, and evaluate how these components have been reshaped by both colonial and postcolonial activities. For the purposes of this study, therefore, I will consider culture as dynamic conduct, idiosyncratic to human beings, which holistically encompasses the lifestyle of a particular group of people. This intricate lifestyle, which includes such aspects as a specific community's language, beliefs, wisdom, philosophy, system of governance, material possessions, etc, is unavoidably influenced by the community's past experiences and aspirations. It is this lifestyle of a specific people that enable them to exist distinctly from any other people on the face of the earth. For this reason, culture is the epicenter of any people, and no attack on a people - physical or otherwise - can circumvent an affront on their culture.

CHAPTER 2
LANGUAGE AND CULTURE

Introduction

Language stands at the center of any community because it is the medium of expression, communication, interaction, and identity among members of that culture. In *Decolonising the Mind: The Politics of Language in African Literature*, Kenyan novelist and political activist Ngugi wa Thiong'o writes that, "[l]anguage, any language, has a dual character: it is both a means of communication and a carrier of culture" (13).

He argues that language is also "the basis and process of evolving culture" (14), because it is the medium through which a community expresses and transmits its cultural materials. It is for this reason that Thiong'o concludes: "If people lose their language, they lose the most important instrument in the definition and production of their own culture" (qtd. in Rodrigues 162).

Thiong'o's position on the relationship of language with culture echoes that of Frantz Fanon, who argues in *Black Skin, White Masks* that,

>...[e]very colonized people - in other words, every people in whose soul an inferiority complex has been created by the death and burial of its local cultural originality - finds itself face to face with the language of the civilizing nation; that is, with the culture of the mother country. (18)

Fanon places language at the center of colonization, and emphasizes its role in cultural indoctrination. This indoctrination is part of language because, in his words, "[e]very dialect is a way of thinking" (25). Hence, he concludes, "[t]o speak a language is to take on a world, a culture" (38). Fanon provides, as an example, a man from the Antilles who chooses to pursue excellence in speaking a foreign language to the exclusion of his indigenous one. Because one's adoption of a foreign language amounts to "a dislocation, a separation" (25),

>...[t]he Antilles Negro who wants to be white will be the whiter as he gains greater mastery of the cultural tool that language is. (38)

With the foregoing, this chapter will examine how language has enabled postcolonial societies to either preserve or forego their traditional cultures. In undertaking this task, I will take into account the fact that most precolonial societies used language not only for communication but also as a means of education and retention of history through oral traditions. This chapter will analyze some of the elements of oral literature that are present in the works under investigation, and assess their relevance as a means of cultural preservation, transmission and identity. Moreover, because colonial powers introduced to their colonies Western education, which they based on foreign languages, it is necessary to assess the impact of this education not only on indigenous languages but also on the identities of the colonized. Furthermore, I will include in this chapter a discussion of colonizers' effort to alter the histories of their colonies. The issue of foreign language in law will also be inescapable in Mahasweta Devi's *Chotti Munda and His Arrow*, where many members of the Munda community are sent to jail because of their failure to understand India's contemporary legal system, which is inherited from her erstwhile colonial master. Consequently, this chapter will designate specific sections to the evaluation of language and history, language and education, language and law, and oral literature as a means of cultural preservation.

2.1 Language and History

Because language is the medium through which history is both preserved and transmitted, the interaction between history and language is of significant importance. In *The Souls of Black Folk*, W. E. B. Du Bois argues that what makes any ethnic community distinct from others is its existence as,

> ...a vast family of human beings, generally of common blood and language, always of common history, traditions and impulses, who are both voluntarily and involuntarily striving together for the accomplishment of certain more or less vividly conceived ideals of life. (178)

Du Bois's stance emphasizes the relationship between such a community's historical past, language and cultural norms, and depicts these factors as crucial to the community's self-definition.

The Historical muddle in *The God of Small Things*

Thus, the novels show that language is a vehicle for conveying history. Chacko, in Arundhati Roy's *The God of Small Things,* says that the formerly colonized peoples have been locked out of their own history, hence losing their identity and becoming "Anglophiles" who are "[p]ointed in the wrong direction" and "trapped outside their own history and unable to retrace their steps because their footprints had been swept away" (51). It might be for this reason that Anuradha Dingwaney Needham writes that history occupies a crucial position in *The God of Small Things.* She states that the novel,

> ...presents history (most often, although inconsistently, with a capital H) as a dominating, oppressive force that saturates virtually all social and cultural space, including familial, intimate, and affective relationships. (372)

Chacko's argument that a people's history can be compared to an old house with ancestors "whispering" inside best captures the connection between history and language. His notion implies that a people's history is passed from the older generation to the younger, and that this transfer requires communication. Therefore, because colonized communities "have been invaded by a war" that bars them from accessing their own undiluted history, they have to "see shadows" instead of the ancestors, and hear only "a whispering" whose meaning they are unable to decode (52). By stating that the war that prevents colonial and postcolonial populations from accessing their true history is one "that captures dreams and re-dreams them" (52), Chacko alludes to the efforts of former colonial powers to hijack and distort their subjects' histories. Chacko further says:

> Our dreams have been doctored. We belong nowhere. We sail unanchored on troubled seas. We may never be allowed ashore. Our sorrows will never be sad enough. Our joys never happy enough. Our dreams never big enough. Our lives never important enough to matter. (52)

Undoubtedly, this "doctoring" of a people's dream, which makes them "belong nowhere," is partly conveyed through the replacement of local

11

languages with foreign ones, which alter a community's story, identity, and expression. Chacko's argument that the war has made him and other Indians "adore our conquerors and despise ourselves" (52) is thus to be seen within this systematic erasure of the indigenous communities' histories.

The Double Colonization of Adivasis in *Chotti Munda and His Arrow*

In *Chotti Munda and His Arrow*, the Mundas, one of the oppressed tribal groups, in spite of their inability to read and write, value their history and devise traditional methods of retaining it. A reading of *Chotti Munda and His Arrow* requires an understanding of Karl Marx's concept of the proletariat as the labor force and class conflict. In the introduction to *Makers of Modern Social Science: Karl Marx*, Tom Bottomore argues that the idea of the proletariat is central to Marxism because "[i]n fact, those parts of Marx's theory of class which are elaborated at all fully concern particularly the formation and development of the proletariat in capitalist society" (20). Because, as Bottomore further states, "[t]he transformation of labor power into a commodity is an alienation of man's nature that deforms and cripples him" (15), the economic exploitation of laborers, such as the Mundas in *Chotti Munda and His Arrow*, will also entail the annihilation of their cultural identity.

Chotti Munda and His Arrow covers several decades in the life of Chotti Munda, its protagonist and Munda community's leader, during which India moves from colonial rule to independence and then to the turbulence of the 1970s. The facts that the community's history is passed orally from generation to generation, and that what transpires during cultural events is preserved orally, are emphasized through the assertion that "everything becomes a story in Chotti's life."[1] Devi states that even "without a written language," the tale of Dhani's murder, when he defies the government and returns to Chaibasha, mingles with that of Birsa, the leader of the Munda revolt (1899 -1900) to reclaim their land, and "make[s] Dhani eternal" (23). The discussion of such events does not escape rumor mongering; hence, "[h]istory advances because rumor happens" among the adivasis (21). The "series of stories" - which are the hallmark of Chotti and the Mundas - are thus conveyed through the spoken language.

The government's effort to ensure that Dhani does not tell his story is thus tantamount to stifling the history of the Mundas. Stating that "[i]t's a long story . . . a tale" (9) that he wants to tell, Dhani mourns that he cannot tell it to the Mundas in Murudi because, "t' Munda folk here are broken backed, livin' on t' kindness of t' Diku-Hindus" (9). This statement brings to the fore the colonization of the Mundas, not only by the Europeans but also by other fellow Indian groups that employ oppressive policies and marginalize them because they are outside mainstream of Indian society. The maltreatment of adivasis by other India communities amounts to colonization, because, as Jennifer Wenzel states, "[d]ecades after independence, Hindu attitudes towards tribals are still critically described in terms of the now discredited *mission civilisatrice* [civilizing mission]" (140). The adivasis are thus victims of double colonization, and as evident in the novel, the departure of the British colonialists and the subsequent formation of an independent government has not improved their lot. For this reason, Devi reveals that "[i]n war and independence the life of Chotti and his cohorts remained unchanged" (121-22).

While the "broken backed" are too pre-occupied with survival to concentrate on cultural history, those who are relatively free are unreachable because the government has curtailed Dhani's movements. "They [government officials] won' let me stay in Chaibasha," he regrets, although "[t]here's still people to hear me there" (9). Dhani desires to live and tell his story in Chaibasha where "Birsa's adoptive son Pariba [and] his initiate disciple Sali" (18-19) live, and not far from Sailrakab, Birsa's last battlefield, where he wants to die. His lamentable situation is however an exemplification of the plight of many ethnic communities whose history is suppressed, distorted or replaced with foreign accounts during the colonial and postcolonial periods.

The minister elected to represent Chotti's area demonstrates distortion of history during the post-independence period. He is infuriated by a historical book's claim that "Buddha ate a pig at the house of an untouchable and died as a result" (247). The legislator physically beats author Birij Tewari, tears up the book, and orders that all history books be burnt because such historical writing may make "the untouchables get a swelled head if they hear an untouchable killed a god" (247).

It is ironical that Europeans as well as members of mainstream Indian society may have aided in the cultural preservation of an indigenous community. An attempt to keep a written account of Munda culture is encapsulated in the case of Ronaldson Hugh, the brother of the Provincial Governor's Secretary, who learns Mundari, draws pictures of Munda heroes, writes down their songs and visits their houses to "see the paintings on the wall" (45). Although the authenticity of his work can be questioned, Ronaldson's effort is laudable because Chotti sees in Ronaldson's possession an authentic picture of Dhani Munda "holding high his bow and machete" (45). The validity of Ronaldson's historical account is also evidenced in that Chotti accepts the picture as legitimate and even obtains its copy. There is a chance, therefore, that Ronaldson's forthcoming book, through which he wants "to inform the reader about the Munda villages and the Mundas" (45), will be a truthful preservation of the community's history. The suggestion that there are other writers who are making efforts to preserve the history of the adivasis is also unmistakable in that the Secretary learns from the *Gazetteer* that archery contests "are an ancient tradition; . . . an integral part of adivasi festivals" (59). An example of a mainstream Indian's effort to preserve adivasi culture is exemplified by the fact that the author of this novel is a Bengali, who, in the words of Alaknanda Bagchi with reference to *Bashai Tudu*, "tries to 'write in' the history of the dispossessed, the disinherited, and the displaced adivasis or tribals who have been almost 'written out' of Indian history" (42).

Possibly, an outsider such as Ronaldson does not fully grasp some of the indigenous culture's beliefs; hence, the authenticity of his work notwithstanding, Ronaldson's limitation is revealed when he wonders why Chotti is named after a river instead of being "called Somra, Somai, Somna as Monday [the day of Chotti's birth] is Sombar" (43). However, his knowledge is given credence by Chotti's wife's inquiry when she asks her husband why their son Harmu should be named after an unknown river instead of "Somru" because he is a "Monday's child, Sombar's child" (47). Chotti's response, "[i]f there's another boy name him as ye like" (47), may suggest that in this patriarchal Munda society, the first born son may be given a name that does not follow the naming customs, and that men have the final authority with regards to the names given to first born sons. This gender-based difference in naming may also appear accurate in that Chotti's daughter is named Sukhni because she is "Friday's child" (104).

The redemptive role of authentic history is exemplified by Ronaldson's successful defense of the Mundas when Tirathnath falsely accuses them of stealing his grain during a famine. Ronaldson tells the Secretary that Chotti

14

is of a "quiet, peaceable type," and that he has "gone around and observed" that "the Mundas are a peace-loving people of a happy disposition" (57). Ronaldson can be placed among Europeans who aid the cause of the adivasis by telling their story. Nevertheless, he suffers alongside the adivasis when his brother sends him back to Britain after discovering that he is the one who advised them to seek help from the camping European officer during a famine in their village. He also refuses to distort Munda history by including the pictures of Chotti and Dhani in his book *The Flute and the Arrow*, in spite of the Secretary's order that he must exclude the two pictures in the "damned book" (58). His redemptive role may have caused his death when he is killed by a villager "as he tries to draw pictures of adivasis in Uganda" (58).

Nonetheless, the necessity for the adivasis to write their own history is brought to the fore by the explanation provided by Chhagan Dusad, the *de facto* leader of the low-caste, that his "booklearning" enables him to write the "story tale" (54), when, for the first time, the adivasis are given food by Tirathnath without binding themselves to providing uncompensated labor. This historical occurrence is attributed to Tirathnath's mother's and wife's dread of the mysterious power of Chotti's arrow. The possibility of misrepresentation of facts is heightened by Chhagan's claim that "[t]' manager will cheat like a bastard" if he writes the report because he is "a tick on t' tiger's neck" (54). The incident further suggests that, while the adivasis may retain their cultural identity, Western education is inevitable if they aim to record their own present-day happenings. Indeed, writing is crucial for the Mundas in the light of Bagchi's statement that:

> Historians recording the ancient glories of precolonial India, scholars inscribing the civilizing zeal of the white man's burden in colonial India, and narrators of nationalism(s) in postcolonial India have all chosen to erase/silence the memory/voice of the subaltern. (42)

Orality and History in Segu

Language and history are also seen as connected in Condé's *Segu*. *Segu* is a story that spans cultures, geographical territories and centuries. Beginning in the late eighteenth century during precolonial West Africa, the

15

novel is a deft amalgamation of fiction and history which uniquely assesses the impact of slavery and colonization as well as the changes that emanate from the introduction of both Islam and Christianity. The story traces the different paths taken by the sons of Dousika, a member of the king's council, as they are scattered to different geographical areas through the arrival of Islamic and Christian priests, colonizers, and slave catchers. The novel tracks Tiekoro, Dousika's first born son, as he converts to Islam and pursues Islamic education, which changes not only Dousika's homestead but the local Segu village. The novel also focuses on Naba and Malobali who end up as slaves in Brazil and Africa respectively. The work contrasts the predicaments of those, like Tiekoro, who have embraced foreign religions with others such as Siga and Tiefolo, who borrow certain foreign notions but reject these religions.

In Segu's African traditional society, the griot is depicted as the custodian of the community's heroic exploits. Since kings - who in the case of the Bambara of Segu ascend the throne when their fathers die - are heroes, they are served by several griots who not only record regal feats, but also soothe the kings and act as moderators during council meetings. Tietiguiba, Monzon Diarra's chief griot, moderates the discussion about what is to be done with a White man who has arrived at Segu "to look at the Joliba [river]" (9). The griots are also the custodians of the community's history, which they retain in the form of either song or narrative. Consequently, a griot who sings of Tiefolo's great hunting prowess equates his song with the reaffirmation and authentication of Tiefolo's success: "But hunter, hunter / If I don't sing for you / Who are you? / Does not the word make the man?" (351). The assertion that "the word" is responsible for making "the man" implies that a person's accurate history is connected with his or her true identity. Moreover, Macalou, Monzon Diarra's griot, demonstrates his knowledge of both Segu's history and the king's past when he asks the king: "What would you like me to sing? The story of the founding of Segu? Or the story of your father?" (26). The ability of the griots to compose songs or narratives based on valiant acts also depicts them as traditional creative artists who package the community's secrets in ethnically suitable oral media. Because the songs for this community, just like among the Mundas in *Chotti Munda and His Arrow*, are synonymous with historic records, Condé asserts that nothing can stop a song from "popping up where it is least expected," because a song is as "elusive as air"

(479). Although the songs composed by griots in this novel are depicted as factual, not all griots' compositions may be accurate because, as Delphine Perret and Steve Arkin state, "The griot is the official memory of his people, and yet he doesn't need to be limited to 'the real truth'" (654).

An examination of the languages spoken by slaves and their children also underscores their heartbreaking history. For instance, Eucaristus speaks,

> ...Portuguese and Yoruba, which were his mother's languages; English, the medium of instructon at Fourah Bay College; a bit of French; and the whole lot jumbled together to form pidgin, the lingua franca of the coast. (385)

These languages are a reminder of his past life as a child born in slavery and of his parents' lives in both the slavery and pre-slavery eras. Eucaristus associates the confusion of the languages with that of his own identity: "The Babel-like confusion of tongues struck him as symbolic of his own identity. What was he? He could not tell!" (385).

Writing is also depicted as a means of preserving history. For instance, Eucaristus, a descendant of African slaves, reads about his parents' African homeland in the book *Travels in the Interior Districts of Africa Performed under the Direction and Patronage of the African Association in the Years of 1795,1796 and 1797 by Mungo Park, Surgeon* (Condé 417). The account proves authentic in that it mentions such geographical symbols as River Joliba, which is seen by precolonial inhabitants of Segu as emblematic of purification. In addition, the account movingly enables Eucaristus to reconstruct his identity, and elicits in him weeping "for himself" and "the purity of his Segu ancestors which he had lost forever" (418). Nonetheless, since such writers as Park and Ronaldson in *Chotti Munda and His Arrow* are few, and because writers may never write with authority about another culture, it is necessary that indigenous peoples construct their own cultural stories. Hence, postcolonial authors use writing not only to express ideas but also as a way of preserving their history. In an interview with Barbara Lewis, Condé declares about writing: "But we can write history. It is not only Europeans who can write. We can do it too" (549). Condé wrote *Segu* as "a reflection on the history of Africa and the reasons for the present-day situation of decay and decline" (Lewis 548); however, she declares: "We can write like the Whites. But we must use another method" (549). This declaration implies that while writing must be adopted by the formerly colonized peoples as a medium of intellectual expression, postcolonial writers must adjust both their approach and their message, so that they accommodate postcolonial socio-cultural contexts.

Amending Antigua's Historical Accounts

Similarly, Kincaid, in *A Small Place* accentuates the necessity of the formerly colonized populations to write their own history. She depicts the tourist as reading distorted history in a book,

> ...about economic history, one of those books explaining how the West (meaning Europe and North America after its conquest and settlement by Europeans) got rich: the West got rich not from free (free—in this case meaning got-for-nothing) and then undervalued labour, for generations, of the people . . . but from the ingenuity of small shopkeepers in Sheffield and Yorkshire and Lancashire, or wherever. (9 -10)

The counterargument, "we made you bastards rich" (10), which is made in writing, underlies the importance of writings by postcolonial authors. Like Kincaid's *A Small Place*, postcolonial writings may be an instrument for countering any inaccurate accounts presented by imperial authors. By reminiscing that the historically true source of Western development is the slavery of people of African descent, which she describes as characterized by "suffer[ing]" and "unspeakableness" (10), Kincaid exposes the dishonesty in the book that shows Western prosperity as founded on genuine trade. She further says that the Atlantic Ocean, along whose beaches tourists come to rest, has swallowed up many black slaves (14). This assertion, which suggests that the tourist's visit should be an act of introspection because it is the tourist's forefathers who conducted slave trade along the Atlantic, is buttressed by her revelation that despite its semblance of beauty, the Ocean also "swallows up" sewage from hotels because "in Antigua, there is no proper sewage-disposal system" (14). Since the sewage system, like other systems in Antigua, has been inherited from the British, Kincaid implies that by swimming in the ocean, tourists immerse themselves in the unpleasant aftermaths of slavery and colonialism.

Kincaid decries the replacement of indigenous languages and shows this replacement as taking away the power of an individual to describe his or her past, present and future. Thus, she refers to the loss of indigenous languages as "the most painful" (31) effect of colonization, and laments the fact that the only language that she and other postcolonial writers from the Caribbean region largely use to describe "this crime" of colonial domination is "the language of the criminal who committed the crime" (31). She depicts English as an inadequate means of describing colonialism because "[t]he language of the criminal can contain only the goodness of the criminal's deed" (32). Kincaid suggests that because language and perception are intertwined, "the language of the criminal can explain and express the deed only from the criminal's point of view" (32). Thus, as Jane King says, Kincaid's belief about erstwhile colonialists is that "English is their language and cannot speak for her, only for the English" (896). While this notion is not entirely illogical, the fact that Kincaid writes in English shows that English may be used for the construction of rejoinders to colonization because colonizers, in the words of Jane King, "will only be able to understand her curses in ways favorable to themselves" (896). As if in response to King, Kincaid further argues that, given the different backgrounds between the colonizer and the colonized, it is possible for the colonialist to interpret an English word differently from the meaning implied by the colonized. For instance, she says, the description of an action as "wrong" may mean to the colonizer that an action is improper because "he doesn't get his fair share of profits from crime just committed" (32).

Kincaid therefore re-describes Antigua as "a small island" which was discovered by Christopher Columbus in 1493, and which was "settled by human rubbish from Europe, who used enslaved but noble and exalted human beings from Africa to satisfy their desire for wealth and power, to feel better about their own miserable existence" (80). In re-writing Antigua's history, Kincaid reiterates the humanity and dignity of the Africans who were enslaved on the island, and contrasts them with their slave masters whom she depicts as cruel and exploitative beings. She also reminds the reader that slaves,

...were forced to work under conditions that were cruel and inhuman, they were beaten, they were murdered, they were sold, their children were taken from them and this separation lasted forever. (54)

Kincaid's writings thus demonstrate her ability to, in Achebe's words, correct historical misrepresentations and inform the formerly colonized communities "that their past - with all its imperfections - was not one long night of savagery from which the first Europeans acting on God's behalf delivered them" (*Morning Yet* 72). Nonetheless, as Suzanne Gauch observes, Kincaid's novel is unique in that instead of "challenging the normative rule of big places, *A Small Place* addresses otherness by rejecting it in favor of ordinariness, an ordinariness that levels many of the distinctions upon which self and other are predicated" (910). This "rejection of otherness" is based on colonial wrongdoing, and, as Gauch admits, it requires one to "understand the past that shaped present-day Antigua" (913). *A Small Place*, as Gauch further posits, seeks to "de-historize" Antiguans from "a history that has long deemed them marginal" and attempts to "reformulate [their] relationship to historical events in a manner that attributes to them a measure of responsibility" (917).

While Kincaid hails the colonial powers for building schools and libraries in their former colonies, she laments that it is through these two institutions that the Europeans "distorted and erased [her] history" and created an environment supportive of the "glorification" of their own history (36). The destruction of the library and its current poor state, which make access to books difficult, are symbolic of the destruction of Antigua as well as its people and their culture. Kincaid also shows the history of Antiguans as commodified by erstwhile colonial powers. She cites a case where a slave-trading family's records are auctioned and bought by a foreigner who "then made a gift of these papers to the people of Antigua" (76). This transaction, she says, amounts to "[t]he records of one set of enemies, [being] bought by another enemy, [and being] given to the people who have been their victims" (68).

Kincaid derides the emblems of political power in post-independent Antigua (such as government house, prime minister's office and parliament building) as marks of false freedom inherited from former colonizers. She views satirically the American embassy, which is hailed by imperialists as the "embassy of a powerful country" (11). While the presence of such an embassy signifies cordial trade relations between Antigua and America, it also reinforces the notion that Antigua is a weak country while America is a "powerful" one. This relationship connotes economic exploitation, which is exemplified by the fact that the food tourists eat was grown cheaply in Antigua before being exported to USA and then re-sold to Antigua at high prices.

Protesting Distortions in Kenya's Historical Records

Thiong'o, in *Petals of Blood*, also perceives Kenya's history as misrepresented by Western historians. *Petals of Blood* is set in Ilmorog, an imaginary village in postindependent Kenya. The novel is the story of Godfrey Munira, the son of Ezekieli, whose frustrations after expulsion from Siriana School forces him to flee to Ilmorog, where he establishes a primary school. He believes that working in Ilmorog, a highly underdeveloped village whose hallmark is poverty and illiteracy, will provide the solitude he needs in order to cope with his shattered life. His affluent father, an ardent follower of European culture and religion, is a former collaborator with the British during the colonial period. Ezekieli detests Munira's failure, because he expected the latter to gain Western education and scale the ladder of economic success. By living in Ilmorog, Munira abandons both his children and his wife, who is a staunch follower of his father's colonial values. He succeeds in his self-seclusion in Ilmorog until the arrival of Wanja, a prostitute and Nyakinyua's granddaughter, who ends up cunningly controlling both him and other men, who include Abdulla, a former freedom fighter; and Karega, also a former student at Siriana. The climax of the story is the murder of Chui, an educationist; Kimeria, a business owner; and Mzigo, a senior education official and businessman. Munira is arrested and asked by Inspector Godfrey to write a statement regarding his relationship with Wanja, Abdulla and Karega, and the possibility that the trio is involved in the murders.

In the novel, Thiong'o writes: "Our present day historians, following on similar theories yarned out by defenders of imperialism, insist we only arrived here yesterday" (67). This statement implies, first, that there exist a possibility that today's history - written in format and media that are borrowed from erstwhile colonizers - is distorted, and, second, that Africa

21

has a much older history than Western historians dare to admit. For this reason, Thiong'o argues that authentic history must go beyond "glean[ing] from between the lines of the records of the colonial adventurers of the last few centuries, especially the nineteenth century" (68). The call for Africa to review and rewrite her history is crucial because, as Thiong'o further states in *Barrel of a Pen*, colonial powers deemed Africa as lacking history, because to them "there was only darkness in Africa and as darkness was no subject for history, Africa had therefore no history prior to colonial conquest" (93).

Consequently, as Ogude states, Thiong'o uses fiction to reassert the distinctiveness of Africans as a people, because he believes that "both history and literature invoke the principle of selection and derive their material from specific cultures and historical experiences" (88). Theodore Pelton, in his article "Ngugi wa Thiong'o and the Politics of Language," presents a similar consideration of Thiong'o's works as an attempt to expose the effects of colonization. Pelton deems Thiong'o one who "sees himself not just as writer but also as a revolutionary continuing the fight against Western imperialism" (15), and for whom writing in an African language "is a necessary step toward cultural identity and independence from centuries of European exploitation" (17). Thus, *Petals of Blood* castigates the endemic corruption of post-independent Kenya's economic system, which is represented by Kimeria Chui and Mzigo; while a novel like *Devil on the Cross* is a rallying call for resistance against such a corrupt system.

Preserving South African History through the Spoken Word

Likewise, Zakes Mda, a poet and playwright, demonstrates through *Ways of Dying* that language is a vehicle through which history is preserved and transmitted. Set in the transitional period between apartheid and post-apartheid South Africa, *Ways of Dying* covers only the days between Christmas Day to New Year's Eve. The story revolves around Toloki, a poor and dirty man who sleeps at a waiting room in the city. Toloki is the son of Jwara, a blacksmith who always referred to him as an ugly child. However, Toloki is a good artist whose picture has won an art competition during his school days. He leaves his home in the village in search of a better life in the city, after a bitter quarrel with his father. In the city, after he comes face to face with joblessness and an indifferent government, he ends up becoming a Professional Mourner to eke out a living. One day, he meets with Noria, a former village mate who used to sing songs that gave his father the power to create figurines. Noria has just lost her only son, Vutha the Second, and her shack has been burnt down. Toloki helps her to reconstruct the shack, and together they start a new life. Their tranquility is only disturbed by Nefolovhondwe, who arrives with Jwara's figurines. Nefolovhondwe also brings the message, that back in the village, Toloki's mother and Noria's father are cohabiting after the death of their respective spouses. The figurines become the source of new happiness not only to the couple but also to the settlement community.

The community preserves and conveys its history through the composition of songs. For instance, Mda writes that some of the songs that children sing as they bring water to Noria are those "they have heard from their parents, and their bothers and sisters sing at demonstrations, and at political rallies and funerals" (69). The fact that children learn these songs from parents and (perhaps older) siblings indicates that the songs are a means of transmitting knowledge from older to younger generations. Moreover, that some of the songs are heard at demonstrations and political rallies underlines the fact that songs are part of the media used in making rallying calls for South Africans to resist apartheid.

Undoubtedly, the Nurse's account in a funeral ceremony is an effort aimed at conserving both individual and communal history. The nurse plays this role as s/he gives a verbal chronicle of a deceased's last days, including "how he had a premonition of his death, of how he died, and of what last words he uttered before his spirit left the body" (18). Given the seriousness accorded to such an account, the Nurse's record is expected to comprise "exact details" (18) about the dead, and s/he must "be faithful to the facts" (7). Armed with this cultural obligation, the Nurse at the funeral of Vutha, Noria's son, states audaciously that the boy's death has been caused by his own people. Her statement, which is truthful - because the five-year-old child has been killed by a gang of youths who defend the squatters from attacks by hostel dwellers - underscores the accuracy of a Nurse's testimony.

The funeral itself is a locale for both mourning and politics. As Sam Durrant writes,

> Funerals during the apartheid era were often politicized and many political chants were also songs of mourning commemorating dead or imprisoned heroes of struggle. (442)

Durrant's explanation means that rites, such as those performed by the Nurse and other mourners, reflect the political situation prevalent in South Africa. Consequently, there is enormous probability that mourners of victims of apartheid may use the funeral as a forum for attacking the colonial regime and exposing its evils. This possibility is heightened by the fact that it is not uncommon to have several speakers at one funeral.

2.2 Language and Education

In *Decolonising the Mind: The Politics of Language in African Literature,* Thiong'o writes that,

> ...[t]he choice of language and the use to which language is put is central to a people's definition of themselves in relation to their natural and social environment, indeed in relation to the entire universe. (4)

This declaration associates the role assigned to a language with the messages, notions and values it conveys. This mutual relationship between language and the message it encodes implies that the placement of foreign languages at the center of education during the colonial and postcolonial periods changed colonized peoples' outlook of both themselves and former colonial powers. Indeed, by stripping their subjects of their means of communication and expression, and insisting that these subjects must learn foreign languages - not only in order to communicate with their masters, but also in order to receive formal education, colonialists aimed at placing their subjects in an unfamiliar cultural space where, like children, they had to learn from scratch a new way of life. Thus, Thiong'o concludes that the colonialists took him and other peoples "further and further from [themselves] to other selves [and], from [their] world to other worlds" (*Decolonising* 12). Thiong'o writes that local languages were considered as "primitive" and reiterates the fact that foreign languages "were often seen [by colonial powers] as coming to save African languages against themselves" (7). Because culture during the precolonial era was passed mainly through oral traditions that were embedded in indigenous languages, colonialists aimed at ensuring that only Western notions would be transmitted to future generations.

Encountering the Power of Traditional Religion among the Adivasis

Because language is the vehicle for instruction, education and the language of instruction are interlinked. In *Chotti Munda and His Arrow*, Devi shows that the adivasis do not pursue Western education as taught in schools but receive traditional education through cultural methods. For this reason, the impartation of knowledge to Chotti by Dhani takes place through traditional means. This traditional educational process further emphasizes the fact that education, language and culture are intertwined.

The transmission of cultural secrets from Dhani to Chotti takes place in 1915 - one year after 14-year-old Chotti visits the house of his sister's grandfather-in-law. During the visit, he encounters 80-year-old Dhani, his sister's grandfather-in-law, who keeps to himself and does not interact with the rest of the family. He is said to do "nothing all day" except making "lovely toys for the Munda children" (7). However, Dhani is a prophetic figure who embodies cultural wisdom, because even though he has never learnt any carpentry, he "sat in front of the smithy and put together wooden handles for them" when they make "machetes, floor-knives, scythes, spades, trowels" (7). Perhaps to keep this cultural wisdom pure, "[h]e spoke to no one, . . . cooked his own rice, . . . [and] did not eat mixed meal, ghato" (7). His wisdom is acknowledged by the police constable who asserts that he knows "everythin' after all" (7).

Dhani's education of Chotti begins when he tells the latter that he has "a spellbound arrer [arrow]" and that "if ten birds fly in t' sky, an' ye tell t' arrer get me t' third one, it'll do it" (5). Chotti learns that Dhani is the brother of Lord Birsa, the great warrior who was killed while defending the rights of the Mundas against the government. Dhani is seen as the heir of Lord Birsa's cultural prowess, and is thus barred by the government from ever leaving the area, or from ever holding an arrow. The government's fear of his power, which alludes to the likelihood that Mundas will defy authority and re-assert their cultural power, is revealed by the constable who pleads with him: "Don't go anywhere please, I'll lose my job" (7). The constable further indicates his powerlessness when Dhani retorts that when he "feel[s] like it . . . [he]'ll cast a spell, become invisible and take off!" (7). The constable's response, "Don't, Dhani," reveals his vulnerability as well as the futility of guarding the latter. It is significant that Dhani's threat is conveyed through language; consequently, language is the medium through which cultural power is practiced and the enemy intimidated.

Dhani's next question to the constable is enlightening because it unveils his position among the Mundas: "Why're ye jerkin' t' Mundas aroun' at market and takin' cuts?" (7). The conversation ends with Dhani's warning that Daroga, the police chief, must be told that "takin' cuts" from the Mundas has to stop or "Daroga too will hafta answer" (8). Dhani's warning, which the despondent constable is expected to deliver, indicates that language is a means of defense against cultural oppression. Dhani's verbal warnings, as well as those given by Chotti, not only connote the community's unique identity but also express its readiness to defend this identity against imminent destruction by institutions such as the police and the government.

Further dissemination of cultural education is evident in Chotti's instruction of other Mundas. For instance, he instructs Dukhia, Bikha and Sukha from Kurmi village not only in arrow-shooting but also in the cultural heritage of the Munda community. The role played by Chotti is not to be belittled because, as Sardesai, et al. write, there existed in precolonial India "[t]he traditional intelligentsia consisting of religious thinkers, functionaries, and preachers and teachers in the traditional education system" (100). It is significant that when Chotti initially refuses to train these youth, what convinces him to do so is a vision of Dhani being killed in Jejur market. This vision thus establishes a connection between Chotti's instruction of these boys and the instruction he himself had received from Dhani. Like Dhani, who fights the police in spite of knowing that they have mightier weapons and he is likely to be killed, Dukhia, one of the students, later fights and kills the oppressive manager of Kurmi village and is sentenced to death by hanging. In addition, at the *pahan*'s request, Chotti also secretly provides traditional instruction to all Munda boys, which elicits in him "an especial joy" and "a new excitement" (79).

Language and modern education have become instruments for the oppression of the Mundas. For instance, in Bharat's village, the brother-in-law of the *zamindar* (landlord) who runs the farm "knows Mundari, but speaks Hindi" both to distance himself from those he considers low caste and to ensure that they do not understand his rules. This mendacious barrier enables him to accuse them of breaking laws they do not know. Budha, a resident of Bharat's village, therefore says correctly that Dikus (intruders and exploiters) take advantage of the Mundas because the latter "don' know book-learnin" (107). In spite of his assertion, Budha demonstrates that cultural education is not entirely powerless when he fights the zamindar's brother-in-law and urges his village mates to flee to the mission whilst he remains and burns the village. This annihilation of the village, which is rightly credited to Chotti's arrow because Budha is his past student, causes despondency among the entrepreneurs and government officials.

Budha's explanation that Mundas are exploited because of their lack of formal education suggests that this education is necessary in postcolonial times, because it will enable the adivasis and lower castes both to protect and to defend themselves. The chief reason why these groups are exploited is because they can neither read nor write, and hence they put thumbprints in exchange for food, thereby binding themselves and their descendants to providing free labor during their lifetimes.

Training received in foreign countries is depicted as impractical in *Chotti Munda and His Arrow*. In the novel, Dr. Amlesh Khurana, an elitist Indian who has been trained out of the country, believes "in theory and statistics, not in the reality of the situation," and is portrayed as an incompetent idealist whose main task is "flying from town to town, from university to university, and from seminar to seminar on the globe" (284). His request to visit villages with only Oraons or Mundas, and his becoming "altogether pained and hopeless about India" (288) when he learns that such groups do not exist in seclusion of other adivasis, shows the worthlessness of his theories under the present social conditions. He turns down the government officer's offer to take him to the existing villages because his work is to "survey the projected economic necessity" (287). Although he has limited education, the government official wonders how the government will rely on the work of an "intellectually arrogant project theorist who will cast aside reality and solve national problems on the basis of theory" (289).

His limited approach notwithstanding, Khurana is hired by the Indian government which,

...loves these statistics-based paper theories, on the basis of which it is possible to construct completely unrealistic projects - in the implementation of which millions of rupees can be given to unsuitable persons - which are never implemented or come to no use even if they are. (285)

Thus, the unsuspecting Khurana is a mere pawn in some postcolonial administrators' scheme to give credence to their misappropriation of public funds. This fraud suggests that a section of post-independence political leadership is greedy and corrupt, and thus cannot alleviate the plight of the marginalized Mundas and other lower castes. Indeed, as the magistrate indicates, the corrupt segment of government is in dire need of theorists like Khurana, and it trains them "by removing them from the country" (290).

Khurana claims that he has "done research with a number of working people such as farmer-potters and blacksmiths to prove that these people are tired, tired of their own line of work" (285). He deduces, therefore, that "India does not need agriculture and industry" but "a revolutionary change in people's mindsets" (285). Khurana fails to recognize that agriculture and industry are the main economic activities, and that if the workers are unhappy with what they do, this unhappiness may be caused by such factors as working conditions and pay. In a further irrational rhetoric that casts doubt on Khurana's education, even at a purely theoretical level, his solution to the problem is that "peasants should manufacture paper by hand, fisher-folk should weave mats, potters should run handlooms, weavers make Bengal lights and carpenters wool animal hair" (285). His recommendations appear to be shaped by Western stereotypical notions that tend to remove formerly colonized peoples from industrialization and reduce them to manual producers of local artifacts.

Khurana's perspective on India and Indians thus reflects a neocolonial prism because he has trained in and lived only in Western countries. This view is evident in his consideration of an adivasi archery fair as a mere performance that he can pay to film. Chotti's remark that Khurana's stance on archery contests is analogous to paying a "mango tree and tell[ing] it ta git ya fruit outa season" (298) and re-asserts that the contest is a cultural undertaking with a determined time and value to the traditionalists. Khurana's attempted commercialization of the contest is an effort to prescribe the festival's activities: "It'll have an archery match, witchdoctors will chase spooks, sacrifice a pig to the sun" (298). Since there is no mention of "witchdoctors" in both the adivasi communities and in their archery fairs, the commercialization of the colonies' indigenous cultures, as exemplified by Khurana, greatly alter cultural festivals in an attempt to make them fit the stereotypical "witchdoctor" mentality of would-be Western viewers of such films.

The Values of Western and Indigenous Education to the Bambara

Like Devi, Condé shows, in *Segu*, that there exist cultural education, wisdom and philosophy which are passed orally through songs, narratives and proverbs by the Bambara community. This cultural education also provides evidence of the existence of intellectualism in Africa during the pre-script era. King Monzon Diarra, for example, wisely states that "[a]n evil word is like a stench. It attacks a man's strength, going from the nose to the throat, the liver and the sex" (24). This statement warns that false allegations are destructive to African society. Another example of a wise saying, "Blood is thicker than water" (79), indicates that kinship occupies a prominent position in African communities. In addition, through the fables "of Souroukou the hyena, Badeni the camel and Diarra the lion [that are] told around the fire in the evening" (75), education and important information regarding the community's worldview is passed. It is, perhaps, such references to storytelling that lead Chinosole to conclude that Condé "dares to position herself as storyteller as if she were speaking 'in' Segu away from the earshot of foreigners" (594). Chinosole's supposition is informed by the fact that the author is not from Africa but from the Caribbean; therefore, only a re-visitation of her African past with its traditional culture can enable her to engage in such a narration. Chinosole further argues that, since Condé is a postcolonial writer, she must be deeply rooted "in the most ancient forms and styles of African storytelling" (594)

This cultural education in Segu village, and in the entire African continent, is depicted as threatened by the invasion of foreigners who introduce the written language, thereby changing the mode of instruction. Among the Bambara, writing is expanded by the Islam-practicing Moors who arrive in Segu for trade, but who eventually start establishing mosques. Tiekoro considers writing as "practicing magic" (20), a mystery that makes him leave Segu for Timbuktu and later for Jenne where he seeks university

29

education. Tiekoro's capacity to study shows that Africans, contrary to the belief of foreigners, are capable of intellectual thought. By becoming a doctor in Arabic linguistics rather than in his own Bambara language, Tiekoro symbolizes the Islamic education's efforts to exclude Africans from their language and way of life.

As opposed to indigenous education, which is passed onto all children without prejudice, Islamic education becomes a basis for discrimination against those classified as belonging to lower ethnic or social groups. Thus, in spite of applying himself at the Islamic university in Timbuktu, Tiekoro discovers that it is impossible to become an Islamic scholar because "one had to be well-born" (88) to achieve this privilege. This notion, which ignores the fact that Tiekoro comes from a noble family "whose lineage was lauded by the griots" (47), is a portrayal of the biased attitude of the Moors. When he eventually completes his education and becomes a "doctor of Arabic theology and linguistics," Tiekoro is denied a job at the university in Jenne, but he is given "freedom to open a school" without any financial support (147).

Like Islamic education, Western education is also a means of indoctrination and denigration of the indigenous peoples. The European missionaries, for example, establish Fourah Bay College "to train craftsmen in European techniques of carpentry, masonry, and metal work and create assistants to help in the administration of the colony" (402). Providing training in manual tasks suggests that Africans are incapable of learning intellectually challenging subjects. The only other subject the Europeans add to Fourah Bay College is religious training, which they see as a means of rescuing Africans from their traditions. Even religious training is seen by some Europeans as beyond Africans, which explains why Eucaristus is treated as an animal by onlookers, who exclaim when he goes to England in pursuit of religious education: "He can talk! And he speaks English!" (407). The foreign education that Eucaristus receives in England is not relevant to his own culture. Instead of being provided with books that relate to his African heritage, he is exposed to Western writings including "the novels of such authors as Laurence Sterne, Charles Dickens, Jane Austen and William Makepeace Thackeray" (409).

Merits and Demerits of Formal Education in *The God of Small Things*

The largely successful but threatened traditional system of education among the Mundas in *Chotti Munda and His Arrow* and the Bambara in *Segu* is contrasted sharply with contemporary education in *The God of Small Things*. Roy shows that as a result of this colonial education, the English language is deemed superior to local languages, and its speakers are to be revered and treated with awe. For instance, K.N.M. Pillai, the local leader of the Communist Party, "insisted on speaking to Chacko in English" (259) when the latter goes to his house to ask for help in designing a label for a new vinegar product of Paradise Pickles & Preserves. Pillai also insists that his wife "understands English very well. Only doesn't speak" (264). This insistence on the knowledge and use of English reinforces the colonial belief that English is the language of power and prestige.

Through Western education, Roy points out that Indians have been brainwashed to view any connection with the Western world as a mark of distinction and praise. Association with India's former colonial power is treated highly, and those with British relatives are held in even higher regard. For instance, the Orangedrink Lemondrink Man, who had earlier sodomized Estha, surges with adoration for Papachi's family when Ammu mentions that her son's cousin is arriving from London. Roy observes that "[a] new respect gleamed in Uncle's eyes. For a family with London connections" (104). The same adoratin is exhibited by K.N.M. Pillai when he introduces Rahel to his friend after her return from the United Sates. Roy states that his question: "In Amayrica now, isn't it?" is not genuine because it is asked for "sheer admiration" (123). Similarly, Pillai's unnecessary revelation that his son, Lenin, is "working with foreign embassies" as "German First Secretary" (125) is, similarly, an attempt at soliciting esteem from his listeners.

The treatment of Sophie Mol and her mother, Margaret Kochamma, exemplifies the high esteem accorded to those of Caucasian background. Preparations for their arrival begin long before they leave London, and during that week, nicknamed *What will Sophie Mol think?* Week, Sophie occupies a unique position in the Ayemenem House. Roy observes that she becomes the topic of discussion by Baby Kochamma, Kochu Maria and Mammachi, all of whom have never met her. Perhaps in her attempt to ensure that the family appears "civilized," Baby Kochamma zealously makes certain that the twins speak English. She enforces her directive by eavesdropping on their private conversations, in order to ensure that whenever she catches them speaking Malayalam, she can levy a small fine that will be deducted from their pocket money. Another punishment for speaking Malayalm is making the twins write, "*I will always speak in English, I will always speak in English* a hundred times each" (36). This brisk instruction is an endeavor to make the children conform to Western ethos rather than freely express their feelings in their mother tongue.

Consequently, because of the special position that Sophie Mol, the daughter of Chacko and Margaret, occupies, her accidental death forever changes the course of the family. Roy says of the aftermath of her death:

> The Loss of Sophie Mol stepped softly around the Ayemenem House like a quiet thing in socks. It hid in books and food. In Mammachi's violin case. In the scabs of the sores on Chacko's shins that he constantly worried. In his slack womanish legs. (17)

The "Loss of Sophie Mol" is emblematic of the loss of the British connection to the family, since she is the bond that linked Chacko to Margaret and to Britain. She is thus the lost insignia of India's connection to its overvalued former colonial master. While the death of Pappachi, the family patriarch, is quickly forgotten, and as:

> ...the memory of Sophie Mol . . . slowly faded, the Loss of Sophie Mol grew robust and alive. It was always there. Like a fruit in season. Every season. As permanent as a government job. It ushered Rahel through childhood (from school to school) into adulthood. (17)

Indeed, the "Loss of Sophie Mol" torments the family and determines its fate as Estha is returned to his father, Ammu expelled from the Ayemenem House, and Rahel taken to boarding school. This turn of events is foreshadowed in the contention that punishments for some acts, such as the alleged involvement in Sophie's death, are so big that they are "like cupboards with built-in bedrooms" where one could spend an entire life "wandering through dark shelving" (109).

Ammu also over-values Western culture by insisting that Estha responds with "How do You do?" and not "Finethankyou" to Margaret's

"How d'you do, Esthappen" (138). Her endeavor connotes her belief that the children's ability to communicate well in English is a measure of their self-worth; hence, she expects from them "a smooth performance" which she views as a "prize for her children in the Indo-British Behavior Competition" (139). Although she appears at times to castigate Indians' adoration of Western culture, Ammu seems to be ignorant about the effects of colonization, because she dismisses Chacko's claim that watching *The Sound of Music* is "an extended exercise in Anglophilia" because, she says, the movie is a "World hit" which "the whole world goes to see" (54).

Pappachi's oppression of his wife may emanate from the colonial education he received. He studied for a six-month Diploma in Entomology at Vienna during the era of British rule in India, and the colonial powers gave him the title "Imperial Entomologist" (47). The use of the term "imperial" in his official title perhaps suggests that he is not only working for an imperial power, but that he is the quintessence of imperialism. It is not surprising, then, that he reinforces colonial notions in his family, and his violence against Mammachi is a sign of emasculation. The education's reductionism is also demonstrated by the fact that, although Pappachi is retired and does not need to dress officially anymore, he slouches "about the compound in his immaculately tailored suits" (46), looking "outwardly elegant" but "sweating inside his woolen suits" (47). Pappachi's indoctrination in foreign cultural ideas is further evident in the picture he takes while training at Vienna. In the picture, Pappachi "wore khaki jodhpurs though he had never ridden a horse in his life. His riding boots reflected in the photographer's studio lights. An ivory handled riding crop lay across his lap" (50). From this picture, one can deduce that Pappachi's encounter with the colonizers (which motivates him to dress like a colonial adventurer in India) alienates him from himself, his true identity, and the activities that take place in his environment (and takes him to a distant land that he can only imagine and not inhabit).

Pappachi is also deluded about the real nature of the Whites, and believes that their race is a superior, flawless one which is not capable of evil. Consequently, when his daughter informs him that her separation from her husband has been caused by a White man, he does not believe her, "not because he thought well of her husband, but simply because he didn't believe that an Englishman, *any* Englishman, would covet another man's wife" (42). However, Mr. Hollick, Ammu's husband's White manager at the tea estate, had asked her husband to go away for a while and leave Ammu, his "extremely attractive wife," in his bungalow so that she can "be looked after" (41). Mr. Hollick sexually exploits women because "[a]lready there were a number of ragged, light-skinned children on the estate that Hollick had bequeathed to tea pickers whom he fancied" (41). Contrary to Pappachi's belief, colonial managers, as stated by Caroline Elkins in *Imperial Reckoning: The Untold Story of Britain's Gulag in Kenya*, oppressed, killed, raped and tortured the indigenous peoples in the name of a "moral obligation, to redeem the 'backward heathens' of the world" (5). While Elkins, a historian, writes about the torture of the Kenyan freedom fighters, her mention of other areas under similar colonization such as "East Asia, including Malaya, parts of Borneo and New Guinea" as well as "the prize of India and various islands in the Caribbean" suggests that the "cultural imperialism par excellence" (5) inflicted on Kenyans was meted out to the peoples of these colonies as well.

Chacko, Pappachi's son and an ardent admirer of Western education, also appears emasculated. He lives as though he is still at the university, and his room is "stacked from floor to ceiling with books" all of which he has read, and from which he quotes long passages "for no apparent reason" (38). For instance, he quotes an irrelevant passage from F. Scott Fitzgerald's *The Great Gatsby* when he, Kochamma, Ammu and the twins are leaving for the airport, and he suddenly says: "Gatsby turned out all right at the end. It is what preyed on Gatsby, what foul dust floated in the wake of his dreams that temporarily closed out my interest in the abortive sorrows and short-winded elations of men" (38). Roy observes that everyone was used to Chacko's awkward quotation of extraneous lines because "Chacko had been a Rhodes scholar at Oxford and was permitted excesses and eccentricities nobody else was" (38). Ironically, the association of such a renowned university and the prestigious scholarship with such abrupt quotes calls into question the real worth of Western education, and its relevance in non-Western cultural settings. In fact, his education fails to impart in him the skills needed in running the family's factory. While Chacko must be given credit for using his pension and provident funds, earned at the Madras college, to purchase a bottle-sealing machine, the fact that he presides over the collapse of such a small enterprise is baffling. Roy observes that until his arrival, Mammachi's pickle-making business was "a small but profitable enterprise" notwithstanding the fact that "Mammachi just ran it like a large kitchen" (55). Even though he gives the business a name, registers it as a company, invests in machines, and expands its labor force, the enterprise "almost immediately" begins to decline financially and is kept afloat by "extravagant bank loans that Chacko raised by mortgaging the family's rice fields around the Ayemenem House" (56). While Western modalities of running businesses are not to be entirely dismissed, and because there is no indication that Chacko studied Business Management at Oxford, suffice it by noting that the strategies he employs do not succeed in yielding higher profits for the company.

The education of the twins during their childhood sheds light on the relevance and suitability of postcolonial India's educational system. The children have only been exposed to irrelevant, Western-oriented adult literature. Roy says that "the twins were precocious with their reading. They had raced through *Old Dog Tom, Janet and John* and their *Ronald Ridout Workbooks,*" while "at night, Ammu read to them from Kipling's *Jungle Book*" (57). While credit is to be given to the adults for ensuring that the children, at this early age, have "precocious reading," the real value of the materials they read is doubtful. Like Chacko, the children have started quoting irrelevant scenes from the books; Roy writes about Rahel:

> *It is a far, far better thing that I do, than I have ever done"* she would say to herself sadly. That was Rahel being Sydney Carton being Charles Darnay, as he stood on the steps, waiting to be guillotined, in the Classics Illustrated comic's version of *A Tale of Two Cities.* (59)

Since the children are obviously removed from the cultural setting of such writings as *A Tale of Two Cities,* and are intellectually excluded from adult creative works that describe such themes as "guillotining," they merely memorize the literature and act it out whenever they think it is relevant to their situations. This reduction of children to "players" of works of foreign cultures questions the effectiveness of the educational system bequeathed to former colonies.

That the works being read by the twins are inappropriate is further evidenced by the fact that even Sophie, for whom the materials might have some relevance, is unaware of the existence of some of them. For instance, despite the fact that the six-year-old twins can quote comfortably from William Shakespeare's *The Tempest*, nine-year-old Sophie is not conversant with the play, and therefore informs Baby Kochamma that she is unfamiliar with the work's "Ariel" (Roy 138). Surprisingly, at his tender age, Estha writes a paragraph about Ulysses and Penelope, apparently in response to a reading on Greek mythology. The fact that he can read and respond to Greek myths shows the extent to which the educational system as a whole alienates children from their own experiences and places them into that of others.

Thus, detached from culturally relevant and age-appropriate literature, Estha and Rahel are "deeply offended" (58), when Baby Kochamma's Australian friend, Miss Mitten, gives them *The Adventures of Susie Squirrel*, a children's book, as a present. Although Miss Mitten's action may be arguably termed racist as it may connote her belief that Indian children are incapable of reading more complex works, the children's derision of Miss Mitten is intensified by the fact that they have always been given adult rather than children's books. Further verification of Miss Mitten's high regard for the English language, and by extension a revelation of the extent to which Whites despise local languages, is demonstrated by her ignorance about the name of the local language. She thinks that it is "Keralese" because they live in a state called "Kerala," and is unaware that the language is called Malayalam (58).

The educational system that has been bequeathed to India by the British is further dented by its apparent inability to distinguish success and failure, as exemplified by Rahel's admission into a school of architecture despite her obvious incapability to undertake the course. Roy reveals that her admission into the school is not "the outcome of any serious interest in architecture. Nor even, in fact, a superficial one. She just happened to take the entrance exam, and happened to get through" (18). The reader is dismayed that the admission officials are "impressed by the size (enormous) rather than the skill, of her charcoal still-life sketches . . . [which are] mistaken for artistic confidence, though in truth, the creator was no artist" (19). This situation exposes the ambiguity in the educational system's yardsticks for measuring talent and achievement.

Protesting against the Europeanization of Antigua

Kincaid, in *A Small Place*, extends the discussion on the status of education bequeathed to former European colonies. *A Small Place* is a short epistolary novel in which the narrator addresses an unnamed North American or European tourist who visits postcolonial Antigua. Describing Antigua as a geographically small place, the address informs the tourist that the island has suffered irreparable damage as a result of both colonization and slavery. As a result, despite the former British colony's physical beauty, such systems as infrastructure and sewer are in a deplorable condition.

In *A Small Place*, Kincaid describes an Antiguan school as "a building sitting in a sea of dust" which looks like "some latrines for people passing by" (7). Similarly, Kincaid depicts the Antiguan library as one of "splendid old buildings from colonial times" (9), which were destroyed by an earthquake in 1974. Since the destruction, a sign saying "REPAIRS ARE PENDING" (9), has been hanging on the library but no work has been undertaken more than a decade later. Kincaid reveals that Antigua got independence from the British soon after the earthquake. This description of pillars of Western education as derelict raises doubt about the sustainability of the educational system established by the Europeans in their former colonies because the maintenance of the buildings and other educational facilities requires funds which may be unavailable in poor economies.

Like Roy, Kincaid implies that the education provided to the local students brainwashes them to overvalue European peoples and celebrations over their own culture. Kincaid says of this education: "We were taught the names of the kings of England. In Antigua, the twenty-fourth of May was a holiday—Queen Victoria's official birthday" (30). Antiguan students are taught that the English are "civilized" people who have come to "rescue" them from perceived "primitivity." Postcolonial education is also depicted as a means of indoctrinating the locals so that they fit in Western stereotypical roles of "slaves." No wonder, one of the institutions "that is often celebrated in Antigua is the Hotel Training School, a school that teaches Antiguans how to be good servants, how to be a good nobody, which is what a servant is" (55). Since Antigua is a favorite tourist destination, Antiguans who graduate from the Hotel Training School are expected to serve tourists in the hotels, and their aspiration to attend the school implies that they perceive service to Whites as a noble duty. The reader is therefore not surprised that this education is unable to prepare Antiguans for work within their postcolonial systems. Indeed, the quality of education is depicted as wanting in that librarians in Antigua are unable to assist their clients in locating reading materials. Kincaid bemoans the fact that "most young people seem almost illiterate" (43) in spite of being recipients of this supposedly formal education.

Thus, the system of education that Kincaid describes is designed to glorify European notions and set the Antiguans on the path to Eurocentric values. She states that because the former library now houses a carnival troupe, books have been replaced with costumes. These costumes reek of life before and after colonization: "Some of the costumes were for angels before the Fall, some of the costumes were for angels after the Fall; the ones representing After the Fall were best" (47). That the costumes signifying the postcolonial period are the "best" indicates that postcolonial life is at "best" to be described as unreal because it simulates Western thought.

While recognizing that Antiguans have embraced Western education despite its limitations, Kincaid declares that their ancestors "were not clever in the way" the tourist's were, suggesting that cleverness is determined by the realities prevalent in a cultural location. Kincaid distances indigenous wisdom from its Western version by connecting the latter with cruelty: "[indigenous] ancestors . . . were . . . not ruthless in the way yours were" (17). She shows the tourist as terming the locals' "harmony . . . with nature" as an act of "backwardness" (16), merely because he or she cannot "be in harmony with nature and backward in that charming way" (17). She accuses the colonialists of failing to accept the realities prevalent at the colonies "[a]nd so everywhere they went they turned it into England; and everybody they met they turned English" (24). The colonizers' effort to transform everybody into "English" has far reaching effects on the lives of the colonized, because "no place could ever really be England, and nobody who did not look exactly like them would ever be English" (24). Diane Simmons writes that imperial powers' claim that England "was the center of the universe, robbed colonial children a sense of their own" (65). However, Simmons also shows that this Western education is useful not only because it enables Kincaid to tell her story, but also because it exposed her to classics such as John Milton's *Paradise Lost* and Charlotte Bronte's *Jane Eyre* which have influenced some of her writings (65).

Kincaid also portrays Western education as largely unachievable for most Antiguans as exemplified by the "headmistress of a girls' school, hired through the colonial office in England and sent to Antigua" (29). She bars girls born outside marriage from attending school, thus implying that Black children are illegitimate. Although Kincaid does not indicate who the fathers of these girls are, her description of the action as "a way of keeping Black children out of this school" (29) may suggest that some of the girls are daughters of White men with - obviously sexually-exploited - Antiguan women. The headmistress's action is one of discrimination, because she does not provide proof that there exist a connection between academic success and the marital status of students' parents. Furthermore, her reference to Black girls as "monkeys just out of trees" is an abusive designation of non-Western peoples as being equivalent to animals.

Decolonizing Education in *Petals of Blood*

Similarly, Thiong'o, in *Petals of Blood*, condemns Western influences that are transferred through education. Chui's conduct after returning from his studies in America serves as evidence that education pursued in foreign nations may be indoctrinating. When he takes over as principal of Siriana, the students, in Karega's words, expect him to stop them from basing their identity in "white snows, [and] spring flowers fluttering by on icy lakes" (170). However, Chui refuses to introduce African literature and history in the school, and insists that the Eurocentric curriculum he inherits must be retained.

Thiongo's portrayal of Chui illustrates his argument in *Barrel of a Pen* that,

...[d]epending on who is wielding the weapon, education far from being a means of illuminating reality can be used as a means of masking reality to mystify the relations between man and nature and between man and man. (90)

39

Thiong'o's perception of education as a weapon underscores the liberating nature of knowledge. However, he expresses doubts about the emancipative power of a skewed education administered and centered on foreign lands. Thus, for education to be liberative, students must interrogate and verify ideas rather than merely adopt such ideas. He shows that failure to authenticate concepts makes learners mere narrators of notions they have read in books or heard in class. Such narrators include Karega's Siriana teachers, who "never wanted to confront the meaning of colonialism and of imperialism" (199). These teachers describe the violent struggle for independence as "grisly murders" (199), thus adopting the colonizers perception of African's resistance to colonial domination. It is not surprising that one of Karega's teachers "quoted Governor Mitchell on the primitivity of Kenyan peoples and went ahead to show the historical origins of this primitivity, or what he called undercivilisation" (199). This distortion of Kenya's history, as well as the use of the terms "primitivity" and "undercivilisation," serve as reminders of the colonizers' attitude towards Africans, and highlights Thiong'o's misgivings about African education in the postindependent period. The situation is worsened by the fact that educational institutions during this period are run by European administrators such as Siriana's Ironmonger and Fraudsham. These administrators ensure that students are taught foreign ideologies, which are irrelevant to both their culture and their country's immediate needs. No wonder, as a student, Chui is nicknamed "Shakespeare" (27) because of quoting Shakespearean works with precision.

Thiong'o also portrays the education provided to Africans during the colonial period as substandard. "During the colonial days," he writes, "African teachers could only teach in African schools," which "were of much the same standard: poorly equipped, poor houses, and limited aids" (107). This statement indicates that when Kenya gained her independence from the British, African children continued to receive poor quality education, because African teachers preferred to work in "former Asian and European schools which remained as high-cost schools with better houses, equipment, teaching aids" (107); hence, the African schools remained poorly equipped to provide any meaningful education to the African masses. This situation explains why Munira is unable to recruit teachers, even untrained ones, for his newly established Ilmorog School. The poor quality of education given to children in post-independence Kenya, and by extension the entire African continent, is also represented in the fact that students at the school in Ilmorog perceive their country merely as a big city.

The novel shows that the Western education bequeathed to postcolonial Kenya is inaccessible to most citizens, because only a few students pass the exams that qualify them for college education. Although there are in fact three universities in the country, it is difficult to gain admission, not only because of the prohibitive cost of education, but also due to the unrealistically high academic grades one must achieve at the immediate lower level. This inaccessibility of education means that many Kenyans are unable to gain formal employment, which requires a good education. In addition, even those who join college may be expelled on flimsy grounds. There appears, therefore, to be a deliberate scheme to prevent Africans from attaining university education. The consequences of failure to acquire college learning are revealed in Munira, who David Cook and Michael Okenimkpe describe as living a "shiftless life" by being "a mere beggarly primary school teacher" (94) in an affluent family. Because of his "shiftlessness" and the frustration such a life breeds, he loses self esteem and persistently sees himself as "an outsider, fated to watch, adrift, but never one to make things happen" (Thiong'o 23).

The unachievability of Western education is also embodied in Karega, Munira's former student, who is similarly expelled from college after he and other students refuse to participate in the burial of Lizzy, Fraudsham's dog. Fraudsham wants the students to conduct a formal burial ceremony, complete with pall bearers, for his dog, but the students find his request laughable because, according to African culture, such an honor is given exclusively to human beings. When Fraudsham expels the students for refusing to lead the ceremony, the entire institution goes on strike leading to the expulsion of many others. This trivial matter leads to the ruin of Karega and many other students' dreams. Karega thus ends up first as an untrained teacher in Munira's Ilmorog school, and later as a "roadside boy" who sells "sheepskins, fruits, [and] mushrooms by the roadside" (104).

Education as a Secondary Need in Apartheid South Africa

Unlike other novels in this study, Mda's *Ways of Dying* does not seem to depict formal education as a necessity. The reader is surprised, for instance, that "neither Toloki nor Noria paid much attention to school work from the very first day they were registered at the village primary school," and that "they were not the only children who did not pay much attention to school work" (32). This scenario begs the reader to consider the fact that South Africans are at war during this time, both against apartheid and among themselves. These wars imply that parents are more interested in their families' safety and survival, as well as their country's liberation. The novel portrays lack of opportunities for South Africans, abject poverty among the masses, and soaring insecurity in cities as possible factors that keep parents away from participating in their children's educational activities.

It is also suggested that some parents, especially those from urban areas, take their children to school not to attain formal education but to keep them away from crime. An example is the mother who, despite having left her village, sends her child to the school in the village in order to keep the child away from the city where children "did not want to learn, but preferred to run around the streets, sniffing glue and smoking daga" (43). While the city, especially during apartheid, may be dangerous for children, South African cities, and perhaps most cities, are, in the words of Sara Nuttal, "always moving zones" (741) because they are the sources of changes in a culture or community. Nonetheless Nuttal admits: "The new South African city is still a space where nightmarish divisions may be witnessed and where the fear of crime delimits dreams of truly public space" (741). Crime, such as that evident in *Ways of Dying*, makes it quite unlikely that children in the city will receive formal education.

Nevertheless, Mda portrays literacy as a necessary means of fighting oppression. This portrayal is best exemplified by Shadrack, who, like all other upcoming entrepreneurs, is tortured by police. He is physically assaulted, in addition to being taken to a mortuary, where he is asked to have sex with a corpse. His use of literacy and knowledge of the legal system as a means of fighting back is demonstrated by the fact that he keeps "all the evidence, and full descriptions of the policemen involved" (142). As a result of his daring efforts, one of his attackers is arrested for the torture. That education is a vehicle for resistance against colonial domination is also denoted by the policeman's warning that educated complainants "think they know everything" (143). Although the reader is not convinced that Shadrack will get justice, given that his written statement is bound to "make a lot of important people angry" and there is "no knowing what cannon [such people] must unleash" (142), his victory is at best marked by the fact that the police eventually admit that the van used during his torture was theirs. Literacy is also depicted as tool for communication beyond one's community because, Madimbhaza, the poor but kind woman who adopts abandoned babies or those whose parents are killed in the on-going wars, receives assistance for the first time when "a newspaper, *City Press*" (168), writes about her philanthropic work.

2.3 Language and the Law

In her article "Can the Subaltern Speak?" Gayatri Chakravorty Spivak states that "the history of Europe as subject is narrativized by the law, political economy and ideology of the West" (66). Spivak's placement of law alongside Western political economy and ideology indicates that European legal systems are carriers of Western culture. Her assertion also explains why erstwhile colonial administrators emphasized the establishment of their laws in their colonies. While these laws were obviously the means of punishing those who resisted domination, they were written in colonial languages and there was little effort, if any, to translate them into the local languages. This unavailability of the statutes in a medium accessible to the indigenous communities - even after most colonies gained independence - means that such communities as the Mundas in Devi's *Chotti Munda and His Arrow* are at risk of breaking laws of which they are ignorant. The refusal of the colonial powers to translate these laws into the local languages may also be viewed as an attempt to force these communities to learn the foreign languages.

The Indian Laws and Land Tenure in *Chotti Munda and His Arrow*

Jennifer Wenzel, in her article "Epic Struggles over India's Forests in Mahasweta Devi's Short Fiction," writes:

> The intensification of forest exploitation after independence is a symptom not only of lingering Westernization, but also of basic conflicts within (or between) Indian culture(s) that were unresolved and exacerbated during the colonial period. (130)

43

This exploitation, which is epitomized by landlords and moneylenders in *Chotti Munda and His Arrow*, displaced adivasis who, as the novel indicates, were reduced to laborers. Sardesai, et al. write that "[t]he British laid down the foundation of a new judicial system by establishing a hierarchy of civil and criminal courts . . .; thus, [they] introduced a new system of justice and law in India" (105). Because colonial and postcolonial political administrations introduced a new legal system regarding land tenure, adivasis, who are oblivious of this system, are likely to become its victims.

Consequently, the predicament of the Munda society as brought out by Devi points to the suffering of communities that are not conversant with colonial languages. Indeed, language stands at the focal point of the postcolonial Indian legal system, and, as Chotti says, while Mundas are neither able to find nor pay lawyers, the communication barrier renders ineffectual the necessity of a lawyer to represent them. Devi writes: "Lawyers will tek money, but what he says Munda doesn' understan'," Chotti says, "an' he [lawyer] don' understan' what Munda says, for lawyers understand B when Munda says A an' explains t' contrary ta t' judge. T' judge judges contrariwise" (159).

Thus, since Indian society has embraced English in its legal system, the survival of adivasis without this education appears bleak. Chotti laments that the reason why many members of the Munda, Oraon, Dusad-Dhobi groups are in "je-hell" is because of lack of education; hence, they are "in je-hell fer land rights, but they don' know what they did wrong" (321). Although "je-hell" is literally the community's articulation of the word 'jail,' the presence of "hell" connotes the difficult life the adivasis lead. The adivasis' main obstacle in their attempts to gain formal education is discrimination from the mainstream Indian society. Chotti reveals that whenever adivasis go to school, they are told to "go herd cows"; hence, education "by law [is] f'r ever'one, but not in fact" (150). This revelation questions the selective application of law in post-independent India and other former colonies, and exposes the elite's desire to keep the lower classes lowly and uneducated. A more compelling instance of bias in the application of Indian laws is clear in the S.D.O.'s effort to identify and punish the killers of Romeo and Pahlwan, two youths who have killed many adivasis. While the murderous duo has hitherto gone unpunished, the Sub Divisional Officer (S.D.O.), who is the head of the local administrative subdivision, threatens the Mundas with dire consequences should they fail to reveal their killers.

The use of a language beyond the reach of Mundas is also blamed for the non-implementation of laws apparently passed for their emancipation from exploitation. Such laws are passed to hoodwink international communities, and other defenders of adivasis, that policies that are supportive of bond labor have been abolished. That politicians engage in lies of this nature is evident when Devi points out that "the hollers like 'eliminate poverty,' 'bond labour's illegal,' 'now money lenders' loan for agriculture is illegal' become posters and get stuck on trees and stations and bus-bodies in the remotest parts of the country . . . [while] people like Chotti and Chhagan continue to get ground down" (241). The reader is not surprised that the minister in charge of enforcing the law against bond labor argues that "the government knows full well that if an Act is passed for the welfare of the adivasi and untouchable, it should never be implemented," because the two groups must be exploited for the benefit of the "pillars of government" who include the "landlord, moneylender, landed farmer" (310).

The Prohibition of Indigenous Language in *A Small Place*

Similarly, Kincaid argues, in *A Small Place*, that the use of indigenous languages during the colonial period is severely curtailed, because the European laws prohibit "using of abusive language" (25). This prohibition greatly affects communication among Antiguans for whom "making a spectacle of yourself through speech is everything" (25). In addition, the enactment of this law connotes the colonialists' erroneous view that Antiguans are "primitive" people whose daily communication is characterized by vulgar language. Furthermore, when West Indians go to England, the police have to get "a glossary of bad West Indian words so that they could understand whether they were hearing abusive language or not" (25). Because words perceived as abusive may be used in a non-abusive manner, judging a statement as abusive based on a glossary indicates the Europeans' use of language as a tool for the oppression of the "other."

2.4 Oral Literature as a Means of Cultural Preservation

A study of the place of language among formerly colonized communities is worthwhile, given that such elements of oral literature as songs and narratives may be expected to shed light on enduring aspects of their traditions. It might be for this reason that Chinua Achebe, in *Morning Yet on Creation Day*, argues that the oral works of art developed during the precolonial period were created "for the good of that [precolonial] society" (29). Giving an example of *mbari*, an Owerri Igbo cultural festival dedicated to Ala, the Earth goddess, involving the construction of a house of images by selected men and women, Achebe writes that art *"belongs to all and is a 'function' of society"* (34), thus implying that such a festival belongs to the entire Igbo society. Since, as Achebe further posits, "[o]ur ancestors created their myths and legends and told their stories for a human purpose" (29), a scrutiny of such forms of oral traditions as songs and oral narratives may be expected to uncover the cultural beliefs of that particular society.

Why "Everything Becomes a Story" in *Chotti Munda and His Arrow*

The novels show that oral literature is a vehicle for cultural transmission. In Mahasweta Devi's *Chotti Munda and His Arrow*, the adivasis are depicted as using language as a means of retaining and disseminating information about their heroes and cultural beliefs. The novel professes that Chotti, by coincidence, receives instruction from Dhani Munda, the brother of Lord Birsa who was murdered while leading an insurgency against the domination of the Munda people. Dhani's instruction is founded on the community's arrow-shooting prowess, a practice that has been retained from the past because it was the means by which the community engaged in warfare, hunting for food and sporting contests. Although Chotti initially desires to use it only in securing victory during arrow-shooting contests, he and the community realize that both this traditional skill and his arrow are saturated with cultural power that will push him to the position of a leader, not only of the Mundas but also of other adivasis and low-caste Hindus.

Oral literature is a means of cultural preservation; Devi states that because "Munda language has no script, . . . they turn significant events into story, and hold them as saying, as song" because "[t]hat's their history as well" (23).[2] In an interview with Spivak, Devi explains the use of song by the Munda community:

> They compose the stream of events into song. By being made into song, into words, they become something . . . a continuity. Their history is like a big flowing river going somewhere, not without a destination. (xi)

Devi's statement supports Achebe's argument on the importance of oral traditions, and outlines two of the functions of these traditions among Mundas as: celebrating their heroes, and preserving their history. (The place of language in the retention of history has already been discussed.) The Munda society uses stories to inform future generations about the community's past heroic acts, challenges and achievements. For instance, the song they sing at the fair when Chotti is prohibited from participating in archery contests for three years presents an account of Chotti's past triumphs. The song reminisces:

> Ye raise t' bow, ye hit t' target
> Makes Daroga mighty afraid, mate -
> Ye go to Gormen and tell 'em our plea
> Makes Daroga mighty afraid, mate -
> So they didn' letya play yer arrer.
> Ye taught Dukhia Munda ta shoot
> Dukhia the bonded slave, mate -
> Dukhia cuts t' manager's head off
> Makes Daroga scared, mate -
> So they didn' let ya play yer arrer.
> Which Munda knows t' bowspell?
> Only ye, mate -
> Which Munda is Gormen buddy?
> Only ye, mate -
> So they didn' let ya play yer arrer. (84)

In the above song, "gormen" refers to the government, while the *daroga* is a police superintendent. In order to interpret the government's action, it is necessary to refer to how the police force was created in India. Sardesai, et al. write that when the British established the *Zamindari* system, the

47

zamindars (absentee landlords) were allowed to collect taxes for the colonial administrators and perform police duties until Governor General Cornwallis "established *thanas* (police posts), each of which was kept under a *Daroga* or superintendent, assisted by fifteen to twenty constables" (Sardesai, et al. 106). Because the police, even when they were Indians, were appointees of the colonial power, Sardesai, et al. conclude that the police force "became an instrument of oppression of the people particularly during the struggle for independence" (106). Since arrow-shooting, which embodies the Mundas' power, is connected to their traditional festivals, the government's attempts to stop such festivals amount to an attempt to re-shape their identity, exert control over them, and perhaps re-direct their history. The above song demonstrates, however, that the Mundas are aware of the reasons why Chotti is banned from competing in the fairs, and denotes that their success is imminent despite the ban imposed on their leader.

The mention of Dhukia Munda in the song underlies the fact that Chotti's students will demonstrate the community's cultural invincibility. Hence, the government's banning of archery contests in Kurmi village and forbidding villagers from visiting Chotti after Dukhia murders the village manager indicates the its fear of this society's traditional might. Further attempts to stop the community's festivals in Kurmi - as evidenced in the new manager's order that the hunt festival be banned because "the Mundas of Kurmi village are most pigheaded" (89) - are not expected to succeed in intimidating the Munda people. Consequently, one may infer that demeaning cultural festivals and authority figures such as the pahan, and depicting the Mundas of the village as irrational and backward is a demonstration of the colonization of adivasis by the larger Indian society and the post-independent government.

The Kurmi village manager's reaction to the local pahan's song signifies his fear of the community's cultural power, especially when the manager and his guard run in fear of a mere "hunt festival song in the voice of an emaciated old man in a deserted village" (94). Although the pahan holds a spear as he sings about the community's past exploits, it is clear that he - the only one who remains in the village after his community flees to the Christian mission in fear of the manager's brutality - cannot muster any energy to fight and "the manager and the sentry begin running for fear of the unknown" (94).

This cultural power is also evident in the climax of the fight between the adivasis and the members of the postcolonial bourgeoisie. In the fight, the S.D.O. has ordered all adivasis to attend an archery contest through which he wants to identify the killers of Romeo and Pahlwan. Chotti's order that everyone must attend the contest and ensure "[t]here's singin' and dancin' before t' arrer play" (360) underlies both the Mundas' pride in their indigenous culture as well as their readiness to defend it. Because it is his students, Disha and Upa, who have killed Romeo and Pahlwan, Chotti takes responsibility for the killings and dares the S.D.O., Tirathnath, Chatha and the police to punish any Munda for the necessary murder of the two terrorists. He warns that none of them will "stay alive" if they "raise terror" on the Mundas in retribution for the murders (363). Most importantly, Chotti shows that while the S.D.O. and local traders draw power from the government authority and from guns, his power emanates from the adivasi cultural beliefs. Devi creates a similar scenario in *Bashai Tudu*, where the novel's protagonist and defender of his people's labor and land rights, Bashai, leads adivasis in a war against the combined force of the police and the army, using traditional weapons like bows and arrows. Cultural beliefs are also evident in that the omniscient narrator of *Chotti Munda and His Arrow* asserts that Chotti "waits, unarmed. As he waits, he mingles with all time and becomes river, folklore, eternal" (363). This assertion also brings out the notion that adivasi culture flows like a river, from generation to generation, to have far-reaching effects on whosoever stands in its way, and that the culture is so interminable that it is not to be abandoned despite the sophistication of modern life. The fact that "a thousand adivasis raise their bows in space and cry, No!" (363) also underlies the enduring power of bows and arrows, their traditional weapons.

The Enduring Griot in *Segu*

Condé's *Segu* also shows orality as a means of cultural preservation. In her article, "Maryse Condé as Contemporary Griot in *Segu*," Chinosole demonstrates the orality of the novel by asserting that even "the opening lines of *Segu* are the words of a griot" (593). Chinosole's conclusion is influenced by Condé's use of the word "speak" in the line: "Speak of Segu outside of Segu, but do not speak of Segu in Segu" (Condé 3), which implies that the novel is a diasporic writing because the author resides outside Segu.

Oral literature especially becomes a manifestation of cultural identity among those who have been captured and enslaved in foreign countries. In "Cultural Identity and Diaspora," Stuart Hall writes that despite the cruelty of slavery in the Americas, enslaved Africans did not give up their African identity. He asserts:

> Apparently silenced beyond memory by the power of the experience of slavery, Africa was, in fact, present everywhere: in the everyday life and customs of the slave quarters, in the languages and patois of the plantations, in names and words, often disconnected from their taxonomies, in the secret syntactical structures through which other languages were spoken, in the stories and tales told to children, in religious practices and beliefs in the spiritual life, the arts, crafts, musics, and rhythms of slave and post-emancipation society. Africa, the signified, which could not be represented directly in slavery, remained and remains the unspoken unspeakable "presence" in Caribbean culture. (398)

Hall's statement implies that certain core aspects of African culture pervaded all spheres of the slaves' lives, and that these core aspects were passed, among other means, orally through naming, storytelling, verbal expression, and music. Hall's observation regarding the preservation of African culture during slavery is demonstrated by Naba, an African who is enslaved in Brazil. Naba tells his son Kayode that he (Naba) speaks three languages: "Two are the languages of my heart - Bambara and Yoruba. The other is the language of our servitude - Portuguese" (207). Naba suggests that the children born in slavery, whose medium of communication is only the slavemaster's language, have a language that connects them to their cultural identities. Wyatt Tee Walker, an African American priest, agrees that individuals in the diaspora retained their culture through oral traditions. Walker writes that,

> ...[t]he slavocracy forcibly stripped away much of the personhood of the African but the *oral tradition* kept intact some measure of their *human-ness* by means of what they could remember from the Mother Country. (19)

Thus, Condé demonstrates, through such characters as Naba, that even during slavery, transplanted Africans made every effort to maintain their own culture. However, for people who have been uprooted from their communities, this language may not be verbalized because it is the "language of heart." The fact that this language remains unvoiced justifies Arlette M. Smith's argument that the concept of exile in Condé's novels is to be taken as "a condition shared by all the people engaged in their quest for a demanding ideal that remains unattainable; it is then viewed as an intrinsic part of the human condition, as the fate of anyone who feels inescapably constrained by adverse circumstances" (386-7). Naba's desire to retain his African identity is to be understood within Smith's declaration because he had never contemplated leaving Segu, the homeland which gave him his cultural identity and provided him with a chance to develop into a great hunter like his half-bother, Tiefolo. His "adverse circumstances" emanate from his becoming a victim of abduction and subsequent sale into slavery, first in far-off African lands, and eventually in Brazil.

Funeral as a Medium of Cultural Preservation in *Ways of Dying*

In *Ways of Dying*, Mda employs the rite of burial to bring out the notion that oral literature is a medium of cultural preservation. An understanding of orality as it is brought out in funerals throughout *Ways of Dying* is reminiscent of Sam Durrant's article, "The Invention of Mourning in Post-Apartheid Literature," where he states:

> Funerals and associated rites of mourning are often thought of as one of the most traditional ties of community, providing an opportunity not only for members of the community to come together, united in common purpose of remembering the dead and ensuring their passage to the next world, but also for the affirmation of the very idea of community itself, the sense of being-in-common that is produced on the one hand by the universal fact of mortality and on the other by the cultural specificity of the mourning rites enacted and the shared beliefs about the nature of the cosmos to which these rites testify. (441)

Durrant's argument thus thrusts the funeral not only as the single most important indicator of the community's culture, but also as its preserver, because most burial rites may be preserved due to their power to bring together members of a community. The Nurse, anybody who was the last person to see a deceased alive, is the center of any funeral in *Ways of Dying*. Consequently, the Nurse may be seen as a storyteller, who helps both in the transmission and maintenance of the society's cultural knowledge. Although the Nurse merely tells how a person died, the community's cultural norms, both past and present, find expression. For instance, the reader learns through a Nurse that when a member of the community dies, the hair of all relatives must be trimmed. The Nurse explains:

> First of all, all the male children must have their hair cut in the order of seniority . . ... After the male children, the grandmothers will have their hair cut, also in order of their seniority. They are followed by the female children. (157)

Through the Nurse, the reader is also introduced to the confusion created by a mistress, when, during a funeral, a brother of the deceased beats his father to death for allowing a mistress's children to be shaved before legitimate children. This tragedy might imply that the idea of having a mistress is uncommon in the community's traditional culture, because it causes confusion in an apparently common ritual. The crucial role of the Nurse in the funeral may further explain why any member who takes up the role of a Nurse becomes transformed. Toloki sheds light on this sudden change when he reveals that his school principal, who acts as the Nurse during the funeral of his schoolmate, "was no longer the principal that Toloki knew. He was completely transformed, and his voice was not the voice he used at school, where he was always angry and did not hesitate to make the cane work on the buttocks of naughty boys and girls" (44).

Stories, which are passed orally from generation to generation and from place to place, are also a medium of cultural preservation. The novel states: "Since we never had anything to do with the mountain people, we only know about events there from stories that people told" (32). The narrator's use of "we," not only in this section but throughout the novel, implies first, that he or she represents the community and, second, that the author is using storytelling as a writing technique. Indeed, Mda's use of storytelling as a technique is not uncommon because, according to Michael Chapman, postcolonial South African writers are increasingly employing the convention as a means of shaping identities. Chapman argues that storytelling in literary history is "an attempt to capture, reorder, and even reinvent a sense of the self in the society" (86). The fact that information is passed orally from person to person in the community is further reiterated in the following statement:

> We know everything about everybody. We even know things that happen when we are not there; things that happen behind people's closed doors deep in the middle of the night. We are the all-seeing eye of the village gossip. When in our orature the story teller begins the story, "They say it once happened . . .," we are the "they." No individual owns the story. The community is the owner of the story, and it can tell it the way it deems fit. We would not be needing to justify the communal voice that tells this story if you had not wondered how we became so omniscient in the affairs of Toloki and Noria. (Mda 12)

Although Toloki's decision to become a Professional Mourner is initially an act of survival, because he enters the profession after he observes that "Nefolovhodwe had attained all his wealth through death," and therefore decides "that he too was going to benefit from death" (133), he realizes that death is painful and only those, like Nefolohodwe, who have alienated themselves from their people can exploit its agony. His style of mourning is different from that of other mourners, because he wears special mourning attire and invents special sounds. While the sounds which Toloki makes during mourning are meaningless and even Noria, who eventually becomes his partner, agrees that she "needs to attend more funeral with Toloki in order to thoroughly grasp the profound meaning that he draws from the depth of his soul" (162), Durrant justifies these sounds as necessary inventions by arguing that "rather than constituting a culture's most entrenched and unchanging traditions, mourning rites often reflect the instability and adaptability of colonized cultures, especially where communities are responding to new forms of death and dying" (441-42). Since apartheid results in many brutal deaths among the Blacks, Toloki's way of mourning may connote the impact of apartheid on the local communities. The fact that he is invited to funerals in his "professional" capacity, and that one woman says that she invited him to mourn at a funeral because he "added an aura of sorrow and dignity that we last saw in the olden days when people knew how to mourn their dead" (109), speaks about the community's appreciation of this manner of mourning.

Conclusion

From the works under study, it is clear that colonial powers, through the use of foreign languages among other tools, attempted to annihilate indigenous cultures as they existed in precolonial societies. Furthermore, the colonizers' educational systems, which were built on foreign languages and culture, became the main arena where concerted efforts were made to substitute precolonial cultural identities with foreign ones. However, the indigenous cultures were never completely lost; instead, colonized peoples took on other identities while retaining their own. Thus, oral traditions, which were the means by which precolonial societies expressed and maintained their cultures, were retained and are still evident in postcolonial literature (although these oral forms may express postcolonial rather than precolonial notions). Since the former colonies inherited Western legal and educational systems, Western education is necessary for one to express and defend oneself in the postcolonial era, and for one to survive in the contemporary world, which is rife with such concepts as globalization. Moreover, language and formal education are inevitable because they are the tools through which formerly colonized peoples will re-assert their identity as non-Westerners, and re-write the histories that were distorted during colonization.

CHAPTER 3
COLONIAL RELIGIONS: FORCE OF SOCIETAL DISINTEGRATION

Introduction

The novels under study show colonial religions as one of the tools used by colonizers in their attempts to erase the cultural systems of those they colonized. Colonial powers considered traditional religions as "primitive" and sought to replace them with Christianity. However, works such as Maryse Condé's *Segu*, Ngugi wa Thiong'o's *Petals of Blood*, Mahasweta Devi's *Chotti Munda and His Arrow*, and Zakes Mda's *Ways of Dying* depict these traditional religions as having intrinsic value. Although Islam is not a Western religion, its followers' demonization of the indigenous religion in *Segu* resembles that of the European missionaries. The previous chapter argues that Western educational systems were the main arena where precolonial cultural identities were substituted with foreign ones. The novels that show that these educational systems were founded on foreign religions include *Segu*, *Petals of Blood*, *Chotti Munda and His Arrow*, and Arundhati Roy's *The God of Small Things*. Because foreign names accompanied conversion to the new religions, naming became an extension of the foreign religions' attempt to re-shape the colonized people's cultural identities. Colonialists and their collaborators also re-classified members of the community based on their acceptance or rejection of these religions. The novels that show colonial religions as the force of cultural breakdown include *Segu*, *Petals of Blood*, *Chotti Munda and His Arrow*, *The God of Small Things* and *Ways of Dying*. Jamaica Kincaid's *A Small Place* will not be included in this chapter because it lacks adequate information on religion. Consequently, this chapter will dedicate specific sections to the discussion of the intrinsic value of indigenous religions to their followers, education as a means of religious conversion, and foreign religions and cultural breakdown.

3.1 The Intrinsic Value of Indigenous Religions

In his essay, "Christianity," Richard Gray reports that initial efforts to evangelize Africa bore little fruit due to Africans' rejection of the missionaries, combined with the fact that missionaries often suffered from tropical diseases. However, he writes, religious activity in Africa was heightened by developments that took place in Africa at the turn of the nineteenth century when,

> [s]teamers, railways and bicycles were removing problems of access; advances in tropical medicine enhanced the chances of survival; [and] the constraints imposed by tribal warfare or by recalcitrant African rulers were being removed [by colonial administrators]. (141)

By collaborating with colonizers, missionaries proved their perception of Africans as a lowly race that was only fit to be oppressed, exploited and re-directed.

This colonial stance was, however, not restricted to indigenous culture and religions in Africa. In *Colonization and Christianity: A Popular History of the Treatment of the Natives by the Europeans in All Their Colonies*, William Howitt writes: "For more than a thousand years, the European nations have arrogated to themselves the title of CHRISTIAN!" (1). His statement implies that since all invaders - preachers, traders and politicians - identified themselves as Christians, Christianity impacted the Europeans' perceptions of those whom they colonized.

Howitt reveals this colonial perception:

> We talk of all other nations in all other quarters of the world, as savages, barbarians, uncivilized. We talk of the ravages of the Huns . . ..We shudder at the war-cries of naked Indians, and the ghastly feasts of Cannibals; and bless our souls that we are redeemed from all these things, and made models of beneficence, and lights of God in the earth! (1-2)

As Howitt suggests, the missionaries opposed what they perceived as idol worship and ungodly rituals in indigenous religions. This attitude towards indigenous cultures and religions gives credence to Dibinga wa Said's claim that "[t]he missionaries are the most effective agents of white imperialism, colonialism, and neocolonialism . . .. They collaborated in the colonial, barbaric, demonic and inhuman conquest of Africa" (505). While wa Said's assertion may appear to signify, quite inaccurately, that there is nothing good in Christianity, his statement is credible because some of the Europeans who invaded the regions under investigation in this study did so purely for the purpose of proselytizing. Howitt discusses in detail how unreligious the colonization of Africa, India, the Caribbean, and other regions was:

> We call ourselves civilized, yet we are daily perpetrating the grossest outrages; we boast of our knowledge, yet we do not know how to live with one another half so peaceably as wolves . . .. We talk of the heathen, the savage, and the cruel, and wily tribes, that fill the rest of the earth; but how is it that these tribes know *us*? They know us chiefly by our crimes and our cruelty. (6-7)

Suffice it to state that Christianity colonized indigenous peoples by use of every means possible to "rescue" the latter from their cultures. Howitt's disclosure explains why, in *Orientalism*, Edward W. Said considers colonization of other peoples by European nations as having been influenced by "innumerable speculations on giants, Patagonians, savages, natives, and monsters supposedly residing to the far east, west, south and north of Europe" (117). This colonial motivation amounted to a desire to expand Christianity, which was seen as capable of rescuing the "savages" and "monsters" from imminent destruction. Unfortunately, Said writes, "all such widening horizons had Europe firmly in the privileged center as main observer . . . [because] colonies were created and ethnocentric perspectives secured" (117). Like other scholars, Said thus considers missionaries as having been a colonial force that attempted to annihilate the religions and cultures of the "other."

However, indigenous religions, which had existed for centuries before the arrival of colonial religions, had inherent value. In *Psychology and Religion*, Carl Gustav Jung writes that religion is "a consciousness which has been altered by the experience of a numinosum" (6). He states that rituals of any religion are crucial because they are "[t]he practice and the reproduction of the original experience" (6), and that such rituals "are carried out for the sole purpose of producing at will the effect of the numinosum by certain devices of magic nature, such as invocation, incantation, sacrifice, meditation and other yoga practices, self-inflicted tortures of various descriptions and so forth" (4-5). Therefore, he concludes:

> No matter what the world thinks about religious experience, the one who has it possesses the great treasure of a thing that has provided him with a

source of life, meaning and beauty and that has given a new splendor to the
world and to mankind. (113)

In Jungian terms, therefore, colonialists' view of indigenous languages as
"barbaric" and as deserving to be replaced was synonymous with taking
away the latter's means of spiritual solace.

"Fetishism" in *Segu*

Traditional religion occupies a remarkably prominent position among
the Bambara in Condé's *Segu*. John S. Mbiti, an African scholar, argues in
African Religions and Philosophy that "Africans are notoriously religious"
because "[r]eligion permeates into all the departments of life so full that it is
not easy or possible always to isolate it" (1). This notion is evident in *Segu*
where the Bambara traditional religion pervades every sphere of life.
Because, according to Mbiti, the precolonial African "is immersed in a
religious participation which starts before his birth and continues after his
death" (19), the invasion of both Islam and Christianity envisages the
destruction of an entire way of life.

Consequently, *Segu* shows colonial domination (through the region's
invasion by Islamic and Christian adherents) as largely based on fighting
the indigenous religion, which the author simply calls "fetishism," although
the term has negative connotations. *Segu* shows both Christian and Islamic
proselytizers as claiming that their religions are superior to "fetishism"
through their consideration of the latter as an unsophisticated, superstitious
and powerless set of beliefs.

However, the traditional Bambara beliefs brought out in *Segu* uncover
an organized but complex religious system. As Tiekoro, Dousika's son,
reveals, the community believes that "the world was created by two
complementary principles, Pemba and Faro, both offspring of the spirit"
(90). The chief god is "Faro, who watched over the smooth running of the
universe night and day" (12). Worship to Faro takes different forms, such as
the sacrifice of a white cock "in case of emergency" (12) during the initial
stages of the delivery of Sira's baby. In this religion, each homestead must
have sheltered altars at "a secret place accessible only to the fetish priests
attached to the family" (12-13), as well as to the family head and few
respected women. In Dousika's compound, for example, the altar contains:

a block of wood called a *pembele,* a representation of the god Pemba, who by whirling around had created the earth while the god Faro took care of the sky and waters. Around the *pembele* were red stones representing the family's ancestors, together with *boli* or fetishes made of every kind of material: hyenas' and scorpions' tails, bark, tree roots, all regularly sprinkled with animal blood and acting as concentrated symbols of the powers of the universe, designed to bring the family happiness, prosperity and fertility. (14)

Each of the items in this altar represents what Gibreel M. Kamara terms, in his article "Regaining Our African Aesthetics and Essence through Our African Traditional Religion," the "three tenets [of African Traditional Religion]—God, ancestors, and a never-ending world" (508), because the *pembele* represents God, stones represent the ancestors, while *boli* represents the universe.

This traditional religion has a chief deity and other deities, as well as a place of worship. The rules on who may conduct sacrifices, and how these sacrifices are to be offered indicate that worship is not conducted in an arbitrary manner. In addition, at the center of the religion are the priests who, as exemplified by Koumare, Dousika's family priest, are the mediators between worshippers on the one hand, and the gods and spirits on the other. The presence of a deity as well as rules on how this deity may be worshipped proves that the traditional religion is comparable to other religions if one is to consider Kamara's argument that the pillar of any religion is a Supreme Being (508).

In "Aspects of African Traditional Religion," John Pobee discusses the presence of "a triple-forked branch set upright in the ground" (2) in traditional African religion as practiced mainly in West Africa. The branch, which he also refers to as "the God- tree" (2), was sometimes used an altar by the Ashanti of West Africa but was mostly "symbolic of the people's dependence on God" (2). The presence of such a tree signifies that trees could be used both as altars and as emblems of the Supreme Being. This usage enables one to understand why the Bambara community in *Segu* adores the *dubale* tree, which is believed to be connected with the lives of the unborn, the living, and the ancestors. Condé reveals that the tree occupies a prominent place among the Bambara because "the placentas of many of their ancestors had been buried [under it] after a safe delivery" (4). In addition, "[a]t night the spirits of the ancestors hid in its branches and watched over the sleep of the living" (4). The tree is also significant in the promotion of the community's cultural ideologies in that "[i]n its shade the women and children sat to tell stories, the men [sat] to make family decisions. In the dry season it gave protection from the sun. In the rainy season it provided firewood" (4). The *dubale* tree, it may thus be concluded, is a traditional religious guide that provides explanations regarding life and death, offers direction in decision-making, and imparts believers with religious knowledge.

Kamara further writes that any African traditional religion is valuable to its followers because "[a]s in the case of all religions, [the] African Traditional Religion operates on moral codes that the followers must abide by to ensure a just and amicable society" (508). To signify the centrality of moral values in the African traditional religion, Kamara defines the religion as "the observance of rules of conduct in the way the individual conducts his or her daily life, the practice of rituals, and the recognition of the ever presence of the living-dead (ancestors) to allow the person to coexist in harmony with other members of the community and nature" (503), so as to please a local deity. If Kamara's understanding of a religion is applied to *Segu*, one will conclude that the Bambara traditional religion is legitimate because it has set certain regulations for its adherents. It is for this reason that Nieli, Dousika's second wife, is expected "to mutter the customary prayer" (12) during Sira's delivery irrespective of her hatred for Sira. That Fale, Monzon Diarra's father, is so haughty that the gods punish him with "an ignominious death" in which "[h]is horse had thrown him in the middle of a swamp, where he'd struggled for hours before drowning" (10), indicates that those who are not faithful to the teachings of the religion may be punished.

This religion permeates all spheres of the traditional Bambara society. For instance, the birth of a child takes a religious angle, because the child is seen as a reincarnation of a dead family member. Consequently, the midwife is both a religious and medical figure in this community. Pobee concurs that birth is a religious occurrence in such West African communities as the Ashanti because it "is considered the intersection of the spirit-world with the world of men and as such a crisis point which calls for spiritual help, not only for the safe delivery by the mother but also for the survival of the child" (14). It is not a wonder that Souka, the midwife who assists Sira during childbirth, is the wife of a traditional priest and is "herself in communication with the tutelary powers" (Condé 12). As expected of a *bara muso*, a first wife of the head of the homestead, Nya delivers invocations to the ancestors to give the baby "an easy journey" (Condé 12). When the baby is eventually born, she is required to offer "to the family *boli* an egg laid by a black hen without a single white feather, and some antelope's hearts" (Condé 17). The accompaniment of these rituals by invocations signifies that Bambara traditional religion allows communication between deities and members of the community.

In the traditional Bambaran culture, as evidenced by the case of Sira's newborn son, Malobali, naming is a religious undertaking. When Malobali is born, Souka lists "all the physical details that would enable Koumare to say of which ancestor the baby was a reincarnation" (Condé 19). The fact that it is Koumare, the family's priest, who must decide the newborn's name, underlies the religious significance of this rite. Naming also requires the consideration of several factors, as for instance, Malobali is so named because he is born "after an elder son who was stillborn" (Condé 17). The consideration of Malobali's stillborn brother during naming echoes Susan M. Suzman's observation that even among the Zulu, and indeed among many other African societies, "[t]he giving of a name to a child had significance within the larger family, with the consequence that the child was rarely the focus of his or her name" (254). Suzman's statement implies that even though a child such as Malobali partly derives his identity from his name, his name also reminds both him and the Bambara community that he has had a stillborn brother. It is thus not surprising that Pobee describes the Ashanti naming ceremony as "the rite of incorporation into a dual kinship" (14) because it connects the living and the dead.

Condé shows water as emblematic of sanctification in the African indigenous religion. When Nya wakes up, her first task is to sprinkle "her hut with water and fumigat[e] it to drive away any spirits lingering on into daylight" (33). It is only after this purifying act that she can proceed to take a bath and thereafter prepare breakfast for her family. The use of water was common in many precolonial African rituals as evidenced by the presence of a pot of water called "the God-water" in "the God-tree" planted in Ashanti compounds (Pobee 2). Among the Bambaras, however, water is also the home of gods because the river is a "favorite home of the god Faro" (Condé 42). Given its religious significance in this community, water is thus rightly regarded as "the essential element"; because "[e]very time he reenters it, a man is regenerated" (Condé 42). In addition, water is viewed as a crucial component during the early stages of human development because in it, "a child takes on life and shape in its mother's womb" (Condé 42); thus, it symbolizes the amniotic fluid.

Death does not visit the African family unless it is willed by the gods and ancestors. The African religion's priest warns the family of imminent deaths of its members. As exemplified by Koumare, priests know those who will die even when such individuals are far away from home. Moreover, when these individuals die away from home, it is the priest's responsibility to receive a message from the *Urubu* of death, a bird that carries such messages, and to ensure that the soul of the deceased is reincarnated through a yet to be born baby. For instance, Koumare foretells the deaths of Naba and Malobali although the two are living far away from home, just as he does that of Dousika who resides in Segu.

The power of the traditional African religion is further evident in that its priests accurately predict events not only for family units but also for the entire community. Koumare, foresees that in Dousika's homestead, "One son was arriving [Malobali by birth], another going away [Tiekoro, in pursuit of Islamic education]! The father was rising, [and] then falling!" (23). Koumare also predicts that Tiekoro, Naba and Malobali will leave Dousika's homestead and "be regarded as hostages or scapegoats, to be wantonly ill used by fate so that the family as a whole might not perish" (42). In yet another case of foretelling the future, Fane, another priest, envisages that of the youth who have defied Koumare and were lost in the Kangaba region, only Naba will not return to Segu. This prophecy, which corresponds with Koumare's, is fulfilled when Naba is captured as a slave while the rest are safely returned home by a search party. Fane has ordered the formation of the search troupe and prophesied that the troupe will be led to the location of the lost youth by "the tracks of the gazelle" (68). Accordingly, crowned cranes - described as "holy birds" which are "the source of language" (72) - appear during the journey, and a herd of gazelles emerge to lead the troupe as griots entreat the birds to speak. Traditional priests hold extra-ordinary powers, which may be equated to Christianity's claim for the existence of miracles. Koumare, for instance, is so powerful that when he swims in the

Joliba river, "[c]rocodiles and other aquatic animals, sensing his power, made way for him" (42).

Furthermore, African traditional divinities protect their worshippers even when such worshippers leave their motherlands. The divinities are responsible for sending to Malobali "a toothless old man, his legs covered with ulcers but apart from that apparently quite robust" (245) - a disguised ancestor who helps him to flee imminent trouble after he rapes Ayaovi, an Ashanti girl. The disguised ancestor urges Malobali: "Run, Bambara, run! They're after you!" (243), and then vanishes. A similarly disguised ancestor visits Siga when he is torn between Fatima, his lover, and her manipulative mother, Zaida. Before vanishing, the ancestor advises Siga to abduct Fatima and return to his Segu village.

The traditional religion as practiced by the Bambara also keeps relatives united and informed of the predicament of their family members. This unifying nature of the religion enables Siga to know that Nadie has committed suicide by throwing both herself and her daughter into a well. Similarly, Naba, despite being enslaved thousands of miles away from Segu, sees the "*urubu* of death" sent to warn him that death is about to strike his family (207). Condé also writes that Naba's soul leaves his body during sleep and goes "to meet people and things" when it meets "the soul of his father as it left his body" (199). Likewise, the *urubu* travels from Brazil to Segu to inform the family that Naba has been sentenced to death in a foreign land, and that his soul is "in danger of having to wander forever in the desolate waste of the damned, unable to find reincarnation in the body of a male baby or to become a protecting ancestor, later a god" (217). The possibility of a soul wandering if the ancestor is far away from home may be elucidated by Pobee's discussion on ancestors as perceived by several West African communities. Describing ancestors as "those of the clan who have completed their course here in the land of the living," Pobee states that they are akin to "elder brothers of the living at the house of God" (7). Pobee writes that not all dead community members become ancestors because "[t]he man who in life was morally bankrupt is disqualified from being an ancestor; so is the one who dies tragically or through some loathsome disease such as leprosy or madness" (7-8). Since those who die in slavery do so "tragically" due to their condition, it may be necessary that their souls, as evidenced among the Bambara, are brought back to the community. Pobee's conclusion that "[t]he ancestor is the one who lived to a ripe old age and in an exemplary manner or did much to enhance the prestige and standing of the family, clan and tribe" (8) may further explain why those who die in slavery do not qualify to become ancestors, unless, as is the case in *Segu*, priests perform certain rituals.

Even in foreign lands, traditional Bambara religion ensures that its core beliefs are maintained. Hence, ancestors make certain that Malobali meets and marries Romana, his late brother Naba's widow, in accordance with the Bambara cultural laws that require widows to be inherited by their husband's younger brothers. However, Delphine Perret and Steve Arkin, basing their argument on the fact that Malobali's mother is not a Bambara, consider this marriage as resulting from Malobali's blindness because "a mixture of blood seems to provoke a failure of vision and finally a curse" (656). Nonetheless, these critics admit that the marriage falls within Bambara customs (656), a fact acknowledged by Malobali when he marvels "at the foresight and perseverance of the ancestors" (279), who take him through "so many seas and deserts and forests" and concoct a "series of adventures" (Condé 280) that lead to the union. Nonetheless, the new family faces imminent disintegration because Malobali - a follower of traditional religion who disguises himself as a Catholic - has not experienced the kind of slavery and betrayal experienced by Romana, a returning slave and devout Catholic.

Precolonial Religion in *Petals of Blood*

While the indigenous religion presented in Thiong'o's *Petals of Blood* is not as comprehensive as its counterpart in Condé's *Segu* (because Thiong'o's work largely concerns itself with the post-independent Kenyan period), the former offers several insights with regards to the Agikuyu people's indigenous religion. Central to these revelations is the Ilmorog community's reliance on Mwathi wa Mugo, a traditional priest who is deemed to have "spiritual power over both Ilmorog ridge and Ilmorog plains," as he is the one "who advised on the best day for planting seeds or the appropriate day for the herdsmen to move" (17). Mwathi, described as "the stick and the shade that God uses to defend" (114), also provides security because Muturi the blacksmith can only make spears and knives at the former's homestead, "for in beating and bending iron with bellows and hammer, he [the blacksmith] must be protected from the power of evil and envious eyes" (17).

In *Ngugi wa Thiong'o: An Exploration of His Writings*, Cook and Okenimkpe describe Mwathi wa Mugo as "the occult priest, most extraordinary of men, who is portrayed by Ngugi with a rare double-edged irony, ambivalence and scepticism which call into question the validity of fundamental metaphysical beliefs of the Ilmorog villagers, perhaps of Africa at large" (93). Cook and Okenimkpe's argument might appear to be credible because no one in the village acknowledges having ever seen the priest. However, such a stance dismisses the Gikuyu and indeed all Africans' traditional religion without considering its purpose and effectiveness. Further evidence that Cook and Okenimkpe's position is stereotypical may be inferred in their use of the terms "occult" and "metaphysical beliefs" in their description of the traditional religion.

The fact that Mwathi wa Mugo is still a force to be reckoned with even in the post-independent era is evident in that he provides fruitful advice during the famine. He foretells that Ilmorogians will only be saved from imminent death by the sending away of Abdulla's donkey. Although villagers initially think Mwathi alludes to sacrificing the donkey, they eventually realize that the donkey must be sent to Nairobi together with a delegation from the village. This act, which combines the old and the new - for Mwathi represents precolonial Gikuyu religion while Nairobi represents post-independent urbanity - signifies that lingering elements of Gikuyu traditional religion will be realized in ways that accommodate postcolonial economic and political situations. Although the destruction of Mwathi's compound by road workers might, perhaps, be evidence of what Cook and Okenimkpe call the "disintegration of Ilmorog" (94), it is instructive that the action leads to the uncovering and preservation of emblems of Mwathi's power. Indeed, the road workers discover that "Mwathi was a guarding spirit: he had been sitting on a knowledge of many seasons gone: rings, metal work, spears, smelting works" (Thiong'o 266). This discovery forces the government to spare the site and convert it to "an archeological site" (Thiong'o 266), thereby preserving a compelling symbol of the Gikuyu traditional religion.

Wanja's failure to conceive, despite her grandmother's taking her to Mwathi, warrants attention. To begin with, she fails to follow Mwathi's decree that she must have a sexual encounter in the moonlight on the night that the new moon appears - she grows impatient on that night and ends up having sex with Munira in her hut. Moreover, her inability to conceive even after Mwathi's advice may be because as a prostitute, she has defiled herself with foreign values; hence, the indigenous divinities represented by Mwathi will not come to her aid.

As demanded by African communal culture, children, including those of an oppressor, are to be treated well. While Ezekieli is mean even to his own children, Mariamu, a traditionalist and laborer on his farm, is kind to all children including Ezekieli's. Munira, now a grown up and an Ilmorog teacher still remembers Mariamu's kindness, especially "his childhood escapades to tea and to charcoal-roasted potatoes in Mariamu's hut" (15). Unlike other laborers on Ezekieli's farm, Mariamu "never went to church," although "she stood out as holier than all others and more sincere in her splendid withdrawal and isolation in her hut surrounded by five cypress trees" (15). Mariamu's benevolence to Ezekieli's children elevates her to a Christ figure who loves her tormentor in spite of the suffering he inflicts on her. In addition, Munira's assertion that she "was very pious in an undemonstrative way: her piety simply lay in how she carried herself; in how she talked; in her trembling, total absorption in her work" (47), perhaps serves as a contrast between the genuinely pure indigenous religion and the hypocritical version of Christianity represented by Ezekieli. She is also a fearless laborer who dares to protest against "failure to be paid in time" and who remains "respectful to Ezekieli but never afraid of him" (15).

The Indomitable Indigenous Religion in *Chotti Munda and His Arrow*

Unlike information provided about the traditional religions practiced by the Bambara community in Condé's *Segu* and by the Gikuyu in Thiong'o's *Petals of Blood*, details of the indigenous religion in Devi's *Chotti Munda and His Arrow* are scanty, perhaps because this novel's primary goal is to show oppression - mostly economic - of adivasis by mainstream communities in post-independent India. Nevertheless, the novel shows the Mundas, the primary group of adivasis referred to in the text, as having a traditional deity, priests, legends, rituals, and strong beliefs especially about morality. The Mundas are "worshippers of god Haram" and "[f]ollowers of a priest, the pahan" (2). The community is guided by its religion in all its endeavors. At the center of the community is "the pahan or priest [who] is the chief of the village community. They sit with the pahan and settle any problem that comes up" (34). It is for this reason that the pahan resolves that the Mundas should boycott working for Baijnath, the landlord and moneylender, in protest of his referring to Bisra as "moneylender" (33). Like Mwathi in *Petals of Blood*, the pahan guides the Munda society and determines what activities are to be undertaken or abandoned. The pahan similarly asks the Mundas not to "gie bonded labour for a thumbprint, f'r abit of rice," otherwise, he warns, "[t]his bonded labour won' be quit in ten generations" (48, 49).

Contrary to the exploitative moneylenders, adivasis are hardworking, honest people who reject the economic policies borrowed from the British. Indeed, moneylenders are, in the words of Sardesai, et al., swindlers who "exploited the cultivators not only by charging high rates of interest but by certain deceitful measures such as false accounting, forged signatures, etc." (113). William Howitt also depicts moneylenders as extending the colonial exploitation of Indians which started when missionaries "who professed to believe the commands that they should not steal, covet their neighbour's goods, kill, or injure . . . [became] the most covetous, murderous, and tyrannical of men" (202-3); unlike the colonialists, however, the moneylenders who exploit Mundas are fellow Indians. Since, as Lalaji, Baijnath's son and the new moneylender, says, "Adivasis work for incredibly low wages. Don't like bickering" (32), the moneylenders take advantage of the Mundas' pious nature. The adivasis reject the depravity among adherents of the colonial economic and political policies that are prevalent even after independence.

Although the pahan is its undisputed spiritual guide, the community is a flexible society which accommodates the likelihood of a god's reincarnation as a human being. Dhani, and later Chotti, is seen as such a reincarnation. Indeed, Devi reveals that a god had prophesied that he would "be born again in t' belly of a Munda mother, [as] Dhani" (16). It is thus not surprising that Chotti recognizes Dhani as "t' god Haramdeo of archers" (9).

Behind Dhani's power is his arrow-shooting acumen. In an interview, Devi tells Gayatri Chakravorty Spivak that she creates "an arrow that Dhani Munda wants to hand over" as "a symbol for the person who will carry on that continuity" (xi). The continuity she alludes to is with regards to the "[a]rmed uprising led by Birsa Munda from December 1899 - January 1900" (377). The arrow-shooting lessons that Dhani gives to Chotti thus signify the transfer of this divine power. Moreover, Dhani's instruction of Chotti indicates that irrespective of the threat their religion faces from Hinduism, Christianity and the government, it will not be easily silenced. Chotti's "glowing face" (9) during instruction perhaps indicates that arrow-shooting will remain a powerful pillar of the religion that will "glow" and save the besieged society. Chotti's position as a spiritual leader is further enhanced when he marries Sugana Munda's daughter; this marriage is important because Sugana is a pahan. Like Dhani, Chotti is more powerful than a priest because "although there is a pahan, it is upon him [Chotti] that the task of leading Chotti's Munda society is devolving" (51), and because in times of crises, "even Dusad-Ganju-Chamar-Dhobi will obey him if need be" (51). Unlike the pahan, who only provides spiritual guidance to Mundas, Chotti emerges as a political figure of all the oppressed groups, including low-caste Hindus. The epic trip, similar to the one taken by Ilmorogians in Thiong'o's *Petals of Blood*, which adivasis and low-caste Hindus of Chotti village take to Tohri in search of government intervention during a famine, confirms Chotti's stature as a mystical figure.

Chotti's arrow is credited with the community's most successful revenge missions in the face of political corruption and injustice, which permeate post-independent India. Indeed, the arrow is praised for killing Tasildar Singh, the manager who beats and banishes Puran Munda. Puran, Chotti's former student, mysteriously kills Tasildar who is just "[o]n horse back" and "[a]n arrow pierced his back" (143). Moreover, when "Budha, Gaya and two other Mundas [both Chotti's former students] fire their settlements as they leave" (120) for the Dhai mission, the arrow is credited with starting the fire. The indomitable power of the indigenous religion is perhaps most evident towards the end of the novel when landlords, moneylenders and government administrators threaten hundreds of adivasis with terror in response to the killing of Romeo and Pahlwan, two members of the Youth League who have brutally killed several Mundas. Chotti takes responsibility for the murder and dares the administrators to "raise terror" (363). In a final show of his religion's power, "he becomes god Haram, lights up his countenance with a transcendental smile" (360), and declares that neither the administrators nor the police will "stay alive" (363) should they punish anyone for the murder of Romeo and Pahlwan.

Besides arrow-shooting, other elements of the Munda's traditional religion are fear-instilling. For instance, the manager, whose cruelty drives the Mundas of Kurmi village to the Tomaru mission, "is afraid of a hunt festival song in the voice of an emaciated old man in a deserted village" (94). The old man is the village's pahan who - in an act of self-sacrifice and utter defiance against both post-independent India's exploitative economic system and the lure of Christianity - has refused to join his fellow villagers in leaving his village and religion for the safety of the Christian mission. The fact that the manager, despite being guarded by a sentry, runs away "for fear of the unknown" (94), shows that the pahan and the religion he represents are to be dreaded even when most vulnerable. The pahan eventually offers himself as a sacrificial lamb when he enters the forest that is infested with wild animals. This entry, Devi states, "is symbolic," because "[w]ith it, at the meeting point of night and dawn, the tale of the Mundas of Kurmi village comes to an end" (96).

The Creative Power of Traditional Religion in *Ways of Dying*

Although Zakes Mda's *Ways of Dying* does not illustrate a comprehensive traditional religion like that described in *Segu*, the novel shows that such a religion exists. Noria, who is referred to as "a child of the gods" (45), is the medium of traditional African deities. Because she "sang for the spirits that gave Jwara the power to create the figurines," without her song, Jwara could not create the "images of strange people and animals that he had seen in his dreams" (29). In "Aspects of African Traditional Religion," Pobee identifies singing as an activity that accompanies work in the African society. He writes:

> *Singing*, now and in the past, is central to the lives of most Africans. When an African works on his farm, he sings; when he goes fishing, he sings. When a carpenter or a mason hammers away, he sings. In songs are laid bare *homo Africanus* in his hopes and fears, his joys and sorrows. (3-4)

Noria's song appears meaningless because she started singing for Jwara when she was seven. Nonetheless, the song had supernatural powers because whenever she sang, "[e]ven the birds forgot about the beetles, and

71

joined the bees hovering over the workshop, making buzzing and chirping sounds in harmony with Noria's song" (29). Mysteriously, Noria also becomes pregnant despite the fact that she has "eschewed all contact with men" (149). In a demonstration of reincarnation, the child, when it is born, resembles the one she had had before, and even has the same birthmarks.

Jwara's spirit orders Nefolovhondwe, an affluent man, to deliver his figurines to Toloki. Nefolovhondwe's obedience implies that despite his adoption of Western culture, ancestors still hold power over him. Mda informs the reader about Nefolovhondwe's powerlessness in the hands of Jwara's spirit:

> Nefolovhondwe thought that he would resist and win. How could he be defeated by a poor man like Jwara? With all the people he dealt with in his day-to-day life, his word was final. He was idolized and almost worshipped by people who were in awe of his millions. He was even invited to dinners by White people who held the reins of government . . ..
> Then his fleas began to die. In his nightly visits, Jwara laughed and danced, and warned that more fleas would die if Nefolovhondwe did not do what he, Jwara, was ordering him to do. (206)

Jwara's spirit tortures Nefolovhodwe and promises to give him no rest until he takes his figurines to Toloki, his son. Nefolovhodwe's life, with its fantasies and magnificence, is continually threatened by Jwara's spirit. His fleas begin to die, and Jwara "stressed that this was no longer a request, but an order. They were going to duel to the end, until one of them gave up or gave in" (206). As a sign of victory for the traditional African religion, Nefolovhodwe gives in, drives to the village for the figurines, and then searches for Toloki until he traces him to the slums.

3.2 Education as a Means of Religious Conversion

While acknowledging that his family and others in his Ogidi village were Christians, Chinua Achebe writes, in *Morning Yet on Creation Day*, that education was the bait that the missionaries used to lead them to conversion. He writes that although new converts engaged in apostasy, "the bounties of the Christian God were not to be taken lightly - education, paid jobs, and many other advantages that nobody in his right senses could underrate" (115). Without demonizing the ability to write in English,

Achebe castigates the use of education to instill not only a foreign religion but also foreign cultural beliefs. Remembering a few examples of the books he read as a young student, Achebe remarks that other than enjoying the "strange beauty" of *A Midsummer Night's Dream*, he could not decode its title's "magic phrase," which he interpreted as "an incantation that conjured up scenes and landscapes of an alien, happy, and unattainable land" (121). He also admits reading *Ije Onye Kraist*, an Igbo adaptation of *Pilgrim's Progress*, but he could only worry about its "frightening pictures" (121). Achebe argues, then, that the conversion of many Africans to Christianity left them "at the crossroads of cultures" (*Morning Yet* 119). This placement at the "crossroads," he says, "does have a certain dangerous potency; dangerous because a man might perish there wrestling with multiple-headed spirits, but also he might be lucky and return to his people with the boon of prophetic vision" (*Morning Yet* 119). The point, as Achebe implies, is that priests of colonial religions established learning institutions through which they passed their religious beliefs to their indigenous students.

Education, Christianity and Islam in *Segu*

In *Segu*, Maryse Condé reveals that while both Islam and Christianity are to be credited with expanding literacy to Africa, both undertake this task at the expense of the indigenous religion. The two religions' use of education to instill foreign notions is best captured in Kodjoe's warning to Malobali that, like the Arabs: "[t]he English won't take any notice of you unless you're converted to their religion!" (227). This conversion is rightly seen by Malobali as a rejection of his own identity and an adoption of another as, in his words, it amounts to a denial of "the gods of one's fathers, and through them their whole culture and civilization" (228). Although circumstances eventually force Malobali to take up a Christian name and act as a Christian, he swears never to really convert "even under torture" (228). Eucaristus da Cunha, another reluctant convert and descendant of African slaves, questions the motive of converting Africans to Christianity which he equates to "imposing an alien civilization upon it" while in fact "every people have its own civilization, subtended by its belief in its own gods" (386).

Because it bases the transmission of Islamic teachings in its institutions, Islam also uses education to fight Bambara traditional beliefs. In fact, Tiekoro converts to Islam during a period when, as David Robinson observes in "An Approach to Islam in West African History," Islamic teachers are invading the Segu region and using education as a basis of proselytizing (110). Robinson identifies one of these Islamic scholars as "Sidi al-Mukhtar, based in Arawan to the north of Timbuktu" (110) who "trained a whole generation of leaders who fanned out into different regions of West Africa and in turn trained their own disciples" (110). Tiekoro's training in Timbuktu and Jenne thus qualifies him to be one of the leaders envisioned by Islamic scholars like Sidi al-Mukhtar. Upon returning to Segu, Tiekoro forces his community to learn Arabic because, he declares, "Islam is the religion of the future" (Condé 165). His mother reveals that "Tiekoro thinks that now all the boys in the family ought to learn to read and write Arabic" (Condé 165). To achieve this goal, Tiekoro establishes a *zawiya*, an Islamic school, on his family's land. The school attracts boys from the entire community and becomes a center of indoctrination, where children are equipped with Arabic cultural notions at the expense of their traditional beliefs. This indoctrination is clear in Tiekoro's order that the children write the name of Allah on the walls opposite their beds so that it is the first thing they see when they awake (Condé 328). Similarly, he urges them to "speak it with fervor from the depths of [their] souls, so that it may be the first name to issue" from their lips or to strike their ears (Condé 329). If, as earlier stated, African religions pervade all spheres of traditional Africans' lives, it is clear from Tiekoro's teachings that Islam is to replace traditional Bambara religion in these spheres. Tiekoro's role may thus be equated to that of one of Sidi al-Mukhtar's students,

> Sidiyya al-kabir, who returned to Southern Mauritania, established his own school and library at Butilimit, and then trained a new generation of learned Muslims who played important roles in the dissemination of Islam in the Western Sudan. (Robinson 110)

Contrary to Tiekoro's thought that Islam will erase fear, the Islamic schools foreshadow the violence that is to be witnessed when prominent Muslim priests fight for power and territory towards the end of the novel. Tiekoro's teacher, El-Hadj Ibrahima, is a brutal instructor, for he beat "little

Moors and Somonos in his school, whom he also burned sometimes with sticks taken from the fire when their recitations from the Koran really displeased him" (38). Ibrahima's ruthlessness is similar to El-Hadj Baba Abou's whimsical punishment of his students, which is propelled by his obsession with "lofty principles and pre-occupation with God [which] did not make him any the more tolerant of human weakness" (50). Similar ill treatment of students is demonstrated by Cheikou Hamadou, to whose school Tiekoro sends his son Muhammad. Hamadou puts his students "on public charity, begging from door to door for their food, sleeping on the bare floor and never washing, as a sign of humility" (337). Muhammad's description of his fellow students as "painfully thin" with "the tight shiny skin that goes with malnutrition" and revealing "scratches and scars on their arms, legs and hands, as if there had been an epidemic of small pox or mange" (338) illustrates the extent of the physical abuse meted on these young learners.

The afore-mentioned mistreatment of children by Islamic teachers sharply contrasts with the humane impartation of education in the African traditional system, in which religious knowledge is transmitted partly through interesting stories told by mothers in the evenings in an atmosphere of nurturing affection. Indeed, educators of the indigenous African educational system are portrayed as charitable and accommodating in contrast with the Condescending indifferent Muslims Tiekoro finds in Timbuktu. To begin with, when he and Siga arrive at the town, they are made to sit on a "wide mud seat built along the front of the house" (47) of Abou, their anticipated host. Abou eventually turns Siga away because he is not mentioned in the letter of introduction that Tiekoro brings from Ibrahima. The cruelty of sending him away with no food or shelter in a foreign land foreshadows the callousness with which Abou treats his students.

In contrast, the African system of education enhances cleanliness and communal hospitality, and treats its students with dignity. It is not surprising that it is his indigenous religion which comes to Siga's aid after he is rejected by Islam. This aid is in the form of a boy who advises Siga to call himself Ahmed and hide his baubles in order to appear as a Muslim. The boy, who has similarly called himself Ismael for survival, promptly gets Siga a job as a donkey boy. Tiekoro also compares this reception by Abou with his parents' reception of visitors in his Segu homeland: ". . . how Nya would take them to the rest hut, send them hot water to bathe in and then provide them with a lavish meal" (47). This contrast shows that despite its shortcomings, the African traditional religion advocates for non-discriminative treatment of human beings unless they are avowed political enemies or captives of war. Islam also appears unreasonable when its clerics beat Tiefolo senselessly as he unknowingly enters a mosque on horse-back. To the credit of Bambara traditional religion, an "incarnation of a spirit sent by Koumare [the priest]" (156) in the form of a servant dresses Tiefolo's wounds during the period of his imprisonment by these Islamic adherents. Furthermore, contrary to indigenous education which is provided to all, Islamic education becomes a means of discrimination. For instance, Tiekoro is looked down upon because members of the Bambara community are not expected to take up "study and Islam" (46). This discrimination, as Tiekoro observes, negates the principles the religion itself advocates, including that "all men were equal, like teeth in a comb" (51).

The Books, the Chapels and the Flag in *Petals of Blood*

Thiong'o's *Petals of Blood* also shows religion as an integral part of Western education in both colonial and early post-independent Kenya. It is not surprising that the administration of Siriana includes principles of Christianity in its largely Eurocentric educational system. It is notable that Thiong'o himself was educated in Alliance High School which, as Carol Sicherman writes, "had been founded by a coalition of missionary groups in 1926" ("Colonial Education" 13). Sicherman asserts that religious schools were common, and that, as exemplified by Alliance, such schools employed what she calls an "ardently Christian ideology" (13) in order to distance students from their (students') cultural influence. She summarizes Alliance as having been "an institution controlled through the colonial examination system, through extracurricular activities, and through the muscular Christianity characteristic of such missionary ventures" ("Colonial Education" 14). Siriana, in Thiong'o's *Petals of Blood*, appears to be modeled along the lines of Alliance because students are expected to salute "the British flag every morning and every evening to the martial sound from the bugles and drums" (29) of the school band. After this colonial ritual, students are required to "march in orderly military lines to the chapel to raise choral voices to the Maker: Wash me, Redeemer, and I shall be whiter than snow" (29). Thiong'o's use of this song, which feigns religious sanctification, may be interpreted as a sarcastic reference to the colonial erasure of African culture.

Furthermore, instead of praying for what is relevant to them, or for their African leaders, Siriana students are required to "pray for the continuation of an Empire that had defeated the satanic evil which had erupted in Europe to try the children of God" (29). In addition, the school's motto, *"For God and Empire"* (27) emblazoned in the school uniform, suggests that the central role of the school is to instill notions about Christianity and the British imperialism. Indeed, Sicherman identifies religion as one of the major components of such institutions, when she declares about Alliance High School: "Religion was central" ("Colonial Education" 14). The difference between Alliance High School and Siriana lies only in time period because Thiong'o was in Alliance during the colonial period, while Siriana is portrayed as postsindependent institution. This depiction, as James A. Ogude suggests, means that "the ills of the colonial state are simply reproduced in the post-colonial state" (91).

The cultural domination associated with Western education notwithstanding, education imparts liberative power. Thus, only those who lack it, such as Ilmorogian villagers, equate research visits to the moon with showing "no fear even of God" and as attempts to go "disturb God in his realm" (81). It may be plausible to infer, then, that if it were purged of its indoctrinating elements, Western education is necessary for post-independent survival not only among Kenyans but also among all formerly colonized peoples because it gives such researchers as Mutuiria, a character in Thiongo's *Devil on the Cross*, the skills to probe African cultural norms and the extent to which they have been destroyed by colonization. In addition, it is literacy that enables Munira in *Petals of Blood* to write the report, thereby enabling the author to tell his tale.

Education and Religious Conversion in *The God of Small Things*

In *The God of Small Things*, Roy discusses various ideas in connection with the use of education for conversion, although they are not brought out in as much depth as Condé's *Segu* or Thiong'o's *Petals of Blood*. As Maria

Sabina Alexandru states , "Even though her writing engages with wider social, political and religious issues, Roy makes it very clear that her subject matter is not 'big mother India' but the 'small things' in people's lives (as the title of her novel points out)" (165). Her adherence to "small things," however, may be partly because she writes from the perspective of Rahel and Estha, Ammu's twins. Nevertheless, the interaction between religion, education and culture comes out vividly when Baby Kochamma makes the twins practice a Christian car song to be sung on the way back from the airport. Roy notes that the twins are required "to form the words properly, and be particularly careful about their pronunciation" (36). Baby Kochamma's efforts to ensure that the children pronounce words with a British accent are evident in the song:

> *Rej-Oice in the Lo-Ord Or-Orlways*
> *And again I say rej-Oice*
> *RejOice*
> *RejOice*
> *And again I say rej-Oice.* (36)

The song, whose theme is joy, also heightens the contradiction of the uncertainty, disaffection, and despair in which the family lives, and foreshadows a bigger contradiction where the death of Sophie Mol, the twins' cousin, will lead to further estrangement within the family.

While credit must be given to Christian denominations for establishing Christian schools, the instruction provided in those schools appears to be so puritanical that it removes Indians from reality. For instance, Rahel is enlisted in a Christian institution where "breasts were not acknowledged," because "they weren't supposed to exist" (18) in such a sacred institution. The education provided in a school like Rahel's necessitates a scrutiny of the origin of Christian institutions in India as well as what informed their establishment. K.S. Sardesai, et al. state that during the colonial period, "[t]he English schools opened by the missionaries were mostly intended as instruments of conversion" (138). Although Rahel's school is not run by foreigners, it is expected that - as in the case of Alliance High School where Thiong'o was educated - such a Christian school is likely to inherit certain elements of colonization. Devastated by both her mother's death and her brother being sent to their father, and perhaps in search of her identity,

Rahel is rightly accused of "hiding behind doors and deliberately colliding with her seniors" (Roy 17) in an attempt to see if their breasts hurt. While Rahel's behavior is arguably unacceptable, it is needful to state that as a girl of eleven, and thus at the threshold of puberty, she suffers as a result of the absence of an adult who would provide information on adolescence.

Christianity as Locale for Education in *Chotti Munda and His Arrow*

Because *Chotti Munda and His Arrow* is set within a community that rejects post-independent economic, social and political systems, the novel does not focus on education as a means by which Mundas are forced to change their culture. Nonetheless, the novel portrays the community's need for formal education, and depicts Christian missions as providers of this education. Whereas in *Segu* characters like Tiekoro willingly convert to new religions and others such as Eucaristus da Cunha willingly leave for Western countries in pursuit of Western religious education, Mundas in *Chotti Munda and His Arrow* perceive the Christian missions as places of refuge whenever their existence is threatened by government officials and moneylenders. For this reason, although Mundas, such as Sukha and Bikhna who flee Kurmi village for the Tomaru mission, are likely to be recipients of formal education, their presence in the mission is driven primarily by the desire to escape from the cruelty of Kurmi village's manager.

Furthermore, in spite of the fact that Mundas who acquire Western education through missions do so by coincidence, education among the Mundas appears emancipative rather than destructive. For instance, when lamenting that Mundas are cheated because they "don' know book-learnin'" (107), Budha acknowledges that "[t]' Mission teaches book-learnin' too" (107). While Budha does not openly call on Mundas to go to the missions in pursuit of formal education, his statement shows this pursuit as a possible undertaking if the community is to acquire skills of emancipation against their oppressors. In addition, the fact that the aged pahan of Chotti village installs a successor who "as a result of living close to a Christian Munda village . . . has learned to read and write Hindi" (122) implies that education is necessary among the Mundas of post-independent India, and that this education is acquired through proximity to Christians. It is expected that such a successor will not only use his education to resist such exploitative practices as using thumbprints to commit oneself to many years of labor, but he may also encourage Mundas to pursue formal education.

3.3 Foreign Religions and Cultural Breakdown

In *Morning Yet on Creation Day*, Achebe writes that in Ogidi village where he was born, the division between Christians and non-Christians was "much more definite . . . than it is today," and that this schism resulted in some of the members of the village, including Achebe's family, being referred to as "'the people of the church' or 'the association of God'" while others were known as "the heathen or even 'the people of nothing'" (115). Achebe's revelation of the religious partition in his home village exemplifies the contribution of Christianity towards the destruction of kinship and communal ties existent in precolonial societies. This theme of familial disintegration also finds expression in Achebe's *Things Fall Apart* where the practices that bind the African society "have fallen apart" and the clan "can no longer act like one" (176). Achebe fervidly indicts Christianity for this severance, as it emanates from the fact that "a man can now leave his father and his brother. He can curse the gods of his fathers and his ancestors, like a hunter's dog that suddenly goes mad and turns on his master" (*Things* 167).

Familial and Societal estrangement in *Segu*

Unlike the case in *Things Fall Apart* where Christianity is the religion that foments rebellion in the Umuofia community, the "falling apart" in *Segu* is initially fuelled by Islam, which divides the Bambara ethnic community. In an assessment of the influence of Islam in Algeria, Ricardo Rene Laremont writes in *Islam and the Politics of Resistance in Algeria: 1783-1992* that the Islamic community "is a community in which its political discourse and political institutions that emerge from that discourse are founded upon a vision emphasizing justice as substantive rather than procedural, that justice has origins in a moral order that is derived from religion, and that its delivery is possible through the application of scriptural laws" (1). Given Laremont's perception of an Islamic community, one would expect that the invasion of Islam in a region such as Segu in Condé's *Segu* amounts to colonization because Islamic teachers aim not only at converting the Bambara to Islam but also at substituting their traditional legal system with an Islamic one.

The decline of the community begins with the fall from grace of Dousika's family, which in turn has its genesis from the demotion of Dousika from the king's council. Nevertheless, Dousika attributes this demotion to Tiekoro's abandonment of the local religion for Islam, and views Samake and his lieutenants as mere "instruments of a higher anger aroused by his own son"(35). The extent to which foreign religions will annihilate the African traditional family unit is evidenced in the paradox that Tiekoro is the eldest son who should be "the very one who ought to have been his pride" (35).

Condé's *Segu* depicts kinship ties as crucial to the African society. Indeed, some decisions, such as the one involving Tiekoro's impending journey to Timbuktu, require that both the living and the dead be consulted. For this reason, Koumare consults Dousika's late father and grandfather and informs Dousika of their resolution to let Tiekoro leave. This resolution, as Koumare asserts, connotes the ancestors' foreknowledge of the imminent destruction of the indigenous religion by Islam. One's ancestors play an important role in his life; hence, the living are required to relate well with both their living and dead family members. The latter are in the form of spirits that roam at night "taking revenge for the neglect of the living and trying to communicate with them through dreams" (Condé 32). In addition, the fact that each member of the community is known by the family name indicates that families are the building blocks of the community - the community exists because families exist.

While African traditional religion values and functions within the aforementioned kinship ties between members of extended families, Islam negates these kinship ties and re-classifies members of the community as either Muslims or heathens. Koumare prophecies that the Islamic god will break up relationships within the African society because Allah:

> ...would be like a sword. In his name the earth would run with blood, fire would crackle through the fields. Peaceful nations would take up arms, son would turn away from father, brother from brother. A new aristocracy would be born, and new relationships between human beings. (42)

This predicted culpability of Islam with regards to breaking the family unit is best captured in the change that takes place in Tiekoro, who looks down upon his community's cultural practices after switching to Islam. He views his brother Tiefolo, a hunter, as "a boor who covered himself with gris-gris to track down animals that had never done him any harm," and as one whose reputation for bravery was "tantamount to a reputation for stupidity" (351). Moreover, before conversion, he "had looked up to his father as a god. He had admired him much more than the Mansa," but "started to think of him as a barbarian and an ignorant drinker of *dolo*" when "the achievements of the Muslims had begun to acquire importance in his life" (22). Tiekoro directs similar contempt towards Koumare, his family's priest, whom he considers as "a middle aged man, almost old, with a bristly unkempt beard, his body hung with the heads of birds, deer's horns wrapped in red cloth, cows' tails and a grayish goatskin. A regular scare crow" (43). This view of non-Muslim community members as "barbarian" grows into a wedge that divides the families and by extension the entire community. In an attempt to introduce a new type of kinship, Islam as exemplified by Tiekoro's lesson to his son, Muhammad, teaches that "[b]elievers are brothers even when separated by kinship or space, because, through religion, they share the same origin of faith" (467).

Islam also causes physical separation because converts are expected to travel away from home in pursuit of Islamic education. This separation interferes with the traditional family structure. Indeed, the departure of Tiekoro not only affects Nya and adds to "her resentment" of Dousika, but also affects his brother Naba who becomes "a kind of orphan" (59). As expected in a culture in which older children mentor the younger ones, Naba "had grown up in his elder brother's shadow, learning to walk by holding on to his legs, learning to fight by thumping his chest, learning to dance by watching him perform in the evening amid a circle of admiring girls" (59). By showing the new friendship that Naba establishes with Tiefolo upon Tiekoro's departure as responsible for Naba's disappearance, Condé indicates that Islam stands guilty of the capture and eventual enslavement of Naba. Indeed, had Tiekoro not left for Timbuktu, Naba would not have ventured into hunting which is blamed for his capture.

Upon Tiekoro's return to Segu, he is appointed member of the king's council in charge of Islamic affairs. This appointment alters the power structure in both the family and the community. The power of Diemogo, the family *fa*, dwindles, as he is overshadowed by Tiekoro. In addition, instead of submitting to Diemogo, Nya consults with Tiekoro from whom she solicits advice "about all that was going on: betrothals, marriages, name-giving ceremonies and dowries" (327). Islam also drives a wedge between Tiekoro and Siga, as Fatima, Siga's Islamic wife, values Tiekoro more than Siga who has remained a follower of traditional religion.

Although Siga eventually becomes the *fa* of the family when Diemogo dies, he is unable to hold the family together, because, as Condé states, the family and community are threatened with the influx "of new ideas and values [which] lurked everywhere" (425). Siga's suffering from elephantiasis during his tenure as the family's *fa*, which makes him "go slowly, taking very small steps" (425), is thus emblematic of the broken cultural order.

Islam's interference with relationships within the African society is not limited to families and single communities. While inter-tribal differences already exist in pre-Islamic Africa, such differences are based on political rather than religious schisms. For instance, Segu politically and economically dominates the region, and the Bambara people have conquered their neighbors such as the Fulani. However, as Tiekoro learns when he goes to Jenne, the Fulani people have embraced Islam and now use it to fight their enemies.

The invasion of Segu by El Hadj Omar also portrays Islam as a force of cultural disintegration. In his essay "An Approach to Islam in West African History," David Robinson refers to El Hadj Omar as "Al-Hajj Umar" and recognizes him as the pioneer of an "imperialist" jihad in the region (114). Robinson states that Omar's actions emanate from his appointment as the "chief agent for the dissemination of the Tijaniyya order," an order which "made strong claims as a superior revelation and brotherhood" (114). Robinson's information enables *Segu's* reader to understand the motive behind Omar's wish to annihilate Bambara traditional religion worshippers alongside Muslims who do not adhere to the Tijaniya brotherhood.

Although Omar is escorted out of the village and Tiekoro condemned to death, Soumaworo's prophecy that Omar's visit will spell trouble for Segu is confirmed when red rains fall, and a wide crack appears on the walls of the local king's quarters on the day Omar arrives in Segu. Condé asserts that "there was no need for fetish priest or expert in the occult to interpret these signs" as it is obvious that Omar "would bring bloodshed to Segu" (358). Indeed, after the initial ejection from the village, Omar later presides over murders all over the region surrounding Segu. Thus, contrary to being the peaceful religion that Tiekoro seeks, Islam replaces the slaughter of animals with the slaughter of human beings. Condé states that, among others, Omar has all menfolk slain in Guemon-Banka, the whole population killed in Baroumba, and the king and the whole population killed in Kaarta (469). So heinous are these killings that Muhammad, Tiekoro's son, finds "himself hating a God who manifested Himself through fire and sword" (470). Islam is also responsible for the death of Tiekoro's brother, Tiefolo, who is killed by Alhadji Guidado for resisting the destruction of the altars of his traditional gods.

Nonetheless, the sudden death of Mansa Demba, the Segu king who has allowed the destruction of some of these altars, may be an indication that local divinities are indomitable beings who, as Condé states, respond "swiftly and strongly to the insult offered them" (478). The destruction of Tiekoro's *zawiya* may also denote that the local religion will not be fully annihilated, and that despite making serious forays into Africa, foreign religions will not go unchecked.

The new religions also introduce hitherto unknown race-based discrimination. Siga, for instance, wonders why "a black skin made you a creature apart" (196) because "[t]he Bambara [like all other African communities] were as strong, proud and creative as any other people" (196). Worse still, those who have been exposed to racial discrimination practice it against their fellow Africans. For instance, unaware that Malobali is her late husband's brother, Romana welcomes Father Ulrich and Father Etienne into her house but tells Malobali to "stay outside" (257). This treatment, despite Father Ulrich's casual proclamation that Malobali "is a child of God, too" (257), reinforces the racial discrimination learnt by Romana from the Whites during her enslavement in Brazil. Furthermore, that the priests do not condemn Romana's action further highlights their implicit approval of this prejudice. One may conclude that Romana's bias against Malobali emphasizes the colonial attitude that has replaced African hospitality that was evident in her during the early stages of slavery. This "traditional hospitality" (263) is demonstrated by Modupe's mother, who receives Malobali after his eviction from Romana's house.

As mentioned above, Condé's *Segu* shows that the arrival of Islam, Christianity and slave trade leads to the allocation of new names to members of the Bambara community. The question of an individual's name becomes paramount when one considers Gayatri Chakravorty Spivak's argument in "Poststructuralism, Marginality, Postcoloniality and Value," where she makes two crucial declarations: first, that "[p]resumed cultural identity often depends on a name" (198) and, second, that "[t]he feeling of cultural identity almost always presupposes a language" (199). Spivak's assertion suggests that since one's name, its meaning, its pronunciation, and its source say something about his or her culture, substituting an individual's name is tantamount to substituting his or her cultural background.

Consequently, it is necessary to discuss naming customs among the Bambara, and to evaluate the effect that change of names had on indigenous cultures. Suzman writes that "[c]hildren in many African societies have meaningful names - unlike their Western counterparts, whose names are primarily labels" (253). Although Suzman's article refers to the naming customs among the contemporary Zulu community of South Africa, her statement emphasizes the importance that Africans assign to their names. The gravity of the destruction of this elaborate naming system during Malobali's imposed conversion to Christianity is revealed when a White priest changes his name to Samuel merely "[b]y [merely] pouring a drop of water on his forehead" (Condé 254). This unsolicited change of name is connected with language, for the priest also forbids him from using his language and teaches him French, "the only language he considered worthy" (Condé 254). Condé equates this removal of one's cultural name and indigenous language to condemnation to "the strongest and subtlest of all jails" (254).

To be fair, the White priest who imposes Christianity on Malobali is to be commended for rescuing him from the sea. Malobali is fleeing the Ashanti kingdom after raping Ayaovi, an eleven-year-old Ashanti girl. The man he finds at the fort promises to help him escape but hands him over to the ship's captain, an apparent slave trader, who binds him and readies him for sale as a slave. Believing that he is aided by traditional divine powers, Malobali manages to untie himself and jump into the sea where the White priest finds him "on the sand - naked, chilled to the bone, weak, terrified"

(253). That the priest enslaves him and subsequently forces him to become a Christian instead of trying to help him return to his home, however, purges him of any messianic qualities.

Similarly, Naba is casually re-named Jean Baptiste "during a semblance of baptism in the chapel of the fort" (97) in the West African Coast. This baptism, Condé reveals, is to signify control over the select slaves who are assigned domestic chores. The "domestication" of slaves who work for slave traders at the fort is contrasted with "the human cattle bundled into slave houses," which is merely "a nameless, suffering mass, waiting to be sent to the Americas" (97). Condé further explains that for slaves to be accepted as worthy to work for the fort officials, they are "baptized and given Christian names" (97). The officials thus imply that the second group, devoid of any names is "untamed," while the forced Christianization of the former is a mark of purification from African traditions.

Although Christianity appears as the justification for the change of slaves' names, Trevor Burnard argues that all slaves had to have their names changed: "White owners had made a determined effort to rename their slaves - part of the transformative process whereby Africans became their property" (329). Giving the example of Thistlewood, a slaveholder in Jamaica, Burnard writes that most slaveholders knew that Africans had names "to which they assigned near magical importance"; therefore, the fact "[t]hat names were so important to Africans might have been good reason for whites like Thistlewood to assume control over them, thereby announcing their mastery" (330). Consequently, the change of names such as those of Malobali and Naba signifies their masters' desire to obliterate their African cultural heritage which is deemed uncivilized. Moreover, the tradition of changing converts' names has no solid biblical foundation.[1] The baptism ceremonies conducted for slaves like Malobali, are likely to be sham procedures because their main drive is to alter slaves' identity. Baptism, in such instances, serves a commercial rather religious purpose because it precedes or accompanies slavery.

Given the above discussion, the explanation provided in the novel by Reverend Mr. Williams, a European missionary, to justify the awkward names that have been assigned to slaves and their children is hypocritical. Williams argues that "[t]he poor devils lost their identity crossing the Atlantic. They had to be called something" (Condé 383). The admission that Africans have lost their culture notwithstanding, Williams's reference to

Africans as "devils" is unjustifiable and in disregard of the Christian ethos he is supposed to propagate. His statement that the slaves "lost" their identity is also hypocritical because the slaves did not actually lose it; instead, they were forcefully torn away from their real "selves" and forced to take up "foreign" names and "selves." Furthermore, his argument that these slaves "had to be called something" is an inaccurate attempt to indicate that the slaves were mere objects and not human beings capable of determining their names. Indeed, that the slaves and their descendants continually yearn to rejuvenate their cultural identity is evident in that, in spite of his possession of a foreign name and Western education, Eucaristus is "obsessed" with a "desire to find the home of his father's family, in Segu, somewhere in the Sudan" (384). As a child of parents who have been alienated from their motherland before their death, Eucaristus is severely estranged from African culture and is thus unable to use "Traore," his family name.

Islam, like Christianity, also imposes foreign names on Africans and indoctrinates them with notions of other cultures. As Siga poignantly observes, "the Muslims always saddle" members of his community "with their names, and so do the Christians" (198). Islam's denunciation of African culture is evident in that, before he leaves Segu for Timbuktu to pursue Islamic education, Tiekoro, under the tutelage of El-Hadj Ibrahima, changes his name to Oumar. This change of name marks the genesis of his removal from his community's cultural beliefs, and lays the foundation for his subsequent work to expunge these beliefs from his own community. His appointment to the king's council as a consultant on Muslim affairs upon his return to Segu also places him at a strategic position that enables him to influence regal decisions in support of Islamic culture. He also establishes a zawiya in the family's compound, where hundreds of Bambara children receive Islamic education.

Colonized peoples may also use foreign names to reap the benefits of both worlds. For example, when Siga changes his name to Ahmed, he states categorically that he does not "want to become a Muslim" (49). His change of name is merely a survival tactic that will make him "look like one" and get a job as a donkey boy. This duality symbolizes a split identity, where one has a foreign name and outward look, but is a follower of the traditional religion. Tiekoro, in spite of his abandonment of the African religion, shows an inclination for its priests' services. Indeed, Tiekoro oscillates between Islam and traditional Bambara religion. For instance, when Abou expels him from his school, he attributes this punishment to his rape of Nadie, a member of his tribe whom he should have protected as required by African culture. He also wishes he can find in Timbuktu a Bambara traditional "priest capable of understanding and interpreting the will of the unseen" (112). Tiekoro's predicament signifies that even those who convert to new religions return to their traditional religions during the time of great need.

This incident also demonstrates the dilemma faced by African converts to both Islam and Christianity as they negotiate their cultural beliefs and the principles of the new religions. Smith explains this double identity as emanating from the fact that "Maryse Condé's characters experience a feeling of mental exile no less acute as their experiential exile . . .. They try unsuccessfully to reach the deeper levels of their psyche from which they feel hopelessly remote" (387). Smith asserts that these character "are both acutely aware of their inner inconsistencies and of their own inability to reach a harmonious psychological and emotional balance" (387). Tiekoro illustrates this "conflict between his heart and his head, between instinctive feelings and intellectual reasoning," because his view of his father as a heathen "didn't mean he didn't love him any more" (22). Islam also forces Tiekoro to pretend that all is well while in reality he rationalizes internal turmoil. When Birame and Molara bring home Olubunmi, Malobali's son, Tiekoro sermonizes away Malobali's death as "cause for celebration" (313), although he is guilty of having forced Malobali to flee the homestead. Indeed, Condé says that despite pretension to the contrary, "Tiekoro was suffering tortures," because he felt responsible for Naba's and Malobali's deaths as well as Nadie's . . .. But the personality he had adopted years ago, that of a sage preoccupied by God alone, clung to him . . .. He couldn't stop himself from saying the words, making the gestures and adopting the attitudes of his double" (315). Thus, Islam, Tiekoro admits, makes him appear "[o]utwardly perhaps a success, but inwardly full of regrets and frustration" (362). The religion fails to be a "refuge, freeing him from the practices that had repelled him in the religion of his fathers" (362), because it causes more pain not only to him but to his family and community. Similar cultural duality is demonstrated by Romana, a staunch Catholic, who turns to her indigenous religion in search of a cure for Malobali. She dutifully buys the black sheep prescribed by Wolo, a traditional priest, leaving bystanders intrigued at the way she "seemed to be led away by the huge animal" (307).

Unlike Siga, who is at liberty to practice his true religion or follow his customs secretly, those who are in slavery are denied the opportunity to practice their religions. Allahina, the boy who feeds Naba after he is captured and sold as a slave, tells the latter that his master has given him an Islamic name although he does not follow Islam. While Allahina is not forced to practice Islam, changing his name is calculated to alienate him from his own religious and ancestral background. Siga's statement that "Naba would lose his name and identity and become just an animal toiling in the fields" (80) indicates that the substitution of slaves' names with those of the cultures and religions of their slave masters is a step in the master's systematic effort at obliterating their subjects' identities, because names connote one's ethnic values, kinship ties, and ethnic affiliation. The fact that a name enables an individual to identify with his or her community explains why "Naba's eyes filled with tears" (105) after announcing his name to Ayodele as "Naba" rather than as "Jean Baptiste." Ayodele, who belongs to the group that is considered nameless, similarly proclaims her name, thereby joining Naba in re-asserting her identity. Consequently, Condé interprets the pair's action as tantamount to building a bridge because they have "named themselves, [and] taken their place in the long line of humanity" (105). This interpretation portends that re-naming a people denies them "their place" as human beings who have a unique civilization and a distinctive destiny.

While Birame, a soldier whom Malobali meets in Ouidah, accuses the returnees of being "a rotten bunch of whited apes who look down on everyone and think themselves superior" (268), the reality is that the slavery experience leaves the victims utterly destroyed. For instance, Ayodele's ability to define herself at the onset of her enslavement contrasts with her confusion and devastation when she is eventually sold to Manoel Ignacio da Cunha, a Portuguese slaveholder. Re-named Senhora Romana da Cunha, Ayodele is not only forced to learn Portuguese, but is also unable to fit among fellow Africans upon her return to Africa. This inability to fit among Africans affirms her destruction—through sexual exploitation and forced labor—as well as removal from her innate cultural and religious customs. Ayodele's predicament is, nonetheless, typical of other returnees whose experiences in slavery have made them inept to co-exist among the people of Dahomey. The description of these returnees by Malobali as "blacks . . . speaking a Portuguese sprinkled with a few words of English and French" (258) demonstrates their linguistic confusion. Through domination and cultural dislocation, the returnees have, as Condé states, "lost all memory of their mother tongue, religion and traditions and adopted with enthusiasm the ways of the white men" (399). Slavery by the Europeans, both at home and abroad, has corresponding effects with regards to the erasure of the subjects' cultural exclusivity. For this reason, although Malobali is enslaved within Africa, he, like Naba, is so removed from his cultural roots that when Modupe, a Yoruba girl, introduces him to Birame, he weeps bitterly when he hears "the sound of his own language again" (258).

Demonizing the "other" in *The God of Small Things*

Roy's *The God of Small Things* also demonstrates that even in the post-independence era, Christianity continues to be a dividing force in both the family unit and the community. In fact, Alexandru says that in the novel: "Arundhati Roy has a lot to say about religion and its power to separate rather than unite people as they are engaged in a worldly competition for power" (174). For instance, Father Mulligan, an Irish monk, is "studying Hindu scriptures, in order to be able to denounce them intelligently" (23). Mulligan's action shows that the study of indigenous religions and culture by adherents of Western religion is aimed at providing a means of fighting the local religions. His action is also not uncommon because even early Christian missionaries to India are recorded to have "discredited themselves by their reckless criticism of Hinduisms" (Sardesai, et al. 138). One such early missionary, Reverend Alexander Duff, lived in India for decades "and had done so much for promoting education and social reform, [but he] lost all balance while assailing Hinduism" (Sardesai, et al. 138). Baby Kochamma and Chacko's consideration of Hindus as backward is thus symbolic of their brand of Christianity's disdain for Hinduism. Baby Kochamma says that the Hindu pilgrims "have no sense of *privacy*," while Chacko responds that Hindus "have horns and scaly skins" and "that their babies hatch from eggs" (82). These statements, which dehumanize Hindus, highlight the extent to which religion has divided Indian society. Moreover, Baby Kochamma's dislike for Ammu's twins partly because "they were Half-

Hindu Hybrids whom no self-respecting Syrian Christian would ever marry" (44), indicates that this division is rife even among members of the same family. Baby Kochamma's statement also implies that religion has become another yardstick by which one's worth and qualification as a member of a certain social class is measured. Kochu Maria, the cook, extends this notion in that she "couldn't stop wearing her kunukku because if she did, how would people know that despite her lowly cook's job (seventy-five rupees a month) she was a Syrian Christian, Mar Thomite?" (162).

According to the article "Christians in Kerala," the Mar Thomite group of Syrian Christians was founded around 1800, when Mar Thoma, a Syrian Bishop, started his own sect within the larger Syrian Christian faith (para 8). The article also indicates that Syrian Christianity itself emerged in 345 AD when "about 400 people migrated from Syria and joined the local Kerala church" which had started as early as 52 AD (para 4). As a Syrian Christian, Maria endeavors to distinguish herself from "a Pelaya, or a Pulaya or a Paravan," and carries herself as "a Touchable, upper-caste Christian (into whom Christianity had seeped like tea from a tea bag)" (162).

Although the Hindu caste system is riddled with many problems because it stigmatizes the Untouchables, the introduction of Christianity to Indian society is portrayed as worsening the Untouchables' predicament. Roy writes that when, during the colonial era, a number of Paravans with the incentives of free food and money "converted to Christianity and joined the Anglican church to escape the scourge of Untouchability," they realized "that they had jumped from the frying pan into the fire" because they were segregated from the rest of the Christians and had "to have separate churches, with separate services, and separate priests" (71). Maria Sabrina Alexandru concludes that this segregation of churches "shows the castelessness of Christianity to have brought nothing more than a reformulation of caste separation" (175). Thus, as it does everywhere else, Christianity during colonial India fails to follow its own fundamental teaching that all humanity is equal.

Christianity as practiced in post-independent India also appears discriminative and judgmental. For instance, while the church is willing to conduct a burial for Sophie Mol, a total stranger from London, it refuses to bury Ammu "[o]n several counts" (154), and she has to be cremated. The "several counts" may include Ammu's sexual relationship with Velutha, an Untouchable (against both Christianity's teachings and cultural norms), her being a divorcee, and perhaps her having married a Hindu husband. Nonetheless, that the church does not probe the life of Margaret, Sophie Mol's European mother who is also a divorcee, indicates its capricious discrimination of those it prejudges as sinful.

Exposing Religious Hypocrisy in *Petals of Blood*

In *Petals of Blood*, Thiong'o similarly depicts Christianity as practiced in post-independent Kenya as a hypocritical religion that removes followers from their cultural reality. This removal is most evident in the fact that Reverend Jerrod Brown drops his African name, Kamau. Jerrod's interaction with Ilmorogians also exemplifies the hypocrisy of Christianity of this period. When the Ilmorog delegation visits his house seeking help for a sick child, Jerrod refuses to help but preaches that "[w]hat the Bible is talking about is not so much a physical illness" but "a spiritual condition" (148). He dismisses the group from his house with a promise that he has "already offered prayers" for the sick child (148). That Jerrod is neither touched by the plight of hungry and tired visitors, nor alarmed by the pain of a sick child, illustrates the incompassionate nature of the brand of religion he practises. Surprisingly, when the plight of the Ilmorogians appears in the newspapers, he calls "on an alliance of churches to send a team to the area to see how the church could help" (185). This action is obviously a gimmick to hoodwink the public that both Jerrod and the church care about the needy. Like his past inaction, however, his belated concern also contradicts Christian teachings, which advocate for genuine concern for the deprived. However, Jerrod's case is not to be used as an indictment of all Christian preachers of this epoch - although there is no other preacher in the text with whom to compare him. Suffice it to say that Thiong'o uses him to symbolize the fact that, since Christianity is a colonial religion, its post-independent adherents are likely to extend its colonial tendencies. Cook and Okenimkpe support this notion by placing Jerrod alongside postcolonial "patrons and administrators of the social system, who are separately and collectively responsible for wrecking the lives of their fellow citizens . . ." (102).

Thiong'o also shows that Christianity changes the way members of the family and society relate to each other. For instance, the meanness of

Ezekieli, Munira's wealthy father, to his children underscores the tyranny evident in colonization. Described as "tall and mean in his austere holiness" (13), Ezekieli "believed that children should be brought up on boiled maize grains sprinkled with a few beans and on tea with only tiny drops of milk and no sugar, but all crowned with words of God and prayers" (14). By feeding his children with a poor diet - perhaps the kind of diet the Europeans used to feed their subjects - and glorifying Christianity, Ezekieli colonizes these children by downgrading them to the level of servants.

When Wanja is beaten by both her parents, allegedly for having a relationship "with pagan boys" (38), after her father sees her holding hands with a boy from her school, Christianity further implicates itself with the introduction of a foreign rule in the determination of one with whom a son or daughter may relate. Nonetheless, as Wanja herself reveals, this beating for an apparently trivial matter indicates an underlying problem, which she describes as the fact that her parents "were drifting apart because of something else that had happened almost at the beginning of the Emergency" (38). That "something," Wanja later explains, is her father's irresponsible reference to the burning alive of her aunt as an act of God's punishment for the latter's assistance to freedom fighters during Kenya's struggle against colonial rule. The family of Wanja's aunt is involved in the activities of the *mau mau*. Since Wanja's parents are Christians, they are collaborators of the colonial masters and are thus opposed to their own people's quest for emancipation. Like Ezekieli, they are blind to the interests of both their child and community.

The religion practiced by Wanja's parents is further portrayed as a sham in that rather than resolve differences, the couple participate in beating Wanja "as a path for their coming together" (38). Wanja attributes her parents' anger to the fact that the "pagan boy," with whom she is accused of being in love, is from a poor family. This view of the boy and the senseless beating of Wanja contradict Christian teachings which advocate for benevolence rather than hatred for the poor. It is this contradiction that Wanja exploits to cause a cessation of the beating when she challenges them: "[You] are people of God: have you no mercy?" (38). Ironically, their hatred for the poor and reverence for the rich prompts their acceptance of Kimeria, the rich man who impregnates Wanja and eventually destroys her life. Consequently, Wanja becomes a sacrificial lamb at the altar of post-independent Kenya's Christianity, with its Western-like affinity for materialism.

Christianity also wrecks the marriage institution as constructed within African cultural understanding. It is a catalyst of disunity in hitherto cohesive families as vividly demonstrated in the relationship between Munira and his wife. Munira's wife initially conforms to the African cultural values. Later, in seeking the deceptive wealth and piety that come with Ezekieli's religion, she converts to Christianity and ceases to relate affectionately with her husband, whom she deems a failure. This obliteration of kinship values leaves Munira's wife aloof, and, as Munira states, drains "her of all sensuality and what remained now was the cold incandescence of the spirit" (16). Aloof, like Ezekieli, Munira's wife becomes a perpetual herald that derisively reminds him of the duty to teach their children nothing but the Bible. When Munira, who lives in Ilmorog, visits her and the children, she scornfully looks at "him with half-severe, half-reproachful eyes" (16) when the children go to bed rather than enquiring of his wellbeing as is generally required by African customs.

Ezekieli himself, however, is a victim of religion-based separation from his family. Formerly known as Waweru, Ezekieli becomes estranged from his father when, against the latter's advice, he converts to Christianity. Waweru's conversion is for selfish gain because, as Ogude writes, he "is portrayed as a man who propagates Christianity because it is rewarding to him and his family" ("Ngugi's Concept" 91). Ogude's assertion is evidenced by the fact that Waweru is a rich man whilst other Kenyans become impoverished during this period of war against colonization. Thus in a tale similar to that of *Segu*'s Tiekoro, Waweru foregoes his African culture and, believing he is pursuing "higher glory," accepts a baptismal name and "divests himself of every robe from his heathen past" (Thiong'o 90). In an indication of missionaries' destruction of African kinship, Waweru, despite agreeing - like Tiekoro - that he is "shin of the shin, blood of the blood" of his father, is enticed by Christianity's claim that only "he who forsaketh his father and mother" (Thiong'o 90) is worthy of the new faith. Of course, eager to instigate disharmony in the African extended family, the missionaries misuse this scripture to enhance their hegemonic tactics.

Religious Delusion in *Ways of Dying* and *Chotti Munda and His Arrow*

Like the other novels, Mda's *Ways of Dying* portrays Christianity as influencing the breakdown of society. When Nefolovhodwe goes to the city, he abandons his wife and marries another one in church. He says of the young girl with whom he lives: "I married her in church before a minister. Unlike the old hag in the village for whom I only paid cattle and was deemed to have married by custom. I am a civilized man . . .. I do things in a civilized manner. I am refined, and I am cultured" (205). While rejecting his indigenous customs, Nefolovhodwe perceives the adoption of Christianity as equivalent to being properly "civilized" and "cultured." That the church appears to support the disintegration of the family and social structures is evident in that there is no effort to find out if Nefolovhodwe has another wife in the village. Moreover, the insinuation that Nefolovhodwe is a Christian informs the reader of the hypocrisy and aloofness of his brand of religion. One is not surprised when Nefolovhodwe dismisses Toloki, who goes to his house in search of employment. Nefolovhodwe tells Toloki that he does not "deal with mundane matters such as people seeking employment," especially when he is "relaxing with [his] fleas" (129).

Shadrack, who operates an unlicensed shop in the squatter camp, takes advantage of the squatters' problems by selling essential groceries at a much higher price. Noria asserts that Shadrack "has been blessed with good fortune because he is a good Christian, and is a member of Amadodana, the men's league of the Methodist Church" (53). However, it is hypocritical that the "good Christian" runs an unlicensed grocery store and sells goods expensively, despite the fact that he has little or no running costs because his store is a shipping container.

In addition, Christianity, as practiced by the Archbishop of the Apostolic Bleed Church of Holly Zion on the Mountain Top, is a commercial venture, where sick people are invited to "get blessed water cheap" (105). The priest is as deceptive as he is hypocritical. Clearly a semi-literate man who misspells the word "holy," the Archbishop also writes "the letters B.A, M.Div., D. Theol. (USA), Prophet Extraordinaire" (105), after his name. His copying of these academic degrees, which he may have seen behind the name of an American priest, highlights his readiness to imitate titles that are used in Western countries. However, his church's practices, which include vomiting and emptying bowels in public, are rejected by the community. For instance, Jwara and Xesibe disapprove of "grown people displaying their buttocks and doing all these strange things in front of children" (107). Paradoxically, the church becomes a mere locale for socialization and immorality, for it is there that "lovers met, and unmarried teenagers made babies" (102).

In *Chotti Munda and His Arrow*, Devi shows Christian missions as the force that destroys Mundas' religion. For instance, the Mundas of Kurmi village, threatened by the cruelty of the area manager, see "[n]o hope but t' Mission" (87) in Tomaru, for they perceive that "[t]here t' mission Mundas live well" (86). Nonetheless, the price these Mundas must pay by escaping to the mission in order to "survive now" (86) is forsaking their "Haramdeo faith" (88) in the false hope that "[o]ne can still return to faith" (86). The end of "the tale of the Mundas of Kurmi village," juxtaposed with the mention of "Joseph Sukha Munda and David Bikhna Munda of Tomaru Mission" (96), emblematizes the destruction of an entire village's religious system because those who have gone to the mission have adopted Christian names. This destruction portends that the survival of a minority group's religion is unlikely in an era during which an Indian political system has adopted the imperial roles of former colonial authorities.

Conclusion

It is therefore evident from this chapter that, contrary to colonial powers' perception of traditional religions as "primitive" and therefore in need of replacement, indigenous religious systems were complex sets of beliefs that were intrinsically valuable to precolonial communities. Of course, just like Christianity and Islam, these religions had their excesses which made followers such as Hindu members of the Untouchable caste and characters such as Tiekoro in *Segu* seek other religions. Writers, however, show that Tiekoro and others who accepted the new religions ended up with a dual identity because they could not completely obliterate their former religions. In addition, because traditional economic activities were destroyed during the colonial period, indigenous people were in need of education which was necessary for employment. Since most of the schools were established by religious groups, such schools became locales for indoctrination and proselytizing. Furthermore, because conversion was always accompanied by the change of converts' names, naming aided in the colonial powers' endeavor to replace converts' identities. Thus, acceptance or rejection of the foreign religions became a new wedge that divided families, clans, and sometimes entire communities. One can also deduce, however, that despite their negative impacts on local communities, foreign religions were not always malevolent. On several occasions, they saved indigenous peoples from imminent danger as emblematized by the case of the Mundas, in *Chotti Munda and His Arrow*, who flee to the mission in order to escape exploitation by landlords; or by that of Malobali, in *Segu*, who is saved from drowning by a Catholic priest.

CHAPTER 4
WOMEN AND CULTURAL PRESERVATION

Introduction

In her essay, "Theorizing the Feminist Novel, Women and the State of African Literature Today," Rose Ure Mezu writes that "the treatment of women is often the gauge of the development of any society" (33). Mezu's statement implies that women occupy a pivotal position in a community's cultural identity, and that any analysis of culture - whether such an analysis focuses on cultural preservation or erosion - cannot ignore the status of women. Generally, feminism is the concept through which the position of women is evaluated, questioned and even revolutionized. However, as Mezu argues, Western "'feminism' has proved grossly inappropriate when applied to Black women" because "[a]lthough African feminism recognizes in Universal Feminism mutual affinities based on gender-specific issues that consign all women to the status of the *other*, *second class*, Western feminism, nonetheless failed to address effectively the specific socio-cultural issues affecting Black women of Africa and the diaspora" (35). To underscore the need for another theory, Mezu concludes:

> Therefore, "feminism" has proved to be a limited terminology that cannot effectively interpret the complex situation of any woman of color - oppressed by both white and black men by reason of her gender, then oppressed along with her black brothers by both white men and white women by reason of her color, while at the same time sorely needing to forge solidarity with her man in order that they both and the race may survive. (35)

Mezu's argument echoes that of Alice Walker's advocacy for "womanism." In *In Search of Our Mothers' Gardens*, Walker, an African American novelist and theorist, defines a womanist as a "black feminist or feminist of color" (xi), and associates womanism with "[b]eing grown up" and "[being] responsible" (xi). Walker's assertion that women are "grown up" and "responsible" is important considering that, as some of the novels in this study will show, women were perceived by men as under-developed in some precolonial societies. Walker further describes a womanist as one

99

who "[a]ppreciates and prefers women's culture, women's emotional flexibility . . . and women's strength" (xi). She further says that womanism is not "separatist, except periodically" because it is "[c]ommitted to survival and wholeness of entire people, male *and* female" (xi). The inclusion of both genders here signifies the common struggle against imperialism in which dominated peoples, both male and female, participate. In addition, the fact that womanism is "[t]raditionally universalist" because it deems "the colored race . . . [as] a flower garden, with every color flower represented" (xi) suggests that womanism not only accepts all races but also enables writers to perceive racism as a means of domination. Thus, Walker identifies two oppressive realities not only for African Americans but for all non-Whites: racism and gender.

With the foregoing, the works under study show that the plight of women was worsened by colonization; consequently, this chapter will scrutinize the domination of women both by imperial powers and by their male counterparts, as well as evaluate women's struggle for emancipation. In *Their Eyes Were Watching God* (1937), Zora Neale Hurston, African American novelist and anthropologist, writes that "de nigger woman is de mule uh de world" (14). Although Hurston here refers to the multifaceted oppression of the Black woman during the era of slavery in America, throughout which the Black woman is suppressed by both racism and male chauvinism, her view finds expression during the colonial period when women were oppressed by both an imperial tyrant and her male counterpart.

Since the role of women in cultural preservation cannot be effectively deduced without referring to the place of women in their societies, it is necessary to evaluate women's second-class status in patriarchal societies during the precolonial, colonial and postcolonial periods. Such an evaluation will show that women play two main roles in these societies: first, they aid in cultural preservation and transmission and, second, they provide healthcare to both the family and the community. All the novels under study will be analyzed in each section of this chapter except Jamaica Kincaid's *A Small Place*. Although *A Small Place* does not present detailed information regarding the place of women in cultural preservation, it makes a few compelling statements regarding this subject; these statements will be discussed together with corresponding ideas from the other texts. Consequently, the chapter will allocate specific sections to the analyses of women's roles in traditional societies, women's second-class status in a patriarchal society, and the emergence of modern women.

4.1 Women's Role in Traditional Societies

As I have already stated, the roles of women in traditional societies are many, but only two of them will be identified in the works under study. These include, first, that women are the reservoirs and transmitters of culture and, second, that women are at the center of their respective communities' healthcare systems because they are expected to ensure their families' wellbeing. These two roles will be discussed in separate sub-sections because the environments in which they are undertaken in each community are different.

A. Women as Custodians and Transmitters of Cultural Knowledge

In "Identity and Its Discontents: Women and the Nation," Deniz Kandiyoti, a postcolonial theorist, acknowledges that women are the preservers and transmitters of culture because they are "the custodians of cultural particularisms by virtue of being less assimilated, both culturally and linguistically, into the wider society" (382). Kandiyoti argues that immigrant women "reproduce their culture through the continued use of their native language, the persistence of culinary and other habits and the socialisation of the young" (382). "Cultural difference," Kandiyoti further asserts, "is frequently signaled through the dress and deportment of women" (382-3). While Kandiyoti's argument is acceptable, it must be pointed out that women, like the entire human race, are not static beings who retain their native cultures to the exclusion of cultural innovations and influences that take place within their dynamic societies.

The works in this study indicate that women are charged with preserving and passing on cultural knowledge. Indeed, women inescapably transmit cultural education to children as they are traditionally the latter's nurturers. They educate children through everyday activities as well as through planned sessions of storytelling. Postcolonial writers demonstrate that even after formal education has been introduced in the

101

postindependent period, the duty of ensuring that children are educated appears largely left to women.

The Wise "Mama" in *Petals of Blood*

In *Petals of Blood*, Nyakinyua and Mariamu embody the roles performed by women in the precolonial period. Mariamu's feeding of all children, including those of Ezekieli, her oppressive employer, demonstrates the African communal view that all adult members in the community must ensure the welfare of all children. In addition, her making tea (without tea leaves) by putting sugar in a spoon and baking it in the fire until it "turned into a sticky mess of syrup" and then pouring it into boiling water (47-48), suggests her preservation of the survival skills existent in the precolonial era. Furthermore, Nyakinyua expresses concern about the plight of the children of Ilmorog village. Comparing Ilmorog - a remote village in the heart of Central Kenya - to a "deserted homestead" (7), Nyakinyua wonders if Munira has come disguised as a teacher in order to take away "the remaining children" (7). It is not surprising that men who interrogate Munira to find out about his intention of teaching in their remote area "staggered back to their homes, but not before reporting their findings to Nyakinyua" (10). That the residents of this village, who are "a bit suspicious of strangers and strange things" (11), consult and trust Nyakinyua as a figure akin to "the mother of the village" indicates their dependence on her wisdom. Her wisdom epitomizes traditional culture, which is unlike postcolonial economic and social systems that take children away from the village. It is this wisdom that Wanja, her granddaughter, comes to seek when she is unable to have a child. Nyakinyua's directing her to Mwathi wa Mugo, the community's traditional priest, indicates her adherence to precolonial means of problem solving. These traditional means may not be adequate in confronting today's dilemma because the priest fails to make Wanja conceive. Women's aforementioned capacity to accept change is evident in Nyakinyua's role in her society. However, Nyakinyua may be aware of the limitations of traditional solutions; hence, her concern about imparting Western education to Ilmorog's children indicates her perception of this education as necessary to the village's future generation.

Furthermore, it is Wanja who, in an act of self-sacrifice, takes up Joseph's position as a bar attendant at Abdulla's store so that Joseph can go to school. Joseph's success in school vindicates Wanja's effort, and shows women as the nurturers of the community's future leaders. Indeed, women, in precolonial, colonial and postcolonial Kenyan society are the ones who raise and educate children, a role that they play with pride because "children, no matter how we neglect them, are what make many a barmaid [or any other oppressed woman] feel human. You are a mother and nobody can take that from you" (250). Wanja's assertion demonstrates the value of motherhood in African world view. As Celine Vandermeersch and O. Chimere-Dan state, "[i]n sub-Saharan Africa, a woman's social status is heavily dependent on reproductive success and a large progeny"; therefore, "sterility tends to be looked upon as a social illness afflicting mainly women who have been disgraced or accused of witchcraft" (662). Vandermeersch and Chimere-Dan further state: "Having no children, a limited number of children, or too few children of a particular sex, are unhappy situations for women. Taking foster children in may be one way of making up for such shortcomings" (662). One who follows Vandermeersch and Chimere-Dan's line of argument may thus conclude that Wanja's endeavor to ensure that Joseph receives formal education may be deemed an act of adoption.

Women as Cultural Mentors in *Segu*

Similarly, Maryse Condé's *Segu* depicts women as the nurturers of children among the Bambara. While the grouping together of women and children in the assertion that "women and children sat [under the *dubale* tree] to tell stories" (4) connotes the lowly placement of women in the community, the fact that women are acknowledged as the carriers of stories, the medium through which society conveyed cultural education, underlines their role as educators in the precolonial period. Women's role as storytellers is significant if one considers the importance of storytelling in most precolonial African communities. Felix Boateng identifies stories, particularly fables, to serve this educational role in traditional African society: "Many of these tales were carefully constructed to inculcate the societies' values into children without necessarily and formally telling them what to do and how to do it" (323-24). Boateng explains that "[a]ll attempts were made to make the storytelling interesting and entertaining" (325), to the learners. He also identifies myths and legends as other types of

103

educative stories because they "not only supplied accounts of the groups' origin, but related precedents to present-day beliefs, actions, and codes of behavior" (326). Based on Boateng's understanding of storytelling, one may conclude that women are not only teachers but also keepers of their communities' history as embodied in myths and legends.

In addition, the fact that Nya is expected to take care of all the children in Dousika's compound shows women as tasked with the duty of ensuring that all children are well-reared. Nya's roles are significant if one considers Arlette M. Smith's argument that mothers are familiar figures in Condé's novels because they are the "symbolic connection between native land and motherhood: both suggest origins, primary source of nurturing, both are seen as the earliest molding forces" (382). Nya's fostering all children is consequential because as Vandermeersch and Chimere-Dan state, "[f]ostering is an expression of persistent traditional kinship solidarity, and it is instrumental in creating or reinforcing ties between individuals or social groups" (659). In "Child Fostering in West Africa," Uche C. Isiugo-Abanihe agrees with Vandermeersch and Chimere-Dan's notion about child fostering: "Most fostering in West Africa takes place within the kinship framework, because children are generally thought of as belonging not only to biological parents but also to the lineage or kinship group" (56). Thus, because Malobali and Sira are sons of Dousika, Nya's husband, they are to be kept within the family and reared alongside Nya's own children.

Childrearing requires one to ensure that children engage in the community's activities, among which education is an integral part. Boateng supports this notion by stating that "traditional African education, unlike the formal systems introduced by the colonialists, was inseparable from other segments of life" (322). Since each activity or ritual in African traditional society was informative, Boateng concludes that "[t]raditional African education was not only there to be acquired, but it was actually there to be lived" (322). If education is perceived in this manner, women are to be deemed as mentors who initiate children into the society's customs.

The Vulnerable Trio in *The God of Small Things*

Arundhati Roy, in *The God of Small Things*, reminds the reader that the educative role of women is not limited to precolonial and colonial times, because women continue to protect and educate their children even in postcolonial societies. Thus, the story of Ammu and her children presents a compelling account of the many roles played by a divorcee in contemporary Indian society. When she returns to the Ayemenem house, Ammu realizes that while she, as an adult, can see beyond the hypocrisy of her family and society, her children are susceptible in "their willingness to love people who didn't really love them" (42) and are thus "like a pair of small bewildered frogs . . . lolloping arm in arm down a highway full of hurtling traffic. Entirely oblivious of what trucks can do to frogs" (42). Aware of this imminent danger, and in spite of her pitiable condition in an environment where she is unwanted, Ammu endeavors to rear and protect them. Roy reveals her efforts: "Ammu watched over them fiercely. Her watchfulness stretched her, made her taut and tense. She was quick to reprimand her children, but even quicker to take offense on their behalf" (42). However, the community's and family's treatment of Ammu, because of her perceived lower status as a divorcee, severely limits her educative role to her children. The family takes control of the twins because, as a daughter and divorcee, Ammu has no jurisdiction over what happens in the Ayemenem house. Worse still, her broken marriage to a Hindu husband was never sanctioned by her Christian family. The vulnerable children become pupils of Chacko and Baby Kochamma, whose interests towards the twins are malevolent. Ammu's fear is justified when the twins are separated. By the time Ammu discovers that she ought to "earn enough to rent a room for the three of them to stay together in" (152), Estha has been returned to his father, Rahel sent to a boarding school, and Ammu herself ejected out of the Ayemenem house. Thus, Ammu and her children's marginalization, as Anuradha Dingwaney Needham states in "'The Small Voice of History' in Arundhati Roy's *The God of Small Things*," emanates from the fact that they "do not belong to the conventional family unit headed by Chacko, Ammu's brother, Mammachi, her mother, and Baby Kochamma" (373).

The Power of Woman-Wisdom in *Chotti Munda and His Arrow*

In *Chotti Munda and His Arrow*, Mahasweta Devi also shows women as playing a major role in the traditional educational system of the Munda community. While Chotti is credited with leading the Munda community through the divine powers he inherits from Dhani Munda, his sister, Parmi, contributes to this transfer of power. Despite being married, she agrees to take care of Chotti during a time of famine. Indeed, it is when he goes to the house of his sister that Chotti meets Dhani, his sister's grandfather-in-law. Moreover, Parmi's information that if Dhani "shoots an arrer, t' police'll catch 'im" (6) arouses Chotti's interest in finding out why Dhani's arrow-shooting would lead to arrest.

Perhaps the strongest indicator that women are the reservoirs of cultural education is most evident in the reaction of the women of Chotti village when Ronaldson Hugh visits their village. Devi states that since no White has ever visited the Mundas, "no one knows what people do or say when such a thing happens" (44). This notwithstanding, women take the lead in making the man comfortable and then introducing their culture to him: "Pahan's wife saves everyone. With easy woman-wisdom. Mundari women smile often. Wife came forth smiling and gave the White guy a string seat to sit on" (44). The reference to pahan's wife's action as driven by "woman-wisdom" suggests both that there exists a version of woman's wisdom and that women are carriers of knowledge. It is not surprising that pahan's wife next invites women to perform a traditional song, which Ronaldson promptly writes down for preservation. Women are thus not only the epitome of the preservation of culture in its oral form, but they aid in its preservation in the written form as well.

The Rescue of Helpless children in *Ways of Dying*

In *Ways of Dying*, Zakes Mda also shows women as attempting to educate their children. Mda indicates that, unlike the communities presented in other novels, child rearing is near-impossible in the abject poverty of immediate post-apartheid South Africa. When Napu, Noria's husband, abducts their son, Vutha, he dresses the child in rags so as to attract the sympathy of passersby as he begs in the city. He and the child have no home and live under a bridge. Eventually, the child dies when Napu abandons him under the bridge for days, only to return and find scavenging dogs fighting for his corpse. Napu is not the only parent who abandons his child; this is a common occurrence in the settlement. These children are picked up by Madimbhaza, who feeds them through her meager monthly pension. As a result, Madimbhaza's shack is referred to as "the dumping ground" because it is where "women who have unwanted babies dump them in front of her door at night" (166). In addition, Madimbhaza collects children who are "victims of the war that is raging in the land" (168) due to both apartheid rule and conflicts between South African communities. Thus, like Mariamu and Nyakinyua, Madimbhaza becomes a "mother" of children who are not her own. Madimbhaza's type of fostering may exemplify what Isiugo-Abanihe terms "crisis fostering," which she says "result[s] from the dissolution of the family of origin by divorce, separation, or death" (57). Such fostering, she continues, entails "improv[ing] the survival chances of children by removing them from the source of a crisis, real or imagined" (57). The help of such women as Noria in feeding and bathing these children as well as ensuring they go to school also highlights the nurturing role of women in this society

B. Women as Providers of Community Health

That Mountain Woman, the Medicine woman of *Ways of Dying*

The novels also show that women provided healthcare for their families. This subject will not be discussed in great detail with reference to Mda's *Ways of Dying*, because it is manifested only once. Noria's mother, That Mountain Woman, is a powerful medicine woman who cures the villagers of ailments caused by wizards and witches (73). That Mountain Woman's practice is not to be doubted considering Daniel A. Offiong's assertion that in traditional African medical system, "greater emphasis is placed on the 'supernatural' rather than on natural causation and treatment of illness and other forms of misfortune" (122). Hence, "[t]raditional healers cure people of their sickness and illness and deliver people from their misfortune" (122). The ailments that That Mountain Woman treats are, however, similar to those that require deliverance as administered by "the Archbishop of the Apostolic Blessed Church of Holly Zion on the Mountain Top" (104). Consequently, That Mountain Woman's practice may be viewed as an alternative to the brand of Christianity practiced by the Church of Holly Zion on Mountain Top. This Christian sect will not be further explained here because religion has already been discussed in the previous chapter.

The Healing Role of Women Among the Bambara

In the essay "The Recovered Voice: Nafissatou Niang Diallo's The *Princess of Tiali*," M'bare N'gom identifies colonization as a force which "contributes to the relegation of women to a secondary role" (266). With regards to precolonial sharing of duties between men and women, and the invasion of Islam into Africa, he writes:

> While traditional society was male-dominated, the division of tasks that prevailed permitted women, nonetheless, to ultimately enjoy a certain degree of independence and a certain political and economic power within the family and the group. The penetration of Islam triggered the "first installments of acculturation" which affected the status of woman who lost almost all of her political and economic power and, from then on, was excluded, from active public life and from the public decision-making sphere. (266)

Thus, Islam, just like Christianity, changed the precolonial system of sharing duties. In *Segu*, Condé shows that the Bambara community assigns to women the duty of ensuring the community's health and well-being. Nya, for instance, demonstrates knowledge of both herbal and religious means of providing care for the sick. During Sira's childbearing, she orders servants to burn certain plants which drive away evil spirits and "help the milk to come" (11). She is also the family's spiritual medium, who is expected to present offerings at the family's altar, and to intercede for Sira because the latter "had already had a still born child the previous rainy season, [hence] extra precautions were needed" (12). Indeed, women, such as Nya, who are "invested with a certain amount of authority" (13) are allowed, alongside priests and heads of families, to enter altars and offer sacrifices.

Although her role is largely medical, Souka the midwife, "the wife of a fetish priest, [who is] herself in communication with the tutelary powers" (12), also combines her trade with religion. Unlike fetish priests who engage in divination of such subjects as the future of members of the family or the community's destiny, the spiritual roles played by women such as Nya and Souka are purely for the immediate healing of the family such as ensuring that children are born safely. Moreover, unlike priests who may spend days and nights consulting traditional divine powers, traditional female healers like Souka merely "look at the shape of a mouth or an eyelid to tell which child would be its parents' pride, and which would drag itself about for years on legs too weak for its body" (16-17). This difference indicates that women's practice might be based on traditional instruction rather than religious involvement. If this notion - which would explain the difference between the spiritual work done by fetish priests and that undertaken by women such as Nya and Souka - is acceptable, then one can argue that the precolonial Bambara community had a comprehensive medical system of which Souka is perhaps a single agent. Furthermore, women stood at the center of the health system, and that all women - as exemplified by the female slaves who bring "powdered vines with which to massage her [Sira's] stomach" (16) - were expected to have basic health skills.

In addition, the manner in which Romana, formerly Ayodele, nurses Malobali to recovery connotes her enduring prowess as her family's healthcare provider. Malobali, who is handed to Romana as "scarcely more than a corpse" (305) after his capture and torture by followers of Guezo, the tyrannical king of the Abomey, is obviously at the verge of death. The fact that Romana is "[a]pparently indifferent to the smell of his open wounds, his vomit and his defecations" as she nurses him and tries "to find all the things the *babalawo* [traditional priest] and doctors asked for, however difficult" (306), indicates that she will go to any length to ensure the medical welfare of her husband. Moreover, that Romana, a Christian returnee to Africa from slavery in Brazil, continues the curative measures of pre-slavery Africa shows that the medical system of precolonial Africa is enduring and is expected to thrive alongside that of the postcolonial era.

Traditional Medical Systems in *Petals of Blood* and *Chotti Munda and His Arrow*

In *Petals of Blood*, Thiong'o further illuminates the notion that women are charged with ensuring their community's health. He writes that, like other women during the colonial period, Mariamu has "to work on her own piece of land; and to keep the home in unity, health and peace" (58). Given that the family was a microcosm of traditional African society, Thiong'o's statement emphasizes the role of women as participants in the community's economic system (by "working on their pieces of land"), and in problem-solving and providing basic healthcare to their families (by ensuring that "unity, health and peace" prevailed). Thus, women were at the heart of the medical systems and general wellbeing of their respective ethnic groups during precolonial times. Thiong'o's further argument that Mariamu, in colonial Kenya, has "to work on the European farms" (58), indicates that colonization also takes the woman away from her core duties, which were the fabric that connected African society; hence, both the family unit and community at large face imminent disintegration.

Unlike *Petals of Blood* and *Segu*, Devi's *Chotti Munda and His Arrow* does not provide in-depth information regarding the Munda community's traditional healthcare system. Nevertheless, that such a system exists, and that women are its pillars, is not in doubt. When Daroga forbids Chotti from participating in archery contests for three years, and he returns home downcast, his wife attempts to treat him: "[She] mixes rough molasses in water and gives it to her husband. Drink a bit, she says, cool yerself. Don' mek such a dark face" (75). Another indicator that Munda women have mastered the art of traditional medicine is the case of Chhagan's mother, whose prowess is even recognized by Tirathnath, a moneylender and believer of modern medical system, who says:

> ...that Chhagan's mother made some herbal paste, and cured Tirath's mother's menstrual problems. Now the thing is to go to the doctor, but Tirath has never seen a physician like Chhagan's mother. As long as Chhagan's mother was alive no one in Chotti village worried about the health problems of women and children. (194)

This statement indicates that adivasis have a medical system at par, or even better than, its modern counterpart. It is thus not surprising that when both Chotti and Daroga get hurt when trying to kill the wild boar, the Daroga's wound, under hospital care, takes a month and a half to heal, while Chotti's hurt foot takes only a week in spite of his refusal to go to hospital.

4.2 Women's Second-Class Status in a Patriarchal Society

In spite of playing essential roles as societies' reservoirs and transmitters of culture, especially as educators and healthcare providers in the family and community, women remain at the periphery of their societies during the precolonial, colonial and postcolonial periods. While they were suppressed in diverse ways during the precolonial period, women became victims of both male chauvinism and racial domination during the colonial period. In addition, the Western-based political and economic systems of the postcolonial era expose women to further oppression. While the postcolonial period has also seen a surge in women's resistance to marginalization, this notion will be discussed in a separate section.

A. The Place of Women in the Precolonial Period

The novels in this study portray women as responsible for continuity, both in the family and community. This consideration is pertinent because it bases the view of the woman on her capacity to have and to nurture children. This perception of women by society stems chiefly from the patriarchal nature of most societies in the world. Mezu states regarding the African situation: "Reasons for woman's neglect and marginalization can obviously be located in a precolonial, patriarchal past where man ruled supreme in the manner of the Roman *paterfamilias*, where the woman was a possession as wife, an object of barter and exchange as sister or daughter, to be defined only in terms of her relationship to the man and never as an autonomous entity" ("Theorizing the Feminist Novel" 33-34). Mezu's argument concerning the position of African women will be expounded through Maryse Condé's *Segu*.

Women in Precolonial Segu

To begin with, the male-chauvinistic Bambara community in Condé's *Segu* treats women as property. In fact, Condé says that men "loved their livestock better than their wives, and sang of their beauty at night around wood fires" (17). Given their perception of women as incredulous beings, men in this community use women as the means of settling their petty scores. For instance, one of the reasons that Samake gives for plotting Dousika's downfall from the king's council is that "twice Dousika had humiliated him [by] luring women away from him by better presents than Samake could afford to offer" (29). This treatment of women as material to be possessed explains their lack of authority in choosing marriage partners.

111

As in the case of Nya, women do not meet their husbands until they have been married through stringent customary marriage rites. Hence, "Nya never saw Dousika until the marriage, not even until she was actually taken into his hut" (58), yet the patriarchal society expects Nya to accept "the stranger who would suddenly have power of life and death over her, who would own her as he owned his fields of millet" (58). Indeed, like "fields of millet," wives, upon their husband's death, are to be "shared out among the brothers in order of age" (142), or may all be given to his eldest brother. It is not a wonder that, upon Dousika's death, Nya is inherited by his brother Diemogo "for whom she had never had any respect" but to whom from now on she owes "total submission and obedience. She couldn't refuse him her body" (220).

Further symbolizing the commodification of women, the Bambara use women as riches to be plundered during war with other ethnic communities. In "Women's and Gender Studies in English-Speaking Sub-Saharan Africa: A Review of Research in the Social Sciences," Akosua Adomako Ampofo, et al. single out the capture and rape of women as one of the major results of war:

> As in other parts of the world, in Africa, women are victims of rape in conflict and war situations such as the civil wars in Rwanda and Sierra Leone. Studies on Africa reveal that rape and the forcible abduction of women are strategies of war that are systematically used to assert power over ethnic groups, by overpowering 'their' women. (693)

It is the realization that "Sira's fate might well have been her own" (11) or of any other woman's that makes Nya accept and sympathize with Sira. Condé vividly describes the rationale for Nya's compassion: "The violence of men, the whim of one of them, might easily have snatched her too from her father's house and her mother's arm, and made her into an object of barter" (11).

When women are captured in war, they become slaves who are prone to be misused as men's sex objects. This unfortunate exploitation of women's sexuality explains why for Dousika says: "It was impossible to count the number of slaves who had taken their turns in his hut at night" (11). The society even allows a man's sons to exploit slaves in a similar manner. Upon conversion to Islam, Tiekoro finds untenable the religion's requirement that he abstain from sexual activity because he "had been used to making love to his father's young slaves ever since he was twelve years old" (83). This upbringing leads him to rape Nadie, a stranger, when, after several days of abstinence, he finds her lighting a fire outside the house of her master, Al-Hassan, in Timbuktu. Tiekoro abandons her, only to return after expulsion from the university. Still, he continually uses her as a sexual item and refuses to find out her family background for fear "that she was not his inferior," because "[h]e needed to despise her in order to despise himself; he wanted to turn her into a symbol of destruction of his hopes" (113).

The sexual exploitation of female slaves annihilates both them and their children. Even after the taxes to free such slaves are paid, lame excuses may be used to retain them in slavery against their wishes. Hence, when Sira's family pays taxes to free her from slavery in Dousika's compound, the latter, "[who] preferred her to his legitimate partners" (11), refuses to let her go. The excuse given is that she is pregnant, and because boys belong to their fathers, the family will not release her until the child has been born and its gender confirmed. The slaves' sons, who must remain in their fathers' homesteads because "boys belong to their father" (128), become victims of prejudice and abuse. This abuse is most unmistakable in that Siga is considered Tiekoro's servant irrespective of the fact that he was "born the same day as Tiekoro, with only a few hours in between" (30). This difference in treatment arises from the fact that "Siga's mother was only a captive whom Dousika must have lain with one day, aroused by the tightness of her skirt over her buttocks" (30). Condé thus laments: "Alas, the hazards of birth! If he'd been born of this womb rather than that, his life would have been quite different" (30). Hence, Siga's entire life becomes "flooded with bitterness" (181) as a result of the community's attitude that extends the mistreatment of female slaves to their innocent offspring.

In a further demonstration of the misery such boys experience, Malobali, Sira's son, is devastated when he learns that Nya, whom he has always accepted as his mother, is only a foster mother. Unknown to him, his mother took her daughter and fled Dousika's compound for her family's home, leaving him behind as required by Bambara customs. Malobali, now equipped with the knowledge of the reasons behind Tiekoro's cruelty against him, eventually flees from the home and ends up as the

113

Christianized slave of Father Urlich and Father Etienne. The impact of the custom-imposed mother-child separation, combined with the abuse of slaves' sons by the legitimate sons, prevent Siga and Malobali from ever developing into mature adults capable of reaching their full potential.

The plight of Sira deserves further scrutiny, because it typifies a woman's life after she escapes from slavery. When Amadou Tassirou marries Sira, he supposes that "he is acquiring a servant, overwhelmed with gratitude" because "she had been the concubine of a Bambara for so long" (136). Tassirou's reason for marrying Sira suggests that women's lives are forever shattered when they are captured during wars and turned into slaves and concubines. In addition, Sira's separation from Malobali devastates her as she constantly thinks of him. Worse still, Bambara culture allows a female slave's former master to stalk and harm her. Sira is stalked by Dousika's soul "thinking up the worst kinds of revenge: entering Sira's womb, there to get into and kill her child; hunting down all her subsequent children and leading them one by one into the grave; occupying her womb completely and making her barren" (139).

In a manner reminiscent of Okonkwo's view of weak men as "*agbala* . . . another name for a woman" (13) in Achebe's *Things Fall Apart*, women are perceived as symbols of weakness in the Bambara community. This may elucidate why weak men, perhaps termed outcasts, are classified together with women as evident in Mansa Monzon's retort to Dousika's inquiry whether Kone has seen the visiting White man: "If you want to see him . . . he's on the other side of the Joliba [river]. With the women and children and outcasts" (10). This grouping of women with children and outcasts indicates men's perception of women as under-developed and thus as unable to reason as full human beings. The perception of women as irrational beings explains Siga's surprise when he sees "Tiekoro weeping, clutching his head in his hands like a child or a woman" (92) after he is expelled from the Islamic university for attempting to rape Ayisha, El-Hadj Abou's daughter. Similarly, men disapprove of Diemogo's weeping during the burial of Dousika because the community believes that "[o]nly women ought to sob and shriek" (146).

Precolonial Bambara community also deems women as the source of impurity. For instance, when Masakoulou and Tiefolo bitterly disagree during the young hunters' expedition in defiance of Koumare the priest, one of the suspected causes of this dissension is that one of the hunters might have "performed the sexual act before they set off" (65). Similarly, before Koumare secludes himself to consult traditional divinities, he abstains "from all sexual intercourse with his wives" to avoid "dissipat[ing] his strength by spilling his seed" (39, 40). Moreover, the inclusion of "some drops of menstrual blood from a woman who'd miscarried seven times" among other paraphernalia used for divination, which include "some warthog's hairs" and "dried lion's heart in powdered form" (40), indicate the society's derision of biological processes, such as menstruation, which are particular to women.

Despite its excesses, the Bambara community assigns specific duties to both men and women. For example, women in Dousika's compound are expected to be "pounding or sieving millet, or spinning cotton," while men should be "chatting together as they sharpened arrows for hunting or whetted farming implements" (4). This implies that women's duties match their perceived role of nurturing the African community, while men's duties connote their functions as providers and protectors of their families. Women in precolonial Segu had their own economy and even a market where they "sold everything that could be sold: millet, onions, rice, sweet potatoes, smoked fish, fresh fish, peppers, shea butter and chickens" (6-7). Condé further writes that "the women milked the cows and made butter which the slaves bartered for millet at the neighboring markets" (17).

Furthermore, in spite of the suppression of women in this patriarchal society, the first wife is highly regarded. Hence, Nya, Dousika's "first wife, his *bara muso*, to whom he had delegated part of his authority and who could therefore address him as an equal" (5), ignores his query on why she had left Sira, his pregnant concubine, unattended. Condé's assertion that Dousika "wouldn't have put up with such offhandedness, verging on impertinence" (5) had it come from any of the other wives, shows Nya's position as that of high privilege. In a community where physical violence is accepted as a way of making women submissive, due to the belief that "to make iron grow straight in the fire, you have to beat it" (106), Nya's action might appear audacious. Nya's privilege, however, is mechanical as Dousika honors her not only because of her position but also out of "respect, almost fear" (6), because as a descendant of a family "related to the ancient ruling family of Segu" (6) she is of a more noble background than him.

115

Indeed, men in the Bambara society have a penchant for using women as a means of improving their nobility. Nieli, Dousika's second wife, was betrothed to Dousika even before she was born. This betrothal took place when Dousika's father, visiting a "Bambara nobleman and noticing that his host's wife was pregnant, he had, in accordance with the custom, asked to have the child for his son if it turned out to be a girl" (12). This practice is however surreptitiously criticized in that Dousika "always dealt justly with this wife who was not of his choosing, but he had never loved her" (12). Consequently, betrothals become synonymous with condemning women to loveless marriages. Irrespective of whether they were chosen by their husbands or by their husbands' fathers through betrothal, women in this polygamous society are not to be loved but controlled.

While the position of *bara muso*, first wife, in this polygamous community should make its holders proud, the roles assigned to this rank take away happiness from its holders. Thus, despite the authority she appears to have as Dousika's *bara muso*, Nya is a victim of marital abandonment. She is treated as Dousika's home manager, because the relationship between them is "one of mere routine"; they share no intimacy and talk about nothing "but the children, managing of the property, the worries of public life" (13). This revelation prepares the reader for her alarming exclamation of "Oh, it's sad, growing old" (13), which appears misplaced considering that she "must be thirty-two" (13). The reader understands her view of herself as old, given that she has been married for sixteen years and has several children. Bearing children at a rather young age and the oppression at Dousika's compound have taken their toll on her and "[s]he'd lost her figure. Her breasts drooped, and the wrinkles of responsibility already emphasized her features" making her look "severe" (13-14).

Furthermore, although Nya appears powerful, her responsibilities are daunting and annihilating. Apart from taking care of her children, and her husband's other wives and their children, she is "the mother" figure to her husband. This notion explains why Dousika, after being embarrassed at the king's council, returns home downcast and is "torn between the grief he felt at her indifference and the desire to clutch at her skirt like a little child" (13). In his moments of frustration, Dousika expects Nya "to pity him, to console him as if he were a child" (35), because, he acknowledges, she is "so strong, [and] the center of his own life" (69). Dousika may appear as an immature husband who relies too much on Nya. He is a weakling and his downfall from the king's council comes as a result of his inability to fight Samake, who influences the king to dismiss him. While this argument would appear credible, because no other man in the text is said to rely in such a manner on his *bara muso*, it might be negated by the fact that Dousika demonstrates authority over his household. In addition, it is clear to the reader that his dismissal from the council speaks more about the inability of Mansa Monzon, the king, to probe accusations before making judgments than it does about Dousika who is being accused falsely.

B. Women's New Pains in the Colonial Period

If women are at the center of any culture, then an evaluation of the relationship between culture and colonization is necessary. In "National Liberation and Culture," Amilcar Cabral writes:

> To take up arms to dominate a people is, above all, to take up arms to destroy, or at least to neutralize, to paralyze, its cultural life. For, with a strong indigenous cultural life, foreign domination cannot be sure of its perpetuation. (53)

Since "it is not possible to harmonize the economic and political domination of a people, whatever may be the degree of their social development, with the preservation of their cultural personality" (Cabral 54), colonization inevitably destroys a colonized people's cultural identity. Economic domination of a people, Cabral therefore concludes, is synonymous with cultural annihilation because,

> ...culture is always in the life of a society (open or closed), the more or less conscious result of the economic and political activities of that society, the more or less dynamic expression of the kinds of relationships which prevail in that society, on the one hand between man (considered individually or collectively) and nature, and, on the other hand, among individuals, groups of individuals, social strata or classes. (54)

Cabral's notion of culture, as it relates to economic and political domination, informs the consideration of colonization as tantamount to marginalization of women. Similarly, it supports the position that the male-dominated postcolonial economic and political systems are also to be regarded as further acts of women's colonization.

Women's Triple Duties in Colonial Kenya

In *Petals of Blood*, Thiong'o shows that in colonial Kenya, women suffered from both male-domination and colonization. This suffering is best captured in Mariamu, Ezekieli's laborer, who complains of being overwhelmed by "her triple duties: to her child Ndinguri; to her husband, and to her European landlord" (58). Thiong'o shows that colonization presented men with new means of suppressing women. By forcing the man to work on their farms, colonialists took the man away from his role as provider of the family. In an evaluation of Ghana's precolonial economic systems, Stephen H. Hymer observes that men had never worked for other people:

> Thus, no member of the community was landless; and, since most belonged to a community, few men were forced, by lack of land, to work for others. The result was a relatively equal distribution of income in which everyone had similar standards of food, housing, and clothing. (34-35)

Although referring mainly to Ghanaian communities, Hymer's observation is true also for Kenya and the other former African territories before the arrival of colonialists. Thiong'o writes that the colonialists destroyed the elaborate traditional sharing of duties because men were taken away "to keep the White man's shambas [farms] alive while theirs fell into neglect and waste" (*Petals* 213). This removal of men from their economic endeavors was the reason why they plundered women's earnings in a false attempt to regain their economic control of the family and society. This situation perhaps explains why Mariamu's husband sells her produce "to the same European farmer, their landlord, who fixed his own buying price" (58). While Mariamu's husband's repressive action is abysmal, one can conclude that colonialism not only reduces the African man but also introduces new ways of female oppression.

The removal of men from their core duties also affected the duties performed by women. In *Petals of Blood*, Thiong'o illustrates how duties were shared in the precolonial Gikuyu economic system:

> For a woman alone can never do all the work on the farm. How could she grow sugar cane, yams, sweet potatoes which used to be man's domain? How break new ground? And how could she smith, make chains, pull wires, make beehives, wickerwork for barns? (213)

This statement suggests that women and men among the Gikuyu, and perhaps in most African societies, tended different crops, the mainstay crops being the sphere of men. Thiong'o reveals that men undertook such activities as the manufacture of weapons and farming tools as well as the cultivation of new lands. Consequently, when colonial settlers forced indigenous men to work on their farms, the latter's duties were left to the women. These women, as exemplified by Mariamu, were overworked.

Wanja's revelation that her aunt, whose house is burnt by her daughter's ex-husband, "used to carry guns and bullets to the forest hidden in baskets of unga [corn flour]" (65), is important because it reiterates women's role in the struggle for Kenya's independence during the colonial era. Men and women played complementary roles in the struggle for independence: while men, such as Wanja's uncle - who is recognized as a "hardcore Mau Mau" - fought in the forests, women supplied them with weapons and food, the two elements that helped to sustain the war. The statue of Dedan Kimathi, the departed enigmatic Kenyan freedom fighter, possesses "breasts . . . as if it was a man and a woman in one," symbolizing that it was "a man and a woman who fought to redeem this country" (161).

Slavocracy and Women Scarification in *Segu*

Unlike Thiong'o, Condé in *Segu* shows how both the capture of slaves and invasion by colonial powers suppressed women. In addition to being "branded [alongside men] on the shoulder with red-hot iron" (106), women captives were also victims of being "raped by sailors" (106) as they were transported to slavery in the Americas. Worse still, women, as personified by Ayodele, became victims of wanton sexual abuse. As a result of physical and sexual misuse during slavery, Ayodele, at only twenty, has a heart "of

119

an old woman, older than that of the mother who bore her, older even than her grandmother's" (203). In addition, she unwillingly carries, during pregnancy, the child of her slaveholder, Manuel da Cunha, with devastating "self-hatred and self-contempt" (203).

Like slavery, internal colonization in Segu makes women victims of sexual abuse because, as Condé writes, White men "took [women], made [them] pregnant, and abandoned [them]" (237). Imperialism also introduces a new type of concubine. While women, as earlier explained, became concubines as a result of being captured in war during the precolonial period, the arrival of Arabs and Europeans introduced a new system of slavery. Were it not for this new trade in slaves, Nadie would not have ended up as a slave of Al-Hassan, a rich Muslim, and subsequently as Tiekoro's concubine. Nadie personifies the suffering that this new trade will cause to women as she foretells that, as a mere concubine who is not recognized by Tiekoro's family, his return to Segu will reduce her to "no more than a piece of cow or camel dung, fit to make a fire, but smelly and despised" (151).

C. Women in the Postcolonial Period

While all formerly colonized peoples fought and continue to fight for total emancipation from their erstwhile colonial powers, Gayatri Chakravorty Spivak argues, in "Can the Subaltern Speak," that women continue to be dominated even within this resistance. She writes that "[w]ithin the effaced itinerary of the subaltern subject, the track of sexual difference is doubly effaced" because "ideological construction of gender keeps the male dominant" (82). Consequently, even in the postcolonial period, women are likely to be victims of both male domination and neocolonialism. In *Barrel of a Pen: Resistance to Repression in Neocolonial Kenya*, Ngugi wa Thiong'o appears to echo Spivak's stance when he writes about a postcolonial elite that "saw the world, they perceived themselves and the possibilities opened out to them, with glasses 'Made in Europe'and which were now permanently glued to their eyes" (80). Thiong'o here refers to post-independence leaders who retain and exploit colonial structures to the chagrin of the masses not only in Kenya but in all former colonies. As expected, postcolonial bourgeoisies use these inherited structures to exploit women, who have been marginalized in such milieus as employment and education.

Gender as Curse in *Petals of Blood* and *A Small Place*

Women of the postcolonial era were further marginalized through the policies inherited by post-independent nations from erstwhile colonial powers. In *Petals of Blood*, Thiong'o illustrates that while the arrival and subsequent departure of colonialists has eradicated the commodification of women in African society so that Ruoro's daughters are not of any "use . . . nowadays" (9), the economic system they have bequeathed to African states has further degraded women and made them, as in the case of Ruoro's daughters, harbingers of "sorrow instead of goats" (9). This sorrow emanates primarily from the sexual exploitation of women by the elite as exemplified by the deception of Wanja by Kimeria, who impregnates and then abandons her. Oddly, even the math teacher, who gets to know about Wanja's sexual escapades with Kimeria, takes advantage of this discovery by asking for a sexual favor in exchange for hiding this information from her parents. Although Wanja repulses the teacher's blackmail, leading to his informing her parents about her relationship with Kimeria, she realizes that her life is already ruined because she is carrying an unwanted pregnancy. As David Cook and Michael Okenimkpe state, Wanja is "a victim of the collusion of social forces" (111). Her parents' demonstration of sympathy upon realizing that their daughter is merely a victim of deception by an older man will not salvage her from imminent annihilation.

During the postcolonial period, men, who are the traditional breadwinners, leave the village in search of employment. Njuguna, for instance, mourns that his sons, who would have helped him till his land and produce wealth, have "gone away to European farms or to the big towns" (9). Similarly, Ruoro mourns that his sons have migrated to towns and only one "occasionally comes back to see his wife Wambui, and even he hardly stays for a day" (82). When men leave the villages, their wives, as represented by Wambui, are not only abandoned but are also forced to take up the daunting task of providing for their families. Worse still, their husbands "sometimes come to see the wives they left behind, make them round-bellied, and quickly go away as if driven from Ilmorog by Uhere [measles] or Mutung'u [small pox]" (Thiong'o 7).

Unlike in precolonial Kenya, where a woman was expected to marry and participate in her husband's and her own commercial activities, women in postcolonial Kenya find themselves unable to survive after the breakdown of precolonial commercial activities. Thus, younger women also migrate to the cities, where, due to exploitation by men, they end up bringing "unwanted children" (7) back to their aged grandmothers. Moreover, women like Wanja end up in prostitution, which she reveals is "not a very beautiful wilderness" (129), because women engage in it for lack of other means of survival. She cites the example of a barmaid who quits prostitution and becomes a housemaid. However, when her employer's wife is away, the man wants Wanja to share his bed (129). She also explains the prostitute's predicament by asserting that when she once gives up the practice and returns home, her father sends her away, stating that he does not "want a prostitute in the house" (130).

In addition, modern economic activities such as tourism are a means of sexual exploitation of women. The clearest evidence of this is the tourist who lures Wanja into his house only to prepare her for an act of bestiality with his dog. The lawyer who rescues her from the streets says that such predicaments are evidence of "what happens when you turn tourism into a national religion and build it shrines of worship all over the country" (134). In Utamaduni Cultural Tourist Center, established at Ilmorog, "[w]omen, young girls, were being recruited to satisfy watalii's [tourists'] physical whims" (334).

Like Thiong'o, Kincaid, in *A Small Place*, depicts tourism in Antigua as the embodiment of an aloofness that makes the visitor "an ugly person" (12) who does not understand and sympathize with the struggles of the indigenous people. Tourism can be considered as the former colonies' dependence on their erstwhile colonial masters because postcolonial governments such as those of Kenya and Antigua invite tourists to boost the local economies. While tourists interact mainly with tour guides and hoteliers, their actions are largely not monitored, and some, such as the one mentioned in *Petals of Blood*, overstay in their host countries and engage in sexual exploitation of local women.

Thiong'o also shows that a new type of neo-slavery, which involves sexual exploitation, will replace initial slavery and colonization. He says of the women at Utamaduni Cultural Tourist Center: "The more promising ones, those who seemed to acquire an air of sophistication with a smattering of English and German were lured to Europe as slave whores from Africa" (334). This new type of oppression of women, and in the modern days even of men, will involve "luring" rather than forced capture or invasion. A similar view of women from countries colonized by Whites is evident in Roy's *The God of Small Things*. When working "at a gas station outside Washington," Rahel encounters pimps, who "propositioned her with more lucrative job offers" (21). The American men's attempts to lure Rahel through promises of a better life appear comparable to similar efforts in the former colonies, thereby suggesting that promises of material wealth have become the bait through which women in contemporary society are ensnared and exploited by men.

Consequently, women's oppression continues even in the postcolonial period. The girl children, and the women they will become, continue to be treated as gratifiers of men's needs. Wanja appropriately compares herself and her fellow female students with their male counterparts:

> But boys were always more confident about the future than us girls. They seemed to know what they wanted to become later in life whereas with us girls the future seemed vague . . . .. It was as if we knew that no matter what efforts we put into our studies, our road led to the kitchen and to the bedroom. (37)

Indeed, that boys such as Ritho, who writes love letters to Wanja, end up spoiling women's lives foreshadows the exploitation the boys will mete on women when they grow up. Wanja is thus angry that "a silly happening . . . a boy's visit . . . a girl's and boy's school affair . . ." (36) should affect an adult woman's life. The perception of women as servants also explains why Munira does not question Wanja when she, a stranger, offers to make tea for herself in his house, and when he goes to school and returns to find "the floor swept the dishes were washed and placed on two sticks as a rack on the floor to dry" (24). It is thus not surprising that even when women work alongside men in modern factories, men are deluded "to think they were better off than women workers because they got a little bit more pay and preference in certain jobs" and because they perceive women's "real job" as lying "on their backs and open[ing] their legs to man's passage to the kingdoms of pleasure" (304). Men in the postcolonial period see women as a source of entertainment. In his expression of fear that Karega will soon "[be] drowned in wine . . . and women" (60), Abdulla, a former freedom fighter, equates women with wine, eliciting from Wanja the complaint: "Abdulla, how can you put women and wine together?" (60).

Women, Wanja further reveals, have become the means by which modern businessmen make money. She cites as an example barmaids who are paid "seventy-five shillings a month"; yet, the male bar owners "expect you to work for twenty-four hours. In the day time you give beer and smiles to customers. In the evening you are supposed to give them yourself and sigh in bed" (75, 75-76). Sometimes, Wanja continues, "you are dismissed because you refused to sleep with your boss" (129). This reality of women being sacked from employment for refusing to give sexual favors to their bosses is the subject of Thiong'o's other writings such as *Devil on the Cross*, whose female protagonist, Wariinga, a young Kenyan lady, is fired for refusing to yield to her boss's demand for sex.

In *Devil on the Cross*, however, Thiong'o shows that women of all professions, not just barmaids, are subjected to this dehumanization. In *Petals of Blood*, the encounter between Wanja and Kimeria illustrates the vicious circle of women's sexual exploitation in Kenya's postcolonial society. This accidental meeting in Kimeria's house takes place when the Ilmorog delegation is on the epic journey to Nairobi. Kimeria threatens to have the entire delegation arrested unless Wanja immediately yields to his sexual lust. Faced with imminent arrest and torture, Njuguna, an elderly man and member of the delegation, surprisingly supports Kimeria's demand, saying that Wanja was "in a way the man's wife" (156). The reader comes to grips with the cruelty of the community's elite as Wanja, in a sacrificial act, gives in to Kimeria's demand in order to have the delegation released.

The Undying Circle of Women Oppression in *The God of Small Things*

Like Thiong'o and Kincaid, Roy, in *The God of Small Things*, also shows White men as considering local women as sexual objects. Ammu's husband suggests that Ammu should accede to the lust of Mr. Hollick, a White man and the tea estate manager, who demands sex with her in exchange for keeping her husband in employment. The proposal by Mr. Hollick signifies the exploitation of local women by Whites who remain in India after the country gains her independence. On the other hand, Ammu's husband's views of her as a pawn to be used in his efforts to keep his employment, juxtaposed with the physical torture he metes out to her when she resists the proposition, shows his failure to treat Ammu as a human being who is entitled to dignity and respect.

Roy illustrates compellingly that the predicament of the woman affects her family, because Estha and Rahel become victims of the mistreatment meted out to their mother both by her family and by society. This vicious circle is expected to continue, and is evident in the way "Rahel drifted into marriage like a passenger drifts towards an unoccupied chair in an airport lounge. With a Sitting Down sense" (19). Given that she grows up "without a brief" (18), Rahel's marriage to Larry McCaslin, whom she meets in Delhi when he comes to collect material for his doctoral thesis, is not expected to last. Her troubled childhood, combined with her separation from Estha, has caused an "emptiness" (21) which even marriage cannot fill.

However, the marginalization of Ammu, by both Pappachi and society, is to blame for the predicament that befalls her. When Ammu completes high school, Pappachi "insist[s] that a college education was an unnecessary expense for a girl" (38), but sends her brother, Chacko, to Oxford University. This gender-based bestowal of education leaves Ammu vulnerable. Furthermore, her fate is already sealed because society views women as only fit for domestic work; hence, "[t]here was very little for a young girl to do in Ayemenem other than wait for marriage proposals while she helped her mother with the housework" (38). Like her "bitter, long-suffering mother" (38), Ammu also depends on her father to raise a dowry if a suitor is found for her. However, her father has just retired from employment and cannot raise enough money for the dowry. Society is also culpable because it bases the identity of a woman on a man, hence, the lack of a surname for Ammu's children because she is still considering reverting to her maiden name. "[Choosing] between her husband's name and her father's name," Ammu realizes, does not "give a woman much of choice" (37), because her identity remains founded on either of the two oppressors.

Roy depicts postcolonial Indian society as continuing the colonization of women. Pappachi's mistreatment of his wife and daughter shows this suppression. A product of colonial education, Pappachi beats his wife, refuses to assist her in the family pickle-making business, which he considers unsuitable "for a high ranking ex-Government official" (46), and will not let her in his Plymouth. In addition, by sitting on the veranda "[i]n the evenings, when he knew visitors were expected" and sewing buttons "that weren't missing onto his shirts, to create the impression that Mammachi neglected him," Pappachi is trying to show that his wife is neglecting him and not fulfilling her wifely duties. For this reason, Roy states that his action "[t]o some small degree" succeeds in "further corroding Ayemenem's view of working wives" (47). Thus, in their attempt to ensure that women remain on the periphery, men block women such as Mammachi from engaging in their own economic activities. This stance explains Pappachi's resentment of "the attention his wife was suddenly getting" (46), for her successful pickle-making, and accounts for the abrupt discontinuation of Mammachi's violin lessons when her teacher, Launsky-Tieffenthal, "made the mistake of telling Pappachi that his wife was exceptionally talented and in his opinion, potentially concert class" (49). As an indication that the girl child awaits a fate similar to that of Mammachi, Pappachi beats Ammu, who spends "cold winter nights in Delhi hiding in the mehndi hedge around their house" after Pappachi has "beaten her and Mammachi and driven them out of the house" (172).

Chacko, Pappachi's son, inflicts his father's colonial tendencies on his mother, sister and female employees. He takes over his mother's business, which he incorporates as a partnership, and informs Mammachi that she is "the Sleeping Partner" (55). Roy also observes that "[t]hough Ammu did as much work in the factory as Chacko," the latter "always referred to it as *my* Factory, *my* pineapples, *my* pickles," because according to custom, "Ammu, as a daughter, had no claim to the property" (56). This rejection of Ammu and her eventual expulsion from the home is indicative of a culture that deems daughters as undeserving of any inheritance, because they should marry and leave their parents' homes. It is this cultural position that Ammu sarcastically terms the "wonderful male chauvinist society" (56), and which Chacko interprets as, "What's yours is mine and what's mine is also mine" (56). However, Ammu's expulsion from the house emanates from her sexual relationship with Velutha, a male of the Untouchable caste. This relationship breaks Hindu society's rigid social rules, which prohibit a "Touchable" female from having any relationship with a member of the Untouchable caste. The distance that members of the Untouchables caste must keep from those of the Touchable caste is clear in that no member of Velutha's family ever enters the Ayemenem house. Indeed, Vellya Paapen, Velutha's father, has to stand in the rain when he informs Mammachi about their children's forbidden relationship. The contempt with which Paravans (one of the groups that comprise the "Untouchables") are treated is also connoted in the fact that "Mammachi could remember a time . . . when Paravans were expected to crawl backwards with a broom, sweeping away their footprints so that Brahmins or Syrian Christians would not defile themselves by accidentally stepping into a Paravan's footprint" (71).

Chacko also exploits his female workers. By calling "pretty women who worked in the factory to his room, and on the pretext of lecturing them on labor rights and trade union law, flirt[ing] with them outrageously" (62), Chacko sexually exploits his female employees. Mammachi supports such exploitation because upon Pappachi's death, "Mammachi was crying more because she was used to him than because she loved him . . . [and because] she was used to being beaten from time to time" (49). Mammachi's action thus connotes her belief that marriage, and men-women relationships in general, should not be propelled by love but by man's whimsical needs. This belief explains Mammachi's approval of Chacko's exploitation of female workers because, according to her, Chacko cannot "help having a Man's Needs" (160). Thus, she has "a separate entrance built for Chacko's room" (160) to ensure that the objects of his lust do not have to go through the house. In addition, she secretly slips money "to keep them happy" (161). While these women may be blamed for letting themselves to be used for "a man's needs," they do it, Roy reveals, because they have "young children and old parents" who need care. Others are victims of their husbands who "spent all their earnings in toddy bars" (161).

K.N.M. Pillai, the leader of the local branch of the Communist Party, also oppresses women and treats them as men's servants. For instance, Kalyani, his wife, calls him *"addeham,* which was the respectful form of 'he' whereas 'he' called her *'edi'* which was, approximately, 'Hey You!'" (256). In addition, when he arrives home, he warmly greets Chacko, but does "not acknowledge the presence of his wife or mother" (258). When he takes off his shirt, he rolls it into a ball and wipes his armpits with it before Kalyani takes and holds it "as though it was a gift" or "a bouquet of flowers" (258). This disrespect for women in contrast with the special regard for Chacko,

127

whom he should be opposed to because he is a capitalist, based on his ownership of the *Paradise and Pickles* factory, indicates that men in this society share patriarchal tendencies, and that their supposed political differences are mere rhetorical arguments devoid of any desire for real change.

The Objectification of Women in *Chotti Munda and His Arrow* and *A Small Place*

In *Chotti Munda and His Arrow*, Devi shows that women are treated as sex objects by some men who do not belong to the Munda society. For instance, Romeo, who engages in the ill treatment of women, is regarded as hero. Devi states that Romeo's real name is Shabankumar, but he "named himself Romeo" after developing a "skill to harass all women from twelve to forty" (254), around the time when he joins the Youth League. The Youth League, according to Anand Sharma, was a movement formed in 1928 by Indian youth with an intention of overthrowing the colonial regime (para. 5). Sharma indicates that the Youth League, also called All India Youth League, had "strong support of [the first prime minister of India] Pt. Jawaharlal Nehru" (para. 5). However, Devi reveals that during Indira Gandhi's emergency rule in the mid-1970s, some members of the group marginalized adivasis and sexually assaulted women. Indeed, Romeo is a killer and a rapist; in one instance, he rapes and kills a woman who refuses "to dance in her birthday suit in blameless joy and innocence of mind" (255). That Romeo can order the woman to engage in such an act shows his attitude towards women: they are entertainers whose bodies he uses as a source of amusement. Devi shows that a section of the post-independent India's administrators support Romeo's colonizing acts because "behind Romeo is the state government, the party organ, Youth League, police, Delhi" (257).

In a censure of the corruption that is evident in postcolonial India's political system, Devi asserts that "the local Member [of Parliament] understands nothing but his 'cut' ["his share"], his whore, and his debauchery" (285). Indeed, the novel shows the political class as corrupt and as opposed to those who would cater for the welfare of oppressed groups such as the adivasis. The "cut" system has been inherited by post-independent politicians from the British colonizers who had "recognized the tribal chiefs as *Zamindars* and introduced a new system of land revenue and taxation of tribal products" (Sardesai, et al 193). The postcolonial oppression of the adivasis has been extended even to parliamentary elections; in one instance, when Mundas of Chotti village go to cast votes, they find that their votes have already been cast. The inclusion of the politician's "whore" in the list of what determines a postcolonial politician's "worth" not only signifies the degradation of women but also shows that possession of women, alongside the rhetoric of postcolonial era politics, has become a symbol of political clout.

The use of a woman as such a symbol is also evident in Kincaid's *A Small Place*, where Evita is said to be a politician's "whore." Described in *A Small Place* as a "notorious woman . . . young and beautiful" (12) who lives in an expensive mansion in Antigua, Evita has enriched herself with the state's resources as a result of being "the girlfriend of somebody very high up in the government" (12). This "relationship with [a] high government official has made her the owner of boutiques and property and given her say in cabinet meetings, and all sorts of other privileges such a relationship would bring a beautiful young woman" (12). Evita's example may suggest that the "whores" become politicians' aides in their quest to loot from public coffers. This example may also indicate that women in postcolonial times use sex and beauty to defraud men, and by extension their own countries. Nonetheless, since these women, as exemplified by Evita, are "young and beautiful," they will be abandoned by politicians when they are deemed old or unattractive.

The aforementioned exploitation of women by modern communities contrasts with the regard for women among the Mundas. For instance, Chotti and all Munda men are depicted as faithful to their wives. In addition, while women even in these tribal groups are considered helpers to their husbands, their assistance, unlike that provided by the "whores," is supportive of their communities' welfare. For instance, when Chotti's wife gets pregnant, a wife must be found for Koel because "[a] bride is needed to help his ma" (42). While marriage in this case becomes a means to get a helper rather than a companion for Koel, the fact that the new bride promptly becomes a member of the family indicates this community's better treatment of women. In addition, Chotti's wife aids her heroic husband's cause for the benefit of Mundas and other low-caste and Untouchable groups. In her interview with Devi, Spivak identifies Chotti's wife as a leader who is "a wonderfully brave, resourceful imaginative woman" ("Telling History" xviii). One is not surprised that when Chotti hides a Naxalite man (who is wanted by the police for leading a protest against exploitative contractors and moneylenders) in his house at night, "[h]is wife says nothing, just feeds him priceless rice, smoked eggplant, pickle" and also gives him food to "[e]at on t' way" (224). Chotti's wife's action is commendable because the Naxalites are fighting for adivasis' land ownership rights. Alaknanda Bagchi explains that the Naxalite movement started at a period "during which the landless *adivasi* peasants rose against the dominant system and soon drew in the urban intelligentsia" (47); eventually, "the urban guerillas took up the cause of the peasants . . ." (47).

Unlike many precolonial societies, where women could become religious leaders, Munda women cannot be pahan. It is for this reason that the pahan of Chotti village is worried because he has "no male chile" because his wife and his brother's wife "breed nothin' but girl chillun" (108). The comparison of girl children with "nothing" shows the lowly position this patriarchal community has assigned to the girl child, and by extension the woman, especially regarding matters of religion and leadership. Another excess of this community is the non-involvement of women in planned marriages. For example, without involving the prospective bride in their propositions, Sugana Munda, Chotti village's pahan, and Chotti's parents determine that Sugana's daughter will marry Chotti. However, this exclusion may not be as insensitive as it appears, for Chotti himself is also not involved. Nonetheless, given that the man in this male-dominated society will be head of the family, the woman is denied a voice in the selection of her future "master" and husband.

Unlike the Bambara community, however, the Mundas have a high regard for mothers. Devi reveals that in "Chotti's society the mother's respect is equal to the father's" (27). Hence, Sugana Munda negotiates his daughter's possible marriage to Chotti with Chotti's mother instead of his father. In addition, the mother's opinion is respected, because Chotti's mother "heard everything and said to her husband, It's no' a bad idea" (27). This opinion, which her husband accepts, culminates in the marriage of Sugana Munda's daughter to Chotti. Another difference between the two communities is that while, among the Bambara a *fa* (a head of homestead) has to be replaced by a male relative when the man who occupies that

position dies, among the Mundas, a woman becomes the head of her family when her husband dies. This difference explains why Chotti's mother is "supposed to be at the helm of the household." Although she is overwhelmed by the responsibility and "looks to Chotti for every little thing" (41), the tendency to depend on Chotti is to be attributed to the latter's divine characteristics that have forced even his father, before his death, to similarly rely on him. Another indicator of the high regard this community has for women is that Mundas do not hunt female animals. This stand explains Chotti's anger when Harmu, his son, kills a female rabbit. Chotti says authoritatively: "Let's not see that agin. T'
fam'ly of life grows larger wit' girl animals, girl birds" (98). The Mundas thus credit women with the growth of communities, because they are the promulgators of life through child-bearing.

Women as Victims of War in Apartheid and Post-Apartheid South Africa

In *Ways of Dying*, which focuses on the last days of apartheid in South Africa, Mda depicts women as victims of men, colonization, and inter-ethnic wars. In "Building a Postcolonial Archive? Gender, Collective Memory and Citizenship in Post-apartheid South Africa," Cheryl McEwan acknowledges that South African women "have often been most marginalised by colonialism and apartheid and excluded from dominant accounts of history" (739). As in Thiong'o's *Petals of Blood*, women, like men, migrate to mushrooming cities in search of a better life. Thus, like Toloki who leaves his home village for the city in the hope of finding "love and fortune" (104), Noria arrives in the city thinking that "she was going to lead a cosy life," because "people in the village, and in the small town where she lived in a brick-making yard, had painted a glowing picture of life in the city" (135). Unfortunately, migrants to the city find no jobs. Noria "had a rude awakening when she arrived" because, contrary to common belief, "[t]here were no diamonds in the streets, nor was there gold"; instead, there was "[o]nly mud and open sewers . . . [unlike] anything she had seen in her life, nor anything she had imagined" (135-36). Since they have fled from abject poverty in the villages, such women have nothing to return to and end up living in deplorable conditions in urban slums.

131

Clearly, the ongoing war between both Black South Africans and the ruling Whites, and between opposing groups of Blacks, exposes women to gender-based violence. Indeed, women become victims of sexual violence. Toloki tells the sad story of a woman who has given birth only the previous day. She and her husband are traveling in a train on their way home from hospital when three gangsters saunter into their carriage and order her to surrender the baby to her husband and follow them. Toloki relates what follows: "The next day, she was found dead in the veld. The gangsters had taken turns raping her, and had then slit her throat" (98).

Women are also taken advantage of when they search for jobs. This exploitation is best exemplified by the case of the poor woman employed by Noria to take care of Vutha. Xesibe, her father, creeps between her blankets at night and threatens to rape her if she continues to resist his sexual advances. Mda sums up her situation: "She was a church woman, and a married woman with a husband and children. The fact that she was in need of a job did not mean that her body was for sale" (90). Unfortunately, the woman ends up without a job. When Noria confronts Xesibe and accuses him of trying to rape the woman, the latter responds by expelling Noria and Vutha from his house. His rendering her daughter homeless signifies his readiness to use wealth as an instrument of female exploitation.

Women are also seen as ornaments to complete a rich man's affluence. For instance, when Toloki visits Nefolovhodwe, a rich carpenter who came to the city from his village, he finds a westernized woman whom the latter introduces as his wife. However, Toloki knows Nefolovhodwe's real wife whom he left in the village when he came to the city. Nefolovhodwe later describes his wife as "the old hag" (205). Toloki is surprised to find yet another woman when he returns to Nefolovhodwe's house to pay for the food he had been given.

4.3 Feminism and Womanism: The Emergence of Modern Women

Women Empowerment in *Petals of Blood*

The writings being evaluated here show that women have attempted to free themselves from the shackles of domination. In *Petals of Blood*, Thiong'o demonstrates that women have started to reject exploitation, and have attempted to become exploiters themselves. Initially a victim of Kimeria's deception, Wanja overcomes her condition as a powerless woman prone to whimsical exploitation by men and grows into a scheming exploiter of men. While she sacrifices herself by engaging in prostitution - a way of life that her society abhors - her development into one who is "somehow sure of her power over men: She knew how they could be very weak before her body . . . [and she could] turn a man into a captive and a sighing fool" (56), indicates that she has not only usurped men's dominant role, which she uses against them, but also proved that men lack the invincibility they claim to possess. Equipped with the knowledge of their vulnerability, she thus bosses around not only the men she serves as a prostitute but others as well. Munira, one of the victims of her authority, is surprised that "his whole being [is] so ready to obey" (47) when she orders him: "and you'll bring me a pound of the long-grained rice" (47). Cook and Okenimkpe describe her as "both the instinctively wise perennial innocent, and the temptress, in spite of herself" (95). The writers further state: "Her physical appeal fits her for the role of barmaid and prostitute, yet she remains insulated from degradation by an acute and shrewd intelligence, an endless zest for life, and unfailing human sympathy" (95). Nonetheless, her childlessness, which drives her to seek even more men, may be considered as a punishment for venturing into social territories that are unacceptable to her largely conservative society. This notion notwithstanding, her childlessness could also be attributed to the exploitation of men, because she has lost the only child she had carried following her sexual encounters with Kimeria.

Thiong'o's writings also show that the modern Kenyan woman has potential to confront male chauvinism and chart a path for her own liberation. When Munira, jealous of the budding relationship between Wanja and Karega, influences the dismissal of the latter, both Wanja and Nyakinyua confront him and demand Karega's reinstatement. Although Karega is not restored to his teaching position, the fact that the women dare to confront Munira signifies their latent drive to resist domination. Moreover, the presence of the two women in the epic journey that Ilmorogians take to the city during the drought, suggests that women can no longer be excluded from political engagements.

Wanja's sagacity in her relationship with Abdulla further proves women's rejection of societal confines. Abdulla initially employs Wanja as a barmaid in his poorly stocked bar; however, he quickly realizes her business acumen and elevates her to a business partner. Indeed, it is her idea that the two should start selling food and *theng'eta*, a type of traditional liquor, to the hundreds of people who come to see the airplane that crashes in their area. Similarly, she and Abdulla acquire land, and subsequently establish a successful business. Although they later lose this business venture to Mzigo, Chui and Kimeria, rich businessmen who secure exclusive rights to brew *theng'eta*, the fact that the success of their endeavor is to be credited to Wanja, who is referred to as "the heroine of the new and the old Ilmorog" (276), demonstrates that women, given a chance, are capable of engaging in modern commercial activities. In *"Anthills of the Savannah* and *Petals of Blood*: The Creation of a Usable Past," Leonard A. Podis and Yakubu Saaka describe Wanja as possessing the "energy and benign influence that suffuse old Ilmorog" (116) and observe that "when she suddenly grows restless and cynical and leaves Ilmorog, things deteriorate" (116).

The Emergence of the Female Voice in *Segu*

In *Segu*, Condé describes women's empowerment that is partly influenced by the arrival of foreigners in Africa. For instance, after being raped by Tiekoro, Nadie begins to find her voice when she rejects the proposal to go and deliver her baby in Segu. Her statement, "But I'd rather stay with you" (114), which she utters while looking Tiekoro in the face, suggests that women in this repressive society have the potential to choose their destiny. Nadie also symbolizes this power of choice by her rejection of Islam "with mute obstinacy" (150) and her subsequent retention of her traditional African religion. However, the fact that her rejection of a new religion is "mute" suggests that women still lack the audacity to express their choices.

Nadie's offering to spin yarn, work which Tiekoro dismisses as "slave's work" (114), in order to support her family points to the emergence of women as providers for their families. Strangely, while Tiekoro dismisses Nadie's commendable efforts, he does not seek work, because "apart from teaching in a Koranic School or becoming a government official, all employment struck him as degrading" (115). Tiekoro abandons traditional work in the villages - because such work appears degrading to educated members of postcolonial societies. The case of Tiekoro and Nadie - whereby the latter "grows more serene" (149), as a satisfied breadwinner, while the former grows "more bitter, anxious and frantic" (148-49) - emphasizes the reversal of roles that colonialism has introduced to Africa. This reversal is also evident in that Malobali is forced to perform "the services of a woman" (252) when he works for Father Etienne and Father Ulrich. Unlike Tiekoro, however, the suffering that Malobali undergoes due to colonization arouses in him appreciation of women as human beings. Thus, when he inherits Romana, Naba's widow, he "discovered for the first time that a woman was a human being, whose complexity disconcerted him." That he "had possessed so many women [but] had never really paid attention to them" (284) emphasizes his change of attitude towards women after his own marginalization by colonialists.

In spite of their oppressive practices, the colonialists are to be credited with granting the African woman a voice. Thus, while Romana regrets losing Malobali in the end, she credits "the whites . . . their customs, their religion" for making her unable "to play [to Malobali] the game of submissiveness, respect and patience like her mother before her" and giving her the courage "to speak to him as an equal, to give him advice, to run him" (300). Thus, as Chinosole argues, while Condé does not depict female characters like Nadie as feminists, she "has given them voice and, through her descriptions, the power of subjectivity, which individualizes" (599) them.

If Romana's refusal to be a passive spectator in the affairs of her family is to be accepted as a positive development, the death of Malobali can be interpreted as the imminent annihilation of men who remain traditional in the face of looming changes. Such men - as further exemplified by Okonkwo, the protagonist who hangs himself in defiance of the changes brought by colonialists in Achebe's *Things Fall Apart* - will not survive. Nonetheless, Eucaristus, Romana's son, attributes his mother's eventual death to "follow[ing] Malobali even to death" (390), and asserts that blessed are "women who are more mother than wife" such as "Virgin Mary" (390). While acknowledging that women are important because they might be the bearers of kings and even divinities, Eucaristus indicts marriage with annihilating his mother.

Siga's mother-in-law, Zaida Lahbabiya, a matchmaker, demonstrates women's defiance. If men sexually exploited women in the precolonial period, women in Zaida's period dare to attempt male sexual exploitation.

Although she is unaware of her daughter Fatima's romantic relationship with Siga, Zaida forces Siga to have sexual relations with herself. Zaida has mastered not only the art of instilling fear into men, but also that of making them her subjects. Moreover, the fact that - unlike in Segu, where women have no say in the choice of their marriage partner - it is Fatima who proposes marriage to Siga shows that women will emerge from domination and choose their marriage partners. The fact that Fatima's proposal is delivered in a written note - "Are you blind? Can't you see I love you?" (182) - marks the genesis of women's emergence from silence, and signifies their potential to express their feelings in writing in the colonial and postcolonial eras. Thus, Fatima's action highlights some of the positive changes that Islam has brought to Africa. Although these changes have not yet reached Segu, women like Fatima, with whom Siga flees to Segu, herald a new perception of women in this village.

Condé also shows that despite the changes that take place in Bambara society, women remain oppressed. Although Nya has immense authority in her homestead, she remains controlled by Tiekoro, whom she sees as occupying "a peculiar place in the family" (313) and to whom she looks up for advice on family affairs, much to the chagrin of Diemogo, the family *fa*. This dependence on Tiekoro, which Siga attributes to the fact that "[a]ll Tiekoro had done was take the trouble to be born first" (321), actually emanates from Tiekoro's possession of foreign education. While foreign education is liberating, it also becomes a new force by which uneducated women like Nya will be dominated. Moreover, the fact that women's voice is not fully exhumed is embodied in that no one asks Modupe, Molara's wife, "what she thought" (314) when she and her husband bring Olubunmi to Dousika's compound. Modupe is "weeping quietly" during the occasion, because having adopted and breastfed the child for ten months after the death of his mother, she has developed a unique closeness to him.

There is further evidence that women have not been fully liberated, because even in the postcolonial era, men associate women with sexual pleasure. For instance, when Samuel, a Christian, promises to introduce Eucaristus, also a Christian and potential trainee as a priest, to a girl whom he says is "perfection itself" (398), the latter inquires: "What sort of perfection are you talking about? The breasts, the hips, the thighs? Do you know if she's good in bed?" (398). These questions suggest that men continue to undervalue women and to base their worth on sex-related organs and functions. Some Muslim men seem to have a similar attitude. Towards the end of the novel, Assa, a young slave girl, "is awoken in haste and told to bathe and scent herself before presenting herself for the stranger's pleasure" (437). Muhammad, the stranger, however turns her away promising not to "defile" her, because he has sworn not to "look at any other woman" (437) except Ayisha whom she hopes to marry. While slaves such as Assa may continue to be sexually exploited by some Muslims, Muhammad's action shows that the religion may help to change men's attitude towards women. Unfortunately for Muhammad, however, Ayisha ends up marrying his friend Alfa Guidado, whom she loves and who she admits "had always been there in her heart" (459). Like Romana, Ayisha rejects the docility expected of the African woman by her society.

Defiance as Trope in *The God of Small Things*

In *The God of Small Things* Roy also indicates that the postcolonial Indian woman will continue her quest for emancipation from cultural norms that severely limit her freedom. Baby Kochamma defiantly displays "a stubborn single-mindedness" (25) by converting to Catholicism from Syrian Christianity in pursuit of Father Mulligan. Her effort, however, amounts to naught after Mulligan leaves and becomes unreachable. Nevertheless, she charts a new path for women of her time and place, not only by attempting to follow the man she loves but also by refusing to seek other men. In addition, she refuses to re-convert to Syrian Christianity. Unfortunately, in spite of her efforts for self-emancipation in an oppressive patriarchal society, Baby Kochamma realizes that she can only be wholly free and provided for if she manipulates the family.

Baby Kochamma's sarcastic description of Ammu's marriage as a "*love* marriage" and as an "*intercommunity* love marriage" (45) deserves attention, because it shows, first, that love is not a basis for marriages in a society which sanctions only arranged marriages and, second, that marriages between members of different communities are not approved. Because the marriage is in reality not preceded by a romantic relationship, Kochamma's statement merely denotes that the marriage defies cultural restrictions. To begin with, Ammu marries the man, whose name remains unknown to the reader, as her means of escape from her oppressive Ayemenem home. Roy informs the reader that "Ammu didn't pretend to be in love with him. She just weighed the odds and accepted," because "she thought that *anything*, anyone at all, would be better than returning to Ayemenem" (39). Consequently, the reader is not surprised that the man turns out to be a liar and a drunkard "with all an alcoholic's deviousness and tragic charm" (40). The failure of the marriage notwithstanding, Ammu defies her community's requirement that a husband be found for her from her community, and that her father pay dowry to the selected husband.

Ammu's attempt to fight back, using "the heaviest book she could find in the bookshelf - *The Reader's Digest World Atlas*" (42), when her husband physically assaults her, demonstrates women's budding refusal to be battered. In addition, her decision to desert him and return to her father's home is a daring effort to explore the choices available to her. While her courageous act is to be commended, Ammu is not expected to succeed in an effort that has not been sanctioned by the society, because, unlike Baby Kochamma, who chooses to forego dependence on men, Ammu has married - and "married the wrong man" (38). Society gives the woman only one chance; hence, at only twenty-seven, Ammu arrives at "the cold knowledge that, for her, life had been lived" (38). As Ammu realizes when she looks at her wedding photographs, her marriage has made her "a foolish jeweled bride," who has "permitted herself to be so painstakingly decorated before being led to the gallows." She realizes that her action amounts to "polishing firewood," and she removes her wedding ring and has a goldsmith melt it into "a thin bangle with snake heads that she put away for Rahel" (43). The bangle may perhaps foreshadow the miserable life that Rahel, and even Estha, will lead as a consequence of their mother's failed marriage.

Although it ends in tragedy, the relationship between Ammu and Velutha indicates that Ammu refuses to accept the peripheral status that her society has assigned to her. Society disliked Velutha only because he is a member of the Untouchable caste. Indeed, Velutha is not depicted as having qualities that the society may otherwise dislike. He is a responsible, caring man who takes time to play with Rahel and Estha and who works faithfully for Pappachi's family. According to Needham, Velutha is "Estha and Rahel's (potentially) surrogate father" (372). Thus, the disgust shown by both her family and the police - her family by first locking her up, and then expelling her; the police by tapping her breast in "[a]n attempt to instill order into a world gone wrong" (Roy 246) - indicates that in Kerala society, caste and class are deemed as more important than love. Consequently, while divorced "Touchable" women like Ammu might perhaps be allowed secret relationships with "Touchable" men - secret, because divorced women are not permitted to have any romantic relationships - society will deal ruthlessly with any actions that break the caste-related taboos. Ammu and Velutha's relationship, as Maria Sabrina Alexandru writes, results from an "unspeakable similarity" since "[al]though seen as fundamentally different by society, because they belong to different castes, Ammu and Velutha identify through sharing a similar marginality" (179). Her eventual death notwithstanding, Ammu's action is acknowledged as one that "made the unthinkable thinkable and the impossible really happen" (Roy 242). One may therefore consider the two lovers as Christ figures whose deaths may be interpreted as redemptive sacrifices that will liberate their society from rules that forbid inter-caste relationships.

In contrast, Margaret divorces Chacko and marries Joe. This freedom of women in Western countries, first to choose whom to marry and, second, to divorce him and marry another, differs sharply with the stance in India. While Ammu's divorce leads to destruction, and Baby Kochamma's life as a single woman is frustrating, Margaret's second marriage foreshadows the contemporary Indian women's struggle for liberty to choose husbands of their choice. In addition, although Margaret, like Ammu, marries "without her family's consent" (234), her divorcing Chacko does not condemn her to misery. This ability to choose, nevertheless, appears catastrophic not only because Joe later dies but also because his death contributes to Sophie Mol's death, because she dies during Margaret's visit to India to "get away" (165) after his death.

Confronting the Oppressor in *Chotti Munda and His Arrow*

Through *Chotti Munda and His Arrow*, Devi reiterates the struggle of women to reject the low position that has been assigned to them by the Hindu community. Consequently, Motia, a low caste-Hindu who is said to "walk with the Munda" and even to "go to their pahan" (179), influences and confronts Tirathnath, her Hindu boss and Chotti village's landowner and moneylender. In one instance, she defends Mundas who have gone to work elsewhere instead of working at Tirathnath's farm. Through her retort, "but work's not behind" (178), to Tirathnath's complaint about missing workers, Motia suggests that her boss's grievance is unjustified, making him abandon any punitive action he might have been fomenting. Furthermore, she warns Tirathnath against blaming Chotti when the adivasis refuse to borrow food in exchange for bonded labor. She cautions him: "Your dad called Chotti's dad 'moneylender' and all this sprang from that. And now you say about Chotti he's 'started mischief'" (50). Her reminding Tirathnath about his father's mysterious death after an encounter with Chotti's late father instills fear in her boss who vehemently denies referring to Chotti as the one who has "started mischief." This denial, however, gives Motia another opportunity to attack: "Look here! You just said it, and now you said 'no' Lord! Or is this too your natural duty?" (51). Her question is a sarcastic rejoinder to Tirathnath's assertion: "To take bonded labour from adivasi and Untouchables is my natural duty" (50).

In an interview with Spivak, Devi recognizes Motia and Rakhin as emblematic of women's struggle for emancipation: "But Motia, in her own way, that Dhobin [washerwoman], who kicked at Tirathnath and went to open a laundry in Patna - that is women's resistance as well" (xviii). Motia also emerges as a potential woman leader alongside Chotti when she, "a dithering oldie" (126), asks Chotti what the community must do in the face of a severe drought. When Chotti responds that the Mundas and their low caste and Untouchable neighbors are to dig holes for water, Motia rallies her fellow women to this cause, saying, "The girls'll come too. You'll shovel sand, we'll throw it far. They'll drink too, why drink yer hard work" (126). This participation shows that while women in marginalized communities may not be allowed to lead such an initiative, they are acknowledged as playing a crucial role. In spite of being married, Tirathnath engages in an extra-marital affair with Rakhin, his washerwoman. Rakhin defrauds him of money and runs off to Patna where she establishes a laundry business. Her action shows that women will resist exploitation and, possibly for their own survival, become exploiters. Rakhin's departure drives Tirathnath to an illness as he "takes to his bed with blood pressure related problems" (276).

Women as Emancipative Force in *Ways of Dying*

In Mda's *Ways of Dying*, women are depicted as the force of liberation in South Africa. For instance, it is women who attempt to seek solutions to the predicament of the slum-dwellers. When Noria invites Toloki to a meeting meant to address such concerns as insecurity, the latter "notices that the people who are most active in the affairs of the settlement are the women," who do all the work and dominate in leadership. He also notices that "[t]he few male residents who are present relish making high-flown speeches that display eloquence, but are short on practical solutions" (172). Malehlohonolo asks at the security meeting: "While our leaders are talking with the government to put things right, the government is busy killing us with its battalion 77, and its vigilantes. What kind of negotiations are these where on the one hand they talk of peace and freedom, and on the other, they kill us dead?" (173). While there is no evidence that Malehlohonolo will get a satisfactory answer to her query, her courage implies that women are ready to confront both colonial and postcolonial oppressive forces. However, as McEwan observes, "Women [in apartheid South Africa] were located in the private realm as supporters of those in the vanguard of the liberation struggle and not in the public realm as resisters of apartheid" (745). This trend is likely to continue in the post-apartheid period because, as shown in *Ways of Dying*, women, as committee members of liberation movements, are not in the main public arena.

Mda also shows that women have embarked on the hard task of rebuilding both themselves and South Africa after years of domination. When Noria visits the settlement's residents to persuade them to stay away from work, Toloki, who accompanies her discovers that "the salvation of the settlement lies in the hands of women" (176). Mda writes:

> Toloki notices that in every shack they visit, the women are never still. They are always doing something with their hands. They are cooking. They are sewing. They are outside scolding the children. They are at the tap drawing water. They are washing clothes. (175)

The women's diligence is contrasted with the men's idleness: "Men, on the other hand, tend to cloud their heads with pettiness and vain pride. They sit all day and dispense wide-ranging philosophies on how things should be" (175). This contrast places women at the center of South Africa's political and economic systems.

South African women also attempt to fight patriarchy, which has relegated them to the periphery of both the family and society. Women Nurses may use the position to fight for their liberation. This is demonstrated by the Nurse who challenges men's behavior by asserting that "Men are dogs, and are known to wander from time to time" (18). In addition, That Mountain Woman is a powerful woman who rules her husband, and the villagers are surprised that a woman can address a man as she does. When Xesibe, her husband, pleads with Jwara to let Noria have time to eat and sleep, she admonishes him: "How dare you, father of Noria, interfere with the process of creation! Who are you Father of Noria to think that a piece of rag like you can have the right to stop my child from doing what she was born to do?" (30). Such tirades elicit from the narrator the comment that, "That Mountain Woman had razor blades in her tongue" (30). By treating Xesibe the way women are treated, That Mountain Woman usurps his position and becomes head of her family; however, she pampers her daughter and fails to protect her from sexual exploitation.

While it is true that Noria's song has creative power and is the force behind Jwara's beautiful figurines, Noria merely gets gifts from Jwara. Jwara's treatment of Noria shows that the girl child, if she has special powers as Noria does, is the object of adoration and exploitation. Furthermore, as Noria grows older, she becomes an object of sexual exploitation by taxi drivers who "would buy her gifts and flatter her" (73). The narrator suggests that Jwara is culpable for Noria's promiscuous behavior: "We were not sure whether it was Jwara who started her on this road. After all, she sang for him from the age of five, and he showered her with expensive gifts in return" (71). While it is not in doubt that Noria's mother mollycoddles her, and thus contributes immensely to her predicament, her nonchalant upbringing of her daughter merely aids the actions of Jwara and other men who take advantage of Noria.

The ability of women to liberate both themselves and others is also epitomized in Noria. She overcomes her past as a victim of male exploitation, and like Wanja in *Petals of Blood*, resists men's exploitative schemes. When she is abandoned at the home of Napu's grandmother, she insists on going back to the city with her husband. In spite of his grandmother's protest that Napu should not "be controlled by a woman" (78), Noria stands her ground and does leave for the city with Napu. Furthermore, stating that she has been "chewed, and then spewed" (144), she turns down Shadrack's request to be his lover. Shadrack, who is relatively well off compared to his under-privileged neighbors in the slums, has earlier told her: "I need you Noria. I have no one to eat my money with" (70). Noria's rejection of Shadrack's offer symbolizes her denunciation of men's view of women as passive providers of companionship or as "eaters" of men's wealth.

Noria also overcomes her traumatic past and emerges as an emancipative figure. Indeed, by housing Toloki, she physically liberates him from the streets with its potent dangers. She also frees him psychologically by treating him like a dignified human being and by helping him overcome his self-perception as "ugly." Her authoritative response: "We must never use that painful word - ugly," when Toloki describes his late father's figurines as "ugly things" (208), typifies this emancipation. Noria's admonition is important because Toloki has been termed ugly all his life - not only by his father, but also by villagers, including Nefolovhodwe who persistently refers to him as "ugly boy" (202). Sam Durrant views Noria as a "potential community leader" (443), and writes as follows concerning her new relationship with Toloki: "Thus the coming together of Toloki and Noria and their collaborative construction of a shack at the heart of an informal settlement suggest the complementarity of artistic and political labour without subsuming the one within the other" (443). Thus, Durrant implies, writing and political activitism are the tools by which the problems of postcolonial South Africa will be confronted.

Conclusion

The above discussion shows that during the precolonial period, women were the reservoirs and transmitters of cultural knowledge in their respective communities as well as providers of healthcare. They also contributed to their families' and communities' labor force, and in some cases they had their own separate economies. Their crucial roles notwithstanding, they were victims of the oppressive practices of their patriarchal communities, especially with regards to the choice of marriage partners. They also had no authority in their families, because they were deemed slaves and property. In communities such as the Bambara, which allowed females to be seized as captives of war, such slaves were sexually exploited and their children never fully accepted into any family. The authors also show that colonization introduced new methods whereby women were oppressed and their plight worsened, as they became victims of oppression both by their male-dominated societies and by colonialists. The novels show that female oppression continues even in the postcolonial period. Some of the economic practices of the post-independence period—such as tourism, the emergence of urban centers, and need for employment—have provided these societies with more milieus for women's domination. Nevertheless, influenced by globalism, education, and changing times, women in communities from India to Kenya to Antigua have embarked on quests for emancipation from male and societal domination.

CHAPTER 5
HYBRIDITY AS A MEANS OF POSTCOLONIAL SURVIVAL

Introduction

The preceding chapters have evaluated the effects of colonization on indigenous cultures especially in the contexts of language, religion and the status of women. These chapters have shown that colonial domination attempted to replace languages and religion, and that this domination worsened the position of the woman within these cultures. The chapters have also shown that because of colonization, peoples of the former colonies were forced to adopt numerous Western concepts and patterns of behavior while still retaining elements of their own indigenous cultures.

In *The Africans: A Triple Heritage,* Mazrui identifies four main stages of cultural integration: first, when two or more systems of values meet and begin "to be aware of each other's peculiarities"; second, when these cultures discover "areas of incompatibility and mutual incoherence"; third, when one culture establishes itself as superior to another and forces the latter either to surrender or to employ "cultural revival and resurrection of original authenticity"; fourth, when there occurs a "cultural coalescence or integration, a fusion of two or more cultures into a new mixed legacy" (239). The fourth stage is perceived as the reality for most formerly colonized communities as they have retained the core aspects of their cultural values while accommodating many colonial notions.

Frantz Fanon takes a position similar to Mazrui's with regards to one culture's adoption of elements of another. Describing culture as "the combination of motor and mental behaviour patterns arising from the encounter of man with nature and with his fellow man" (32) in *Toward the African Revolution: Political Essays,* Fanon espouses the concept of "universality," which involves a decision to "recognize and accept the reciprocal relativism of different cultures, once the colonial status is irreversibly excluded" (44). Fanon thus suggests that the outcomes of colonization cannot be wished away, and that colonized cultures must accommodate inescapable elements of the colonialists' cultures.

In *Culture and Imperialism,* Edward W. Said argues that an examination of the "identity, history, tradition, uniqueness" of a people will involve the placement of these concepts "in a geography of other identities, peoples, cultures, and then to study how, despite their differences they have always overlapped one another through unhierarchical influence, crossing, incorporation, recollection, deliberate forgetfulness, and, of course, conflict" (330-31). Said's statement implies that formerly colonized peoples cannot fully define their postcolonial identities outside the influences of other cultures because, due to colonization and factors such as migration and adoption of Western systems, their identities "overlap" with those of other peoples.

This concept of accommodating foreign cultures within one's own is referred to as cultural hybridity by Salman Rushdie. In *In Good Faith*, Rushdie defends his novel *The Satanic Verses* as comprising "a group of characters most of whom are British Muslims, or not-particularly-religious persons of Muslim background, struggling with just the sort of great problems that have arisen to surround the book, problems of hybridization and ghettoization, of reconciling the old and the new" (4). Because *The Satanic Verses* centers on Muslims who are influenced by both religious and secular phenomena, Rushdie concludes that it "celebrates hybridity, impurity, intermingling, the transformation that comes of new and unexpected combinations of human beings, cultures, ideas, politics, movies, songs" (4). Hybridity is thus to be experienced in postcolonial societies because the religious, political, economic and social systems of precolonial societies have been influenced by colonization. In *Salman Rushdie's Postcolonial Metaphors: Migration, Translation, Hybridity, Blasphemy and Globalization*, Jaina C. Sanga recognizes hybridity as a Rushdian concept, and describes it as "the process or the moment of homogenization when dissimilar entities are combined and exist in complement with each other" (75). Sanga further states that "[i]n terms of culture and contemporary representations of reality, hybridity involves the melange of an incongruous array of genders, classes, nationalities, religions and ethnicities" (75). Sanga's description of hybridity in its broader sense is crucial because it includes gender and religion.

Rushdie's consideration of hybridity resonates with Homi K. Bhabha's definition of national culture. In *Nation and Narration*, Bhabha writes that "[t]he locality of national culture is neither unified nor unitary in relation to itself, nor must it be seen simply as 'other' in relation to what is outside or beyond it" (4). He states that the question of what is within or without a national culture "must always itself be a process of hybridity, incorporating new 'people' in relation to the body politic, generating other sites of meaning and, inevitably, in the political process, producing unmanned sites of political antagonism and unpredictable forces for political representation" (4). Bhabha further argues that the identity of a nation is not a homogenous phenomenon because national culture can only "be articulated as a dialectic of various temporalities—modern, colonial, postcolonial, 'native' . . ." (302). Bhabha's statements portend that the identity of a people or nation must accommodate not only such a people's past, but also the people's contemporary reality. Such an identity is impossible without the "hybridization" of the diverse influences on a people, culture or nation, especially because these countries are not monocultural but multicultural.

Some may argue that the notion of hybridity is another form of neocolonialism because it places less emphasis on colonial oppression and social evils within the postcolony. However, because colonization is irremediable, the survival of postcolonial societies is only possible if such societies redefine their identity in a manner that recognizes both their uniqueness as non-Western communities *and* their inheritance of Western systems of communication, worship, education, and politics, among others. This notwithstanding, the use of hybridity by postcolonial societies must not be deemed an entirely positive affair. While cultural hybridity is a harmless, voluntary process if it is perceived as a fusion of different cultural values, postcolonial hybridity is a painful experience because it is an aftermath of colonial denigration of indigenous values. Thus, as R. Radhakrishnan writes, one must distinguish "between hybridity as a comfortably given state of being and hybridity as an excruciating act of self-production by and through multiple traces" (159). Radhakrishnan's distinction of two forms of hybridity is therefore crucial to the assessment of the adequacy of hybridity to describe the cultural situation of formerly colonized peoples. It will suffice to state here that postcolonial hybridity is painful because, in Radhakrishnan's words, "hidden within [it] is the subject of the dominant West" (159).

With the foregoing, this chapter will assign specific sections to the discussion of the irreversibility of the colonial enterprise, hybridity in language and educational contexts, hybridity in religious beliefs and practices, and the status of women in changing societies. However, not all the novels will be referred to in each section of this chapter because the writer considers the information in some of them inadequate to form a coherent argument. For instance, the section on the irreversibility of the colonial enterprise will refer only to Jamaica Kincaid's *A Small Place*, Mahasweta Devi's *Chotti Munda and His Arrow*, and Maryse Condé's *Segu*; while *A Small Place* will not be included in the discussion on religious hybridity. The section on the status of women in changing societies will refer to Ngugi wa Thiong'o's *Petals of Blood*, *Segu* and Arundhati Roy's *The God of Small Things* because these texts best elucidate the concept of women and hybridity.

5.1 The Irreversibility of the Colonial Enterprise

The novels in this study show that formerly colonized peoples cannot erase colonization and its effects because erstwhile colonizers left behind not only certain elements of their culture but also restructured such systems as political governance, education, and economic activity. Indeed, in *The Africans: A Triple Heritage* Ali A. Mazrui argues that acceptance of some of the colonial notions is unavoidable because the impact of the colonial enterprise is permanent. For instance, he writes, it is Europe that "Africanised Africa" through cartography and mapmaking, which culminated in the fact that "what we regard as Africa today is primarily what Europeans decided was Africa" (101). Mazrui thus reminds peoples of the former colonies that their identification of themselves as African, Indian, or Caribbean is not devoid of imperial undertones. In identifying "imperialism and colonization" as emanating from colonial racism, Mazrui writes that Africans' self-identity remains shaped by this racism, which in the first place enhanced their "mutual recognition of each other as 'Fellow Africans'" (101). Consequently, the irreversibility of certain colonial effects is crucial to understanding the postcolonial identities of former colonies because these colonies can never return to their way of life as it existed in the precolonial age.

Meeting the World through England in *A Small Place*

In *A Small Place*, Kincaid uses her unnamed protagonist to bring out this irreparability. The protagonist laments that he or she, like other formerly colonized peoples, has been removed from his or her real self-identity and forced to adopt another identity. To indicate that neither apology nor the payment of indemnity can replace what colonization has taken away, Kincaid asserts:

> But nothing can erase my rage - not an apology, not a large sum of money, not the death of the criminal - for this wrong can never be made right, and only the impossible can make me still: can a way be found to make what happened not to have happened? (32)

Since "what happened" cannot be undone, Kincaid implies, it is impossible for Antiguans to return to the way of life that pre-dated colonization. Further manifestation of this notion, which Suzanne Gauch terms "entrapment within the signifying system of the former colonizer" (916), is evident in Kincaid's statement: "I met the world through England, and if the world wanted to meet me, it would have to go through England" (33). Kincaid thus professes that there exist fundamental foreign aspects in postcolonial cultural systems. This statement reiterates that Antiguan worldview has been Europeanized because some of the changes brought by imperialism are irreversible. Kincaid further alludes to these lasting changes when she asserts that former colonialists "should, at least, be wearing sackcloth and ashes in token penance of the wrongs committed, the irrevocableness of their bad deeds, for no natural disaster imaginable could equal the harm they did" (23-24).

The reader of *A Small Place* may take issue with Kincaid's assertion that "[a]ctual death might have been better" (24), because such a conclusion implies that the precolonial way of life was flawless. However, the reader must still admit that colonialists did destroy some of the nurturing segments of indigenous cultural systems. Nonetheless, because both precolonial and colonial cultures had strengths and weaknesses, the reader cannot declare that all cultural norms introduced by colonialists were malevolent.

Furthermore, any reader interested in knowing his or her cultural heritage will find offensive Kincaid's assertion that "[a]s for what we were like before we met you, I no longer care. No periods of time over which my ancestors held sway, no documentation of complex civilizations, is any comfort for me" (37). Such readers would like Kincaid and erstwhile colonized communities to "at least care" about their cultural roots, and to appreciate any documentation of their ancestors' cultural values. Although Kincaid appears to reject her traditional past, her statement must not be interpreted as a dismissal of the preservation of precolonial systems through folklore, rituals and other traditional means. Instead, Kincaid avows that, while such records must be cherished and appreciated, their existence in the backdrop of colonial cruelty offers "no comfort" to an individual whose identity has been annihilated. In addition, there are chances that some aspects of culture as practiced in the precolonial period would have changed anyway. Kincaid alludes to the dynamic nature of culture when she writes:

> ...and what is culture anyway? In some places, it is the way they play drums; in other places, it's the way you behave in public; and in still other places, it's the way a person cooks food. And so what is there to preserve about these things? For is it not so that people make them up as they go along, make them as they need them? (49-50)

Kincaid shows culture as a changing phenomenon because members of a community may experience an event gradually, "until eventually they absorb the event and it becomes a part of them, a part of who and what they really are, and they are complete in that way until another event comes along and the process begins again" (53). She implies that culture, as it exists in both the former colonies and in Western countries, is influenced by many events that took place in the respective regions. Her stance appears to echo that of David A. B. Murray who writes, in "The Cultural Citizen: Negations of Race and Language in the Making of Martiniquais," that the colonial impact cannot be overlooked in Martinique, another Caribbean island. Murray argues that Martinique's citizens have to incorporate "certain qualities of French nationalist identity such as individualism . . . [within] an identity that was distinct and liberated from France without fomenting widespread desire for political and economic independence" (79). Hence,

Martinique's citizens have accepted the French political and economic systems, but they still retain their cultural identity.

Nonetheless, the above statement by Kincaid must be purged of two notions. First, that culture is merely about how members of a community "play drums," "how they behave in public" or "how they cook"; such a definition of culture limits it to merely the most visible elements of a community's material life. Second, as much as these visible elements appear as not worth preserving, they deserve conservation because they may reflect deeper beliefs or a community's worldview.

Confronting the Inevitable in *Chotti Munda and His Arrow*

Similarly, Devi, in *Chotti Munda and His Arrow*, admits that despite efforts by the adivasis to retain their traditional culture, changes brought to India both by colonization and independence are unavoidable. Devi depicts the Mundas' prophetic icon, Chotti, as realizing "that with the passage of time the Mundas' way of thinking and talking is also changing" (106). Devi's assertion must not be interpreted to mean that the Mundas' way of "thinking and talking" was illogical before colonial influence. Instead, it is an indication that Mundas have to accommodate certain elements of colonial and post-independence realities. Such realities, as Devi says in her interview with Archana Masih, include loss of adivasis' land because "[f]or any industrial project like dams that come up, tribal land is taken" (para 18). Moreover, Mundas have to contend with such hitherto non-existent institutions as Christian missions, the railway, and the police. The changes are shown as on-going rather than conclusive in that Chotti not only concedes that "[t]' Munda's mood is changing,'" but also predicts further changes through the rhetorical question: "When our kids grow up, who knows what words they'll say, what deed they'll do" (112).

Devi further indicates that the changes that have taken place in India, from colonial times to independence to postcolonial inequities, have forced the adivasis to re-define their identity. Therefore, as Chotti says, "it is clear that the time has come to rewrite old proverbs" (241). If "old proverbs" are interpreted as symbolic of traditional philosophy and orality, then, their "rewriting" amounts to cultural modification that encompasses postcolonial reality. For example the community's saying that the poor, who have

151

nothing to lose in case they are attacked, need not fear a robber, has been modified to the proverb, "It is the naked who must most fear the thief and armed robber" (241), because the poor such as the Mundas are victims of exploitation by moneylenders and other oppressive officials of colonial and postcolonial India. Similarly, the Mundas seek Christian missions for short-term gains - even though they have to give up their religion. The fact that these Mundas must confront colonization and its effects is also evident towards the end of the novel, when Chotti organizes an arrow shooting competition as a political protest against the S.D.O. and the police.

The Imposed Model in *Segu*

Condé's *Segu* similarly implies that despite imminent defeat of Arabic oppressors and European colonialists, the Segu kingdom has been irreparably altered. One of the major indications that the colonial experience and its effects are indelible is embodied in Eucaristus's response to Emma's inquiry as to why he desires to travel to England in pursuit of theological education: "I think the white man's model will impose itself on us whether we like it or not. And soon the world will belong to those who know how to make use of it" (404). Emma has earlier accused Eucaristus of being "so in love with England and the English" as though Africans "ought to imitate them in everything" (404). Eucaristus's response thus indicates his rejection of the notion that Africans should "imitate everything"; he admits reasonably that colonized peoples will need certain core aspects of Western concepts, which he terms as "the model." This interpretation of Eucaristus's argument appears credible given that he tells Emma how he perpetually questions whether "the white man's civilization [is] better than that of our ancestors" (404).

Segu shows this model as inescapable even at the king's palace, which is perhaps the most conservative and most powerful representation of Bambara culture. The gravity of the change that has taken place in the palace is evident in that Da Monzon, the king, has earned the new title of "master of night suns" (132), because he has installed "some big shiny metal chandeliers with candles" so that "there was no such thing as night anymore" (132). Nonetheless, the fact that his African titles, including "master of battle, the long snake that protects Segu, source of vitality, and so on" (132), are retained indicates that the new way of life will not completely obliterate the old. Further evidence that the king has modified his palace so as to accommodate items introduced by Segu's colonial masters is that he has had "a private drawing room built, with European armchairs and low settees covered with Moroccan blankets" (132). The king has also borrowed Islamic attire, including "loose white drawers and a red *boubou* or long tunic" (140), but has retained "a long leather-bound stick and a broad saber" which are recognized as "the only insignia of royalty" (140).

The irresistible changes that have taken place in the palace underscore the accommodation of some of the foreign cultural elements by the Bambara community whose members are unable to resist "[m]anufactured goods from Europe and North Africa" (321). It is thus not surprising that when the king visits Dousika's homestead when the latter dies, the mourners, "in accordance with a recently introduced custom . . . were firing off guns in the dead man's compound, guns he had gotten from traders on the coast" (141). The firing of guns, juxtaposed with the fact that "[c]rowds of griots appeared like a swarm of locusts descending on a field and began to proclaim Dousika's exploits and lineage" (141), shows that this community's rites of passage have been adjusted to allow the inclusion of a foreign way of honoring a deceased hero.

Another demonstration that such imperial undertakings as slavery have forever changed Africa is the fact that the *agoundas*, Africans who have returned from slavery in Brazil, "swathed in silk and velvet out in the sun" (282) during the wedding of Romana and Malobali. Romana is an agounda while Malobali is the slave of Father Etienne and Father Urlich, missionaries to West Africa. The wedding, which is solemnized by Father Urlich, elicits complaints from individuals like Birame who have not tasted the misery of slavery outside Africa. They wonder why the agoundas did not stay in Brazil "[i]f all the agoundas were interested in was perpetuating the memory of Brazil" (283). However, these agoundas imbibed these practices during slavery, which took away their original identities. In fact, these adopted Brazilian practices are emblematic of their freedom, because during the weddings they had witnessed in Brazil, "all they had done was bring in the dishes" (284) because they were not allowed to participate in such activities. "But now," Condé writes, "it was they who danced to the music of waltzes and quadrilles, with an abandon perhaps unknown to the Portuguese" (284). While the agoundas may be criticized for refusing to return to their traditional African ways of conducting weddings, their actions are vindicated by the fact that they might not have taken part in any African weddings, especially if they were born in Brazil or were captured when they were children. In addition, the African rite of marriage, as practiced by those who have never experienced slavery, is likely to change because missionaries such as Father Urlich will introduce Christian weddings. This possibility thus puts both agoundas and local populations on the threshold of imminent cultural change.

5.2 Hybridity in Educational and Language Contexts

Chapter 2 has shown that colonial languages and education were introduced to the former colonies, forcing the colonized peoples to adopt foreign languages and educational systems. For this reason, except Devi, who writes in Bengali, the authors under study write in English. This is not only because doing so enables them to reach an international audience, but also because colonial languages are widely used in their nations. However, the adoption of colonial systems did not in any way obliterate precolonial wisdom, neither did it signify the abandonment of indigenous languages.

The Indigenization of Colonial Language in *A Small Place*

Colonial language may be indigenized by the formation of various local dialects. This possible indigenization of a colonial language echoes Kenneth Ramchand's revelation that speakers and writers of the Caribbean region have adopted diverse types of creolized English. Ramchand argues that "[i]n the twentieth century we have to give up the notion of separate languages (Creole English and Standard English) and we have to envisage a scale" (90). Ramchand says that one of the reasons for the existence of many versions of English among writers is that "coexisting with the new literary growth in the West Indies, and pre-dating it, is a long oral tradition of storytelling and folk poetry in the dialect" (114). Thus, while placing these dialects within the Caribbean cultural history, he identifies them as progressively changing versions of the Creoles emanating from the "bad English" spoken by African slaves and their descendants. It is possible that writers of other regions also use indigenized colonial languages, because, as Gayatri Chakravorty Spivak states in "Can the Subaltern Speak," while "[c]ertain varieties of the Indian elite are at best native informants for First World intellectuals interested in the voice of the Other," even these informants must use elements of their indigenous selves because "the colonized subaltern *subject* is irretrievably heterogeneous" (79).

The stance advanced by both Ramchand and Spivak is significant in understanding the undertones of Kincaid's sarcastic protest that today's young people are unable to answer simple questions "in their native tongue of English" (44). Clearly, Kincaid wishes to draw her reader's attention to the existence of a "native tongue of English" - an adaptation of the colonial language to the local cultural and linguistic norms. This adaptation suggests that while colonized people may recognize that colonial languages have been imposed on them, they can contextualize these languages and create hitherto non-existent dialects. Kincaid's assertion that the tourist has "an accent" (17) may therefore be interpreted as a defense of these indigenized versions of English. Murray similarly shows that Creoles, indigenized forms of colonial languages, are heavily used in Martinique. He writes that while French is Martinique's official language, "[e]ven in public settings and institutions where French is considered to be the proper language of communication, Creole often erupts and disrupts its authoritative position" (87). Consequently, in Martinique, Antigua and elsewhere, colonial languages exist alongside their indigenized counterparts.

Formal Education and Survival in *Chotti Munda and His Arrow*

On the other hand, Mahasweta Devi, in *Chotti Munda and His Arrow*, shows that although there exist an elaborate traditional educational system in the case of Mundas, the effects of colonization and of independence necessitate a review of the indigenous education and its effectiveness in colonial and postcolonial eras. In spite of the perceptible invincibility manifested in the use of cultural education, there is evidence that Mundas' inability to read and write presents an insurmountable setback in their efforts to survive in colonial and postcolonial India.

In "Hindutva, Religious and Ethnocultural Minorities, and Indian-Christian Theology," Sathianathan Clarke identifies adivasis as a group that includes "many more or less homogeneous indigenous communities, which are not obligated to the Indian caste system yet are marginalized by caste

155

communities" (199). Clarke recognizes that "there is a serious threat to their traditional culture and worldview from the forces of modernization and Hinduization" (199). In fact, the adivasis are exploited because they can neither read nor write; hence, without knowing the extent of their commitment, they put thumbprints that bind them and their descendants to providing labor for their lifetimes in exchange for meager amounts of food. In the interview with Masih, Devi agrees that tribals in India need "[e]ducation, at least functional literacy" (para. 20) in order to enhance their interaction with the mainstream Indian society.

The ability to read and write would enable Mundas to understand India's legal system, which was adapted from the British system. Contrary to the Indian legal system, the Mundas settle disputes among themselves by orally presenting their cases to their pahan, who makes judgments. Since colonization has forced the whole of India to have a unitary legal system, the Mundas have become victims of laws that they neither know nor understand. Formal education would provide, first, language skills that would enable communication between Mundas, lawyers and judges and second, knowledge regarding the legal system bequeathed to India by the British. Education would indeed have saved such Mundas as Dukhia Munda, who pleads guilty instead of innocent as advised by the lawyer, and the many members of the Munda, Oraon, Dusad-Dhobi communities who are "in je-hell fer land rights cases, but they don' know what they did wrong" (321). Moreover, the reference to "land rights" is reminiscent of the many rights, both theirs and other people's, that formal education would enable them to access. Indeed, as Devi implies, education would enable them to fight for compensation for their land because "[w]hen [government officials] take land, it is never land for land or money for land, so in this condition [adivasis] become a nomadic migrant mass of people in search of work" (Masih para. 18).

Since non-Mundas are likely to misrepresent facts about Mundas, the latter must acquire literacy so that they can preserve authentic written records about their culture and history. This notion underlies Chhagan Dusad's declaration that his "booklearning" enables him to write the "story tale" (54) when for the first time Tirathnath gives the adivasis food without binding them to bonded labor. In spite of attempts by such White characters as Ronaldson Hugh - the brother of the Provincial Governor's Secretary, who learns the Mundari language, draws pictures of Munda heroes, writes down their songs and records details of their culture - to assist the adivasis, the latter need to acquire the ability to preserve their own cultural heritage. Indeed, Hugh seems to be a lone artist who does not live long enough to write accounts about the adivasis, because he is killed by a villager as he draws pictures of adivasis in Uganda. His death implies that the adivasis in India, Uganda and other former colonies must take up the efforts to preserve their own culture - a feat they can achieve only if they acquire the necessary educational skills.

To prevent further exploitation, the adivasis have to accept cultural hybridity. While they must reject the impurity of some non-adivasi notions such as moneylending, they must retain their core virtues such as humanity, harmony with nature, diligence and honesty, while pursuing certain elements of formal education, which will enable them to resist the exploitation of their forests and minerals.

Moreover, Gayatri Spivak's translation of Devi's *Chotti Munda and His Arrow* connotes a writer's adjustment of English to convey indigenous notions. In her introduction of the novel, Spivak writes: "One of the most striking characteristics of the novel is the sustained aura of subaltern speech, without the loss of dignity of the speakers" (Devi viii). She also refers to Devi's reaction after the latter reads the translated novel: "Gayatri, what I am really enjoying in your translation is how you've shown that dialect can be dignified" (Devi viii). The two writers thus suggest that the style, diction, and sentence structure of English language employed in the novel are appropriate because they effectively portray the nature of communication among the Mundas.

Hybridity, Education and Language in *Petals of Blood*

The notion of hybridity explains such concepts as the "Africanization" of education as emphasized in Ali A. Mazrui and Michael Tidy's *Nationalism and New States in Africa*. Mazrui and Tidy observe that African post-independent governments engaged in "Africanizing teaching personnel, curricular and syllabuses," by ensuring "the rapid decline of missionary control over primary and secondary education, secularization of staff and a corresponding increase in state control of schools," as well as the introduction of "predominantly African history and literature" (304) at some levels of learning. Thus, while retaining colonial institutions, African governments sought to hybridize education by removing certain aspects of Western cultural indoctrination and including concepts of indigenous culture.

In *Petals of Blood*, Thiong'o shows that in spite of the havoc caused by the elite such as Chui, Jerrod and Kimeria, Western education is necessary for survival in today's global society. For instance, the lawyer who helps Wanja, and later the delegation from Ilmorog, admits that he has acquired Western education and is thus "an expert in those laws meant to protect the sanctity of the monster-god and his angels" (163); however, he uses his knowledge to rescue oppressed people who get into trouble with the law. This necessity of Western literacy underlies Thiong'o's own return to the use of the English language in writing his novels, years after declaring that he would only write in Gikuyu. Simon Gikandi points out that Thiong'o could not escape Western influence in his writing: "What did it mean to produce literature and theory in an African language according to the protocols established by American and European institutions?" (195-96). Gikandi questions the rationale of the publication at New York University of *Mutiiri*, a Gikuyu journal, because Thiong'o's immediate audience could not read the work, while Gikuyu speakers resided far away (196). Thiong'o's return to English may be interpreted as his realization that English is important not only as an instrument of protest against colonization but also as a medium to convey information to an educated postcolonial audience.

Abdulla's narration of stories to the children during Ilmorogians' epic journey to Nairobi shows that storytelling, a traditional mode of conveying the community's secrets, is still in use in contemporary African society. Thiong'o's reference to oral traditions elicits from Leonard A. Podis and Yakubu Saaka the conclusion that *Petals of Blood* "offers a radical critique of Kenyan society, calling for a revolution based on the rediscovery of indigenous culture with its communal traditions" (105). These children, who are enrolled in Munira's school, also need formal education; hence, the two educational systems (traditional and current) must exist side by side, and informal teachers, such as Abdulla, must teach alongside formal ones if the African student is to acquire Western education but keep his identity. The case of these children is similar to that of Mundas in *Chotti Munda and His Arrow*, for Mundas must adopt literacy but maintain their use of songs as a means of transmission of cultural history. Further indication that the old means of instruction become an integral part of life in the post-independence era is manifested in the performance of traditional dances on the eve of the circumcision of some of the boys from Ilmorog. Indeed, the villagers' engagement in the rite of circumcision, a mark of transition from childhood to adulthood, shows that traditional rites of passage will not be extinguished.

Undoubtedly, language, as Thiong'o argues in *Decolonising the Mind*, is the weapon that the erstwhile culturally dominated peoples must use to defend their cultural identity and re-assert their existence as groups that are distinct from Europeans. He wonders why many postcolonial African authors write in English instead of their mother tongues. He rejects the European notion that languages such as English, French and Portuguese are to be used in many milieus because they have "a capacity to unite African peoples against divisive tendencies inherent in the multiplicity of African languages within the same geographic state" (6-7). However, African and other writers of formerly colonized territories may find writing in foreign languages inescapable because, as Simon Gikandi implies in "Travelling Theory: Ngugi's Return to English," writing in indigenous languages limits the works' readership (194).

Nonetheless, Thiong'o's position on the inadequacy of foreign languages to solve Africa's problems is consistent with that of Ali A. Mazrui and Michael Tidy who, in *Nationalism and New States in Africa*, write that while foreign languages such as English and French are "invaluable in various ways for modern African development [because they] help to integrate Africa in world culture . . . [and] are politically neutral in the context of Africa's multi-ethnic communities" (300), these languages do not "necessarily help to overcome the crisis of national integration, which is one of the most fundamental political problems facing African countries" (300). While Mazrui and Tidy recognize the necessity of such languages as English as a medium for globalization, they contend that these languages do not enhance communication between people of the same geographical state. They further argue, quite credibly, that these languages are "intrinsically and hopelessly ill-equipped" (300) to meet the challenge of interethnic communication at the grassroots level because they are the preserve of the educated.

Stating that "imperialism continues to control the economy, politics, and cultures of Africa" (*Decolonising* 4), Thiong'o posits that Africans and other formerly colonized societies are nevertheless engaged in "an ever-continuing struggle to seize back their creative initiative in history through a real control of all the means of communal self-definition in time and space" (*Decolonising* 4). He believes that language occupies a pivotal position in mapping a postcolonial self-identity because "[t]he choice of language and the use to which language is put is central to a people's definition of themselves in relation to their natural and social environment, indeed in relation to the entire universe" (*Decolonising* 4). Consequently, an analysis of the use of languages - both colonial and indigenous - in former colonies may show that while in most cases local languages have not been completely erased because they enable local interaction, foreign languages have been adopted as the media for economic, educational and political communication.

Accordingly, language continues to be the means by which Kenyans, through their subversive writings and political protest, continue to resist the evils of the colonial and postcolonial eras. In *Petals of Blood*, when Karega is arrested as a suspect in the murder of Mzigo, Chui and Kimeria, the workers of Ilmorog go to the police station and shout: "*Long live the workers' struggle!*" (4) as they demand his release. When the police ask them to disband, the workers retort:

> Disband yourself . . .; disband the tyranny of foreign companies and their local messengers! Out with foreign rule policed by colonised blackskins! Out with exploitation of our sweat! (4)

Their action not only highlights Africans' refusal of neocolonization but also indicates that language will continue to occupy a prominent position both in a people's assertion of their identity and in their struggle for political and economic emancipation.

Hybridity, Education and Language in *Segu*

In *Segu*, Condé shows that although cultural education is passed orally through songs, narratives and wise sayings among the Bambara people of Segu, literacy, which is spread by both Arabs and Europeans, finds acceptance in the community. This education, with the religions and languages it brings into Segu, appears crucial as the community interacts not only with its immediate neighbors but with far-off peoples. However, Tiekoro and other pursuers of this education realize that they are never wholly accepted by the foreigners even after they successfully complete prescribed courses. This culture-based discrimination emphasizes the need for the educated to aver their humanity as well as re-accept some of their traditional beliefs such as those regarding nobility and kinship.

While Siga realizes that education as provided by Muslims in his area is important, he questions its connection to Islam, thereby rejecting its indoctrinating role. His refusal to "sing praises" of a foreign God combined with his declaration that the Islamic deity is not his God (178), demonstrates his contempt for Muslims' use of education as the arena for conversion of Bambaras to Islam. Siga thus charts a new path for his community by acquiring education while retaining his traditional religion. Furthermore, his daring endeavor to assert the intrinsic value of his traditional religion in a letter to Cheikou Hamadou, Muhammad's Islamic teacher, foreshadows the use of writing to assert the identity of the colonized communities. Indeed, demanding that Hamadou release Muhammad, Tiekoro's son, to the family, Siga writes that his community has the "right to reject Islam" because it is not the religion of its ancestors. Despite rejecting Islam, however, Siga initially accepts a superficial change of name to Ahmed, a change which enables him to get a job, first as a donkey boy and later as a trading assistant. His adoption of the Islamic greeting "*wa aleyka salam*," which "had been adopted even by unbelievers" (424), indicates that he accepts some elements of Islam as long as such elements do not interfere with his fundamental beliefs.

Hybridity is also evident in the many languages that Eucaristus speaks. These languages include Portuguese and Yoruba, which were his mother's languages; English, which is the medium of instruction in College; and French. Clearly, these languages are a reminder of his parents' lives in both the slavery and pre-slavery eras, as well as his life as a child born in slavery and as a student at Fourah Bay College.

Locating the Balance in *The God of Small Things*

In *The God of Small Things*, Roy shows that if cultural hybridity is to be accepted as the means by which postcolonial societies negotiate the turbulent cultural confusion that arises from colonialism, the decline of Pappachi's family may be attributed to adherence to Western values at the exclusion of local ones. Because the Indian society is intrinsically hybrid, local values may include notions acquired from diverse cultural locales. In fact, in "Reexamining Indian Nonalignment: Arundhati Roy's *The God of Small Things*," Anna Guttman writes that "[t]he hybrid Indian culture is both a result and an aspect of the 'environment'" (124). This statement implies that Indian culture is not compellingly aligned to any one particular colonial power. Nonetheless, because Pappachi is a product of colonial education, he glorifies Western culture and refuses to adjust his life to his immediate environment. Thus, he is a culturally maladjusted individual who continues to dress in suits even after he has retired from his executive job.

Pappachi's son, Chacko, the eventual heir of both his father's Plymouth and his mother's pickle-making factory, also demonstrates similar cultural maladjustment. Despite acquiring Western education at the prestigious Oxford University, Chacko emerges as a failure because the bulk of what he has learnt, as exemplified by the long quotes he has memorized from European writers, is not needed in his environment. It is not surprising that he eventually relocates to Canada, perhaps in an attempt to find a locale conducive to the acculturation he has received in England and the Western attitude of his father. On the other hand, Rahel and Estha, Ammu's twins, cannot survive when they are separated both from each other and from their mother because the Western education they receive takes them further away from their Indian identity. Nonetheless, the Pappachi family demonstrates hybridity in its use of language. For instance, despite the fact that both Chacko and the twins quote long passages from the writings of European authors, they largely use the local Malayalam language in their communication within the family.

Digging out the Past in *Ways of Dying*

Likewise, Zakes Mda, in *Ways of Dying*, emphasizes that hybridity is necessary in post-apartheid South Africa. In an indication that the colonial endeavor has left indelible marks not only in South Africa but also in all former colonies, Michael Chapman, in "The Problem of Identity: South Africa, Storytelling, and Literary History," states that "[o]nce secure national identities and nations - homogenous in language, religion, and culture - have now among their permanent citizenry the black Briton, the German Turk, and the Chicano American" (87). For this reason, he continues, colonized peoples must dig up their past oral traditions and combine them with postcolonial education:

> But because in South Africa we lack a shared heritage we are under an obligation - as the West no longer thinks it is - to retrieve our ancient folk traditions. In reminding ourselves of the humanity colonialism and apartheid consistently denied the indigenous people, we are reminded that the stories of the earliest people of the subcontinent - Bushmen and Bantu-speaking Africans - are stories of human sense-making that deserve consideration along with any of the great mythologies of the world. (94)

Chapman's notion that people must rediscover the past is exemplified by the arrival of Jwara's figurines to Toloki and Noria's shack in the city. Indeed, the fact that the figurines, which symbolize past village life, have been brought to the city denotes that life in post-apartheid South Africa will embrace both past and present economic practices. Furthermore, because the figurines were created by Jwara, through the inspiration provided by Noria's song, they also underline the necessity of oral traditions in post-apartheid South Africa. Noria's old song is still potent because when she sings it for Toloki at the shack, the latter, for the first time in his life, is able to draw pictures of human beings.

Toloki's self-assigned job of a "Professional Mourner" also reflects hybridity. Sam Durrant writes that "[i]t is under the pressure of dealing with what anthropologists call 'bad' deaths, those which happen outside the home, in unexpected or unknown circumstances, that mourning rites undergo their most radical reinventions" (442). In line with Durrant's argument, Toloki's sounds, even though they are meaningless, demonstrate hybridity because the traditional mourning rites are adapted to reflect the painful deaths experienced by South Africans of the apartheid and immediate post-apartheid periods. Furthermore, given Durrant's argument, the Halloween party costume that Toloki adopts as his mourning attire is an innovation that allows him to accommodate the impact of colonization on his largely traditional "profession."

5.3 Hybridity in Religious Beliefs and Practices

The introduction of colonial religions to the former colonies forced the colonized peoples to adopt some of these religions. This adoption, however, was not to the total exclusion of their precolonial beliefs; consequently, there arose in the former colonies a mixture of the precolonial and colonial religions. In *Orientalism*, Said argues that the European invasion of the East led to a "confrontation of the gods" (117) as European missionaries attempted to understand Islam and convert its followers to Christianity. The crash of the two religions, Said states, eventually led to "classifications of mankind . . . beyond the categories of . . . gentile and sacred nations" (120). Said continues:

> But if these interconnected elements represent a secularizing tendency, this is not to say that the old religious patterns of human history and destiny and "the existential paradigms" were simply removed. Far from it: they were reconstituted, redeployed, re-distributed in the secular frameworks just enumerated. (120-21)

Said's argument implies that Islam as practiced in the East was re-shaped to accommodate the notions introduced by Christian missionaries and colonial authorities. This trend is expected even in other formerly colonized regions where foreign and indigenous religions were combined.

Accommodating Christianity in *Chotti Munda and His Arrow*

In *Chotti Munda and His Arrow*, Devi depicts the Mundas' religion, which centers on the pahan, as an overarching system of beliefs which determines the community's daily economic and spiritual endeavors, and sets moral rules. In addition, the religion provides such leaders as Chotti with wisdom and powers that adherents of mainstream religions can only ignore at their own peril. The religion's spirituality notwithstanding, it is portrayed as not wholly able to liberate Mundas from colonial and postcolonial exploitation. While certain Christian missions grab land and work in alliance with some corrupt government officials - thus eliciting doubt about their sincerity in helping Indians - these missions may in fact sometimes aid the adivasis. Indeed, such Christian sects as the Baptist missions are credited with feeding the Mundas of Chotti Village during a severe famine and providing refuge to Mundas who flee from oppressive landowners.

Nevertheless, when Mundas flee to the Christian missions they are forced to adopt some aspects of Christianity. As expected, the Mundas who convert to Christianity will not abandon wholly their indigenous beliefs because their conversion is an act of survival rather than that of spiritual conviction. Indeed, the addition of Christian names to Mundari ones, as exemplified by "Joseph Sukha Munda and David Bikhna Munda of Tomaru Mission" (96), highlights both the adoption of Christianity and the retention of the converts' cultural identity.

This conversion for survival is significant because it brings out the possibility that the Mundas' traditional divinity, Haramdeo, is willing to accommodate some of the elements of post-independence realities to ensure the continued existence of his followers. Thus, Devi writes, Haramdeo is taking cognizance of "railway, motorcar, and pichers we hear of in town - that move, that talk," and "he's lettin' his chillun go here and there. Thinkin' go kids go, go to tea garden, go to Mission, plough another's field, go where ye'll live. Otherwise these things cannot happen" (110,111), indicating that the Munda's hitherto rigid indigenous religious system has to accommodate foreign practices if only for Mundas "to live." For instance, Chotti and the pahan take the train for the first time when they take Puran to Latehar after his release by the court on charges of killing Tasildar, the oppressive farm manager. Chotti expresses elation at this new means of transport: "I ne'er thought I'd be on t' rails" (147).

Syncretism in *Segu*

It has been previously stated that cultural hybridity is inevitable whenever two or more cultures encounter one another because, in Stuart Hall's words, "Cultural identities come from somewhere, have histories. But, like everything which is historical, they undergo constant transformation," and they are therefore "subject to the continuous 'play' of history, culture and power" (394). Hall's argument relates to the cultural identities of diaspora individuals who have been moved from their indigenous communities.

In *Segu*, Condé shows that while the sending of Tiekoro to Timbuktu by traditional Bambara religious divinities might appear to indicate the latter's powerlessness, their action is vindicated by the imminent changes that take place in the region. Thus, these divinities' action is not only that of foresight but also a foreshadowing of the changing way in which they will be worshipped alongside other gods whose entry into Segu is unavoidable. To begin with, Tiekoro retains Traore, his family name, even after being renamed Modibo Oumar upon converting to Islam. Furthermore, despite Tiekoro's admission that "the Islam practiced by his family and even by his pupils was only superficial" (360), he does not condemn them. This superficial brand of Islam allows both his family and his pupils to gain the benefits of education, while at the same time practicing their traditional religion. Delphine Perret and Steve Arkin write that a reader of *Segu* "realizes that Tiekoro's system of beliefs, like that of his Islamized descendants, is becoming divided" (655). With the foregoing, Tiekoro becomes the epitome of religious hybridity necessary for the survival of Africans after foreign influence on their traditional religions.

Other members of the Bambara community who convert to new religions retain their African identity. Malobali remains a follower of the Bambara traditional religion in spite of his conversion to Christianity and the change of his name to Samuel. Unlike Tiekoro, however, Malobali emerges as a stronger defender of his culture and religion, perhaps because his conversion is forced rather than voluntary. Malobali, like other converts such as his wife, Romana, practice Afro-Christianity, because they adhere to certain aspects of both religions. In fact, Phiefer L. Browne refers to Malobali as "the nominal Christian, secret fetishist" (184) because of his efforts to blend both beliefs. Thus while such an endeavor as Malobali and Romana's wedding is purely Christian, other undertakings adhere either to traditional religion or combine both faiths. This religious hybridity explains why Romana combines Christian divinities with African ones during her prayers for Malobali's illness. Condé reveals that "[s]he appealed not only to Jesus Christ, the Virgin Mary and the saints in paradise but also to the powerful Yoruba Orisha whom her parents used to appease with palm oil, fresh yams, fruit and blood" (304). Malobali on the other hand teaches Romana's children Bambara culture and even gives them Bambara names.

Given the fact that they have been removed from their African identity, and because they abhor slavery, children of former slaves are forced to take up a hybrid identity. Such children do not fully conform to the Bambara culture and religion although, as exemplified by Eucaristus, they retain their identity as Africans and are continually in search of information about the identity of their ancestors. It is for this reason that in spite of his desire to find the home of his father's family in Segu, Eucaristus is unable to use Traore, his family name, because he is estranged from the African culture.

That the Bambara community eventually has a king named Oitala Ali also highlights the place of hybridity in postcolonial political leadership. The ascendance of Ali to kingship in conformity with Bambara traditions indicates that the community has accepted the fusion of both Islamic and African cultures in its governance. This fusion is also unmistakable in that as Segu's soldiers join their neighbors in the fight against El-Hadj Omar's soldiers, "[t]he fetishists displayed their gris-gris, the Muslims their verses from the Koran" (486). The fact that these two groups join to fight a common enemy means that cultural unity is more potent than divisions wrought by foreign religions. It is also evident that even the Muslims in this group practice an Africanized brand of Islam because "[a]ll [soldiers, including Muslims] had, hidden in their clothes, the talismans their mothers had given them before they set off" (486). This revelation, which comes towards the end of the novel, indicates that core African beliefs such as the use of talismans are not obliterated by conversion to Islam. In "Amadou Hampate Ba and the Islamic Dimension of West African Oral Literature," Gabriel Asfar writes that there existed a level of compatibility between Islam and African traditional religion as practiced by some West African communities; hence, "Islam took hold and grew in sub-Saharan Africa upon the foundations of traditional religion" (142). While this statement does not refer specifically to the Bambara community, it is significant that Muslims who participate in this war carry symbols of Bambara traditional religion.

It may be concluded, therefore, that in spite of owing allegiance to foreign religions, the Bambara soldiers show more loyalty to their community and its cultural interests. This scenario is not surprising when one considers that, in "Christianity, African Traditional Religion and Colonialism: Were Africans pawns or Players in the Cultural Encounter?" Gabriel E. Ezewudo, writes that there exist a "duplicity in African Christianity" (50), because in spite of embracing the religion, Africans retained some aspects of their traditional beliefs. He states that even after conversion to Christianity, Africans retained "some deeply-ingrained cultural mores and tabus" (54), resulting in a combination of the two beliefs. Thus, Ezewudo concludes, "[an African's] allegiance lies more with the clan, and the prescription of the new religion can be compromised" (54-55).

Syncretism in *Petals of Blood*

Thiong'o, in *Petals of Blood*, illustrates similar blending of colonial religion with African cultural beliefs. Abdulla assigns the name of "Joseph Njiraini" (286) to the nameless boy whom he finds roaming on the streets after the boy's entire family was either killed or captured by colonial authorities during the struggle for independence. This name points to a new naming system that assigns both Christian and African identities to African converts. While Abdulla assumes that the boy does or will subscribe to Christianity, the former's action highlights the inevitability of the use of foreign names in postcolonial Africa. This notion appears further plausible in that he has earlier given himself the name "Abdulla" thinking that it is a Christian name. The fact the name is Arabic (hence, it actually denotes Islamization rather than Christianization), indicates that Islamic, Christian and African values will be integrated in a self-redefinition of the postcolonial Kenyan.

Such a re-definition requires the replacement of the brand of Christianity practiced during the colonial era, because the religion advanced by colonialists, and which was adopted by converts such as Ezekieli, forbade its African converts not only from practicing their culture but also from participating in their struggle for independence. However, Thiong'o's portrayal of the adjustment of Christianity in order to meet the needs of postcolonial Kenyans is limited, because, as James A. Ogude writes, "[Ngugi wa Thiong'o's] presentation of religion is one-dimensional. For Ngugi, religion is a tool of oppression - a vehicle for lulling the poor and turning them away from material reality of this world" (104). This fact notwithstanding, the conversion of Munira to a new Christian sect which questions the rationale of his father's refusal to aid Kenya's struggle for political independence heralds the emergence of a brand of Christianity that recognizes the humanity of Africans.

In addition, the consumption of *theng'eta*, a traditional brew made of fermented millet and crushed theng'eta plants, in the post-independence period is crucial because it underscores the persistence of some of the elements of African traditional religion. The brew is a catalyst for communication with the Agikuyu's divine powers. Nyakinyua, the apparent carrier of traditional wisdom and the architect of the initial theng'eta brewing, terms the theng'eta plant "a spirit," and describes the brew itself as "a dream . . . a wish," because: "[i]t gives you sight, and for those favoured by God it can make them cross the river of time and talk with their ancestors. It has given seers their tongues; poets and Gichandi players their words; and it has made barren women mothers of many children" (210). The fact that those who attend the thengeta-drinking ritual reveal crucial information about their identity and aspirations shows the potency of the brew, and vindicates Nyakinyua's assertion that the brew, which is also referred to as "[m]illet, power of God" (211), is to be considered as a spiritual medium. This ritual informs the reader that such traditional practices will continue to exist within postcolonial religious systems.

Multiple Beliefs and Culture in *The God of Small Things*

Roy, in *The God of Small Things*, also demonstrates that Christianity will continue to be practiced in the postcolonial period. However, Christianity exists alongside Marxist ideology, Hinduism and other religions such as Islam - although the latter is not mentioned in the novel. Indeed, Christianity is subjected to some of the beliefs of Hinduism. Because Hinduism pre-existed Christianity in Kerala, Maria Sabrina Alexandru writes that "In a world with a Hindu background, where Christianity and communism are supposed to be instruments of freedom, their supposedly freeing effect is lost on Paravans" (175). Consequently, Christians such as the Pappachi family adhere to the Hindu caste system. This adherence elicits from Alexandru the argument that "[i]n Roy's Kerala, Christianity and Hinduism come face to face. Paradoxically, the mind/body conflict between them is reformulated in such terms that they become mutually supportive with respect to the categories of both caste and gender" (176). This background enables the reader to understand the reason why Kochu Maria, despite her lowly job and wage, insists that she is a Touchable of the Syrian Christian faith.

Religious hybridity in *Ways of Dying*

Religious hybridity is also evident in Mda's *Ways of Dying*. Mda depicts the position of a Nurse, an enduring symbol of traditional religion, as enabling members of the community to practice cultural hybridity. Indeed, the responsibilities of the Nurse are changing. For instance, the Nurse at Vutha's funeral strikes a political tone when he accuses his own people of being behind the child's murder. In addition, a female Nurse uses the funeral to advance a feministic agenda when she accuses men of infidelity (18). The changing role of a Nurse echoes Sarah Nuttal's argument that any definition of the "now" in South Africa must embrace hybridity:

> In setting out to theorise the "now" in South Africa, one is undertaking the activity, as I see it, first, of working out what remains of the past, and how we relate to both the past and its remainders, or its traces in the present; and second, of working out our relationship to that which hasn't happened yet, the world of aspirations, the fictions with which people fill the future. (732)

The presence of the Nurse, even in Christian funerals signifies this duality. Mda writes that during the burial of Vutha, for example, "the church minister says a quick prayer" (9) because there are loud protests at the Nurse's accusation of his own people with Vutha's murder. In spite of the fact that the Archbishop's religion is pervaded by degrading acts such as vomiting and emptying the bowels in the public, his brand of Christianity is a localized version of Christianity. Indeed, his teachings are hybridized because they deviate from the mainstream teachings. In "Traditional Healers in the Nigerian Health Care Delivery System and the Debate over Integrating Traditional and Scientific Medicine," Daniel A. Offiong writes: "Because illness is attributed to mystical forces, traditional healers make sure that preventive measures are available to their clients; they enhance productivity and help people to protect their property; they detect witches and sorcerers; and they mediate between the living and their ancestors" (122). The Archbishop's prayers, thus, tend to emanate from an African understanding of sickness. In "Social Change and African Traditional Religion," John Pobee writes about such sects: "These sects stress healing and exorcism, thereby having a great appeal in the effort to end crises such as tragedy, severe illness, mental breakdown, which traditional society attributed to personal forces of evil such as demons and witches" (8). He suggests that they are symbols of hybridity: "The sects, therefore, are perhaps the most important single institutional evidence for the persistence of the African traditional religion in all the social change that has come about in our modern times in Africa" (8).

Moreover, in spite of the fact that he is an irresponsible and egocentric parent who abandons his son Vutha, Napu's actions suggest hybridity. Because he has no money to pay for dowry, he marries Noria through colonial laws; Noria's parents realize that "there was nothing they could do about it, since he, Napu, son of a nobody, had married their daughter in front of the law" (81). His acceptance of the Western form of marriage, however, does not signify that he has accepted the Western culture in its fullness. Indeed, he resists the name Jealous Down which That Mountain Woman gives to his son. He names him Vutha, a local name, and verbally protests against the name given by That Mountain Woman: "It's an English name! My son will not have an English name!" (83)

5.4 New Wine in Old Wineskins: The Status of Women in Changing Societies

The novels in this study show that women are the reservoirs of culture in their societies. Despite their crucial role, women have remained oppressed by the patriarchy of the precolonial, colonial and postcolonial periods. The cultural changes that have taken place through these periods have, however, modified the roles of women. Consequently, the works show that women embody both the new and the old facets of their societies' cultures.

Preserving the Past and Embracing the Present in *Petals of Blood*

In *Petals of Blood*, Thiong'o depicts women, as exemplified by Mariamu and Nyakinyua, as the preservers and transmitters of culture. For instance, Mariamu's feeding of her community's children portrays her as both one who preserves vanishing cultural knowledge, and as one who passes it to the community. Nyakinyua, on the other hand, not only connects the Ilmorog village to a traditional seer, Mwathi wa Mugo, but also seeks the education of the village's children. Cook and Okenimkpe recognize her educative role in their assertion that "[h]er impassioned tributes to her dead husband's courage and love of honour fill the young with respect for their ancestors and the desire to emulate them in the present" (93). Her search for the reasons why formal teachers do not stay for long in Ilmorog, and her concern that Ilmorog's children do not receive sufficient instruction, show that she also understands the role of contemporary education in uplifting the standards of both the students and the village.

Nyakinyua also provides informal education to the entire village, especially with regards to traditional religious and historical spheres. For instance, she encourages her granddaughter, Wanja, to seek Mwathi wa Mugo's divine prowess in her desire to conquer barrenness. In addition, she teaches the village about the founding of Ilmorog, the effects of colonization on the village, and about possible solutions to the poverty bedeviling it. While Nyakinyua must be hailed for her foresight, a careful reader of *Petals of Blood* will realize that formal education has significantly decimated women's role in the education of society, and in turn society's chances of retaining some of its core cultural values.

Thiong'o illustrates how women have been reduced to playing a peripheral role in what was once their main duty. To begin with, the economic system, as adopted by Kenya from the British, has forced men to leave their homes in search of jobs. Men's departure has in turn forced women to become the new breadwinners and heads of households. While these responsibilities may appear to indicate that women have been empowered - and they have indeed risen to levels that precolonial societies would never have allowed - these duties have jeopardized women's role in the conservation of culture. Consequently, women have lost their space as providers of both education and healthcare to their societies. One may argue that women have not in fact lost these roles as they are being played by female teachers and female physicians, among other professional groups. However, unlike today when these tasks are performed only by the elite, the precolonial era Gikuyu society generally expected all women to provide basic education and healthcare. Thiong'o also demonstrates that the postcolonial Kenyan woman will personify both precolonial and postcolonial cultural experiences. For example, Nyakinyua, despite her advanced age, becomes the undisputed unofficial leader of her remote Ilmorog village. On the other hand, Wanja symbolizes both the marginalization and the emancipation of the Kenya woman from societal patriarchy. Indeed, Podis and Saaka write about Wanja's pregnancy towards the end of the novel: "Amid the misery and disappointments that have nearly engulfed the characters by the end of the book, this occurrence brings a sense of promise for the future" (110). It is thus not surprising that Wanja and Nyakinyua participate in the epic journey the villagers take to the city in search of help during the severe drought; their presence in this trip suggests that they are potential leaders of their male-dominated society.

Women Suppression in *The God of Small Things*

Like other postcolonial writings in this study, Roy's *The God of Small Things* shows that colonialism has brought changes that have in turn led to the emergence of new means by which women in the Malayalam community are suppressed. For instance, Pappachi punishes Mammachi by beating her and by refusing to assist her in the factory. Furthermore, Mr. Hollick, Ammu's husband's supervisor, shows that some Whites who stay in India during the post-independence period consider Indian women as sexual objects. Mr. Hollick's request that Ammu should stay with him for a few days, and her husband's acceptance of the proposal indicates that the economic system bequeathed to India by its erstwhile colonial masters is a catalyst for further exploitation of Indian women.

Furthermore, Indian customs regarding marriage require scrutiny, because they are the cause of Ammu's downfall. To begin with, traditions require a woman's father to raise a dowry for her marriage, thus making a woman's future pegged partly on her father's level of wealth and choice of spouse. Ammu can only flee the oppressive environment in her father's homestead by marriage, which becomes the gateway to her misery. However, although her marriage fails, Ammu opposes her society's customs by choosing a marriage partner for herself. Similarly, her decision to divorce her husband rejects the societal belief that a woman must stay in a marriage even when it is oppressive. Nonetheless, the patriarchal attitude of her society eventually annihilates her when she returns to the Ayemenem house. Ultimately, she chooses to have a relationship with Velutha, a man of the Untouchable caste. The death of both Ammu and Velutha, thus question Indian society's failure to accept romantic relationships between individuals of different castes or socio-economic backgrounds.

The Redefinition of Women's Role in *Segu*

In *Segu*, Condé reveals that some women have attempted to redefine their roles as they accommodate the effects of colonization. While colonization replaces the role of women as the main providers of basic education to Bambara children, women adopt a new role where they influence their children to pursue formal education. For instance, while Nya's role as educator is taken away by the establishment of formal Islamic schools, she takes up a new role in the prevalent educational system when she encourages Tiekoro, and later other children, to seek Islamic education. Equally, Romana urges her son Eucaristus to seek theological training overseas, a feat he embarks on after her death.

Nadie's and Fatima's interactions with their husbands also highlight women's embracing of crucial elements of hybridity. To begin with, by taking up tasks such as spinning yarn, which were perceived as slaves' work during the pre-Islamic times, Nadie foreshadows the contemporary times when work will be evaluated based on its income rather than traditional classifications. Her success, coupled by the fact that she becomes the sole breadwinner during the period of Tiekoro's joblessness, underscores the emergence of women as providers for their families. On her part, Fatima dares not only to choose a marriage partner but also to convey her romantic feelings to Siga in writing. Her action heralds the genesis of women's emergence from silence and foreshadows their potential to assume their own voice during the postcolonial era.

Conclusion

This chapter demonstrates that because members of postcolonial communities have been irrevocably influenced by colonization and the various forces such as education, economic and political systems after independence, they define themselves through hyridity in order to accommodate these influences. For this reason, traditional methods of instruction such as narratives and songs exist alongside or within Western systems of education. On the other hand, colonial languages have been adopted for use in sectors such as education and inter-community communication, while local languages are mostly used in all other environments. In addition, formerly colonized peoples such as those in the Caribbean region may adopt colonial languages but indigenize these languages and purge them of colonizing aspects. Members of postcolonial societies have also combined elements of both colonial and precolonial religions such that even when these members identify themselves as adherents of colonial religions, they retain certain elements of their indigenous beliefs. Last, women are no longer the educators and healthcare providers of their families and communities; as a result, they have either modified these roles or taken up new ones.

Notes

Chapter Two

[1] The assertion that "everything becomes a story in Chotti's life" is found on pages 5, 9, 23, 29, 80, 121, 184, among others.

[2] The assertion that Mundari language has no script, and that the Mundas pass their history by "story and song" is repeated on page 134. This underscores, of course, the importance of oral narratives among the adivasis, and it also shows the adivasis as dangerously dependent on those who have embraced modern policies, especially with regards to the development of Mundari writable script.

Chapter Three

[1] Indeed, nowhere in the Holy Bible is water baptism accompanied by a change of name. Baptism is said to be necessary "for repentance" and in order to "fulfill all righteousness" (Mat. 3: 11,15, NIV). The change of name, on the other hand appears to be the result of a theophany as exemplified in Saul's conversion (Acts 9).

Bibliography

Achebe, Chinua. *Morning Yet on Creation Day*. Garden City:
    Doubleday, 1975.

---. *Things Fall Apart*. New York: Anchor, 1957.

Alexander, Simone A. James. "The Mystic Return: Reconfiguring Home in
    Maryse Condé's *Heremakhonon*." *MAWA Review* 16.1-2 (June-Dec.
    2001): 67-84.

Alexandru, Maria Sabrina. "Towards a Politics of the Small Things:
    Arundhati Roy and the Decentralization of Authorship." *Authorship
    in Context: From the Theoretical to the Material*. Ed. Kyriaki
    Hadjiafxendi and Polina MacKay. New York: Palgrave, 2007. 163-81.

Ampofo, Akosua Adomako, et al. "Women's and Gender Studies in
    English-Speaking Sub-Saharan Africa: A Review of Research in the
    Social Sciences." *Gender and Society* 18.6 (Dec. 2004): 685-714.

Anwar, Waseem. "Transcribing Resistance: Cartographies of Struggling
    Bodies and Minds in Mahasweta Devi's *Imaginary Maps*." *South
    Asian Review* 22 (2001): 83-96.

Asfar, Gabriel. "Amadou Hampate Ba and the Islamic Dimension of West
    African Oral Literature." *Faces of Islam in African Literature*. Ed.
    Kenneth W. Harrow. Portsmouth: Heinemann, 1991. 141-50.

Bagchi, Alaknanda. "Conflicting Nationalism: The Voice of the Subaltern in
    Mahasweta Devi's *Bashai Tudu*." *Tulsa Studies in Women's Literature*
    15.1 (Spring 1996): 41-50.

Barnard, Rita. "On Laughter, the Grotesque, and the South African
    Transition: Zakes Mda's *Ways of Dying*" *Novel: A Forum on Fiction* 37
    (Summer 2004): 278-304.

Bhabha, Homi K. *Nation and Narration*. New York: Routledge, 1990.

Bloom, Harold. *Jamaica Kincaid*. Philadelphia: Chelsea, 1998.

Boateng, Felix. "African Traditional Education: A Method of Disseminating
    Cultural Values." *Journal of Black Studies* 13.3 (March 1983): 321-36.

Boehmer, Elleke. *Colonial & Postcolonial Literature*. New York: Oxford UP,
    1995.

Bottomore, Tom, ed. Introduction. *Makers of Modern Social Science: Karl
    Marx*. Englewood Cliffs: Prentice-Hall, 1973. 1-29.

Bouson, J. Brooks. *Jamaica Kincaid: Writing Memory, Writing Back to the Mother*. Albany: State U of New York, 2005.

Broichhagen, Vera, et al., eds. *Feasting on Words: Maryse Condé, Cannibalism, and the Caribbean Text*. Princeton: Princeton U, 2006.

Browne, Phiefer L. Rev. of *Segu*. Maryse Condé. *Black American Literature Forum* 23.1 (Spring 1989): 183-85.

Burnard, Trevor. Slave Naming Patterns: Onomastics and the Taxonomy of Race in Eighteenth-Century Jamaica." *Journal of Interdisciplinary History* 31.3 (Winter 2001): 325-46.

Cabral, Amilcar. "National Liberation and Culture." *Colonial Discourse and Post-Colonial Theory: A Reader*. Ed. Patrick Williams and Laura Chrisman. New York: Columbia UP, 1994. 53-65.

Cantalupo, Charles, ed. *The World of Ngugi wa Thiong'o*. Trenton: African World Press, 1993.

Chapman, Michael. "The Problem of Identity: South Africa, Storytelling, and Literary History." *New Literary History* 29.1 (Winter 1998): 85-99.

Chinosole. "Maryse Condé as Contemporary Griot in *Segu*." *Callaloo* 18.3 (Summer 1995): 593-601.

"Christians of Kerala." Ananthapuri.com. 8 March 2009. Path: Syrian Christianity.

Clarke, Sathianathan. "Hindutva, Religious and Ethnocultural Minorities, and Indian-Christian Theology." *The Harvard Theological Review* 95.2 (Apr. 2002): 197-226.

Condé, Maryse. *Segu*. New York: Penguin, 1984.

Cook, David, and Michael Okenimkpe. *Ngugi wa Thiong'o: An Exploration of His Writings*. Nairobi: Heinemann, 1983.

Collu, Gabrielle. "Adivasis and the Myth of Independence: Mahasweta Devi's 'Douloti the Bountiful'." *ARIEL: A Review of International English Literature* 30.1 (Jan. 1999): 43-57.

Dasgupta, Subha Chakraborty. "Contesting Polarities: Creating Spaces-Reading Myths in Mahasweta Devi's Stories." *Indian Literature* 47.2 (Mar. – Apr. 2003): 200-5.

Devi, Mahasweta. *Bashai Tudu*. 1990. Trans. Gayatri Chakravorty Spivak and Shamik Bandyopadhyay. Calcutta: Thima, 1993.

---. *Chotti Munda and His Arrow*. 1980. Trans. Gayatri Chakravorty Spivak. Calcutta: Seagull, 2002.

Driesen, Cynthia Vanden . *Centering the Margins: Perspectives on Literatures in English from India, Africa and Australia.* New Delhi: Prestige, 1995.

Du Bois, W. E. B. *The Souls of Black Folk.* 1903. Ed. Henry Louis Gates, Jr. and Terri Hume Oliver. New York: Norton, 1999.

Durrant, Sam. "The Invention of Mourning in Post-Apartheid Literature." *Third World Quarterly* 26.3 (2005): 441-50.

Eagleton, Terry. *The Idea of Culture.* Oxford, UK: Blackwell, 2000.

Edlmair, Barbara. *Rewriting History: Alternative Versions of the Caribbean Past in Michelle Cliff, Rosario Ferré, Jamaica Kincaid and Daniel Maximin.* Wien: Braumuller, 1999.

Edwards, Justin D. *Understanding Jamaica Kincaid.* Columbia: U of South Carolina, 2007.

Elkins, Caroline. *Imperial Reckoning: The Untold Story of Britain's Gulag in Kenya.* New York: Holt, 2005.

Ezewudo, Gabriel E. "Christianity, African Traditional Religion and Colonialism: Were Africans pawns or Players in the Cultural Encounter?" *Religion and Society: Black Creativity & the State of the Race.* Ed. Rose Ure Mezu. Randallstown: Black Academy, 1999. 43-62.

Fanon, Frantz. *Black Skin, White Masks.* New York: Grove, 1967.

---. *Toward the African Revolution: Political Essays.* 1964. Trans. Haakon Chevalier. New York: Grove, 1967.

Farred, Grant. "Mourning the Post-apartheid State Already? The Poetics of Loss in Zakes Mda's *Ways of Dying.*" *Modern Fiction Studies* 46.1 (Spring 2000): 183-206.

Ferguson, Moira. *Jamaica Kincaid: Where the Land Meets the Body.* Charlottesville: UP of Virginia, 1994.

Frederick, Rhonda D. "What If You're an 'Incredibly Unattractive, Fat, Pastrylike-Fleshed Man'?: Teaching Jamaica Kincaid's *A Small Place.*" *College Literature* 3 (Summer 2003): 1-18.

Gandhi, Leela. *Postcolonial Theory: A Critical Introduction.* New York: Columbia UP, 1998.

Gauch, Suzanne. "*A Small Place*: Some Perspectives on the Ordinary." *Callaloo* 25.3 (Summer 2002): 910-19.

Gikandi, Simon. *Ngugi wa Thiong'o.* Cambridge: Cambridge UP, 2000.

---. "Travelling Theory: Ngugi's Return to English." *Research in African Literatures*. 31.2 (Summer 2000): 194-209.

Gilbert, Helen, and Joanne Tompkins. *Post-Colonial Drama: Theory, Practice, Politics*. New York: Routledge, 1996.

Gray, Richard. "Christianity." *Colonial Moment in Africa: Essays on the Movement of Minds and Materials 1900-1940*. Ed. Andrew Roberts. Cambridge: Cambridge UP, 1986. 140-90.

Grayson, Erik. "The Most Important Meal: Food and Meaning in Jamaica Kincaid's *Lucy*." *Journal of the Georgia Philological Association* 1 (Dec. 2006): 212-27.

Guttman, Anna. "Reexamining Indian Nonalignment: Arundhati Roy's *The God of Small Things*." *The Nation of India in Contemporary Indian Literature*. New York: Palgrave, 2007. 115-34.

Hall, Stuart. "Cultural Identity and Diaspora." *Colonial Discourse and Post-Colonial Theory: A Reader*. Ed. Patrick Williams and Laura Chrisman. New York: Columbia UP, 1994. 392-403.

Hawley, John C. "José María Arguedas, Ngugi wa Thiong'o, and the Search for a Language of Justice." *Pacific Coast Philology* 27.1 (Sept. 1992): 69-76.

Hong, Ying-yi. "A Dynamic Constructivist Approach to Culture: Moving from Describing Culture to Explaining Culture." *Understanding Culture: Theory, Research and Application*. Eds. Robert S. Wyer, Chi-yue Chiu, and Ying-yi Hong. New York: Taylor & Francis, 2009. 3-24.

Howitt, William. *Colonization and Christianity: A Popular History of the Treatment of the Natives by the Europeans in All Their Colonies*. London: Longman, 1838.

Hurston, Zora Neale. *Their Eyes Were Watching God*. 1937. Perennial Library Edition. New York: Harper, 1990.

Hymer, Stephen H. "Economic Forms in Precolonial Ghana." *The Journal of Economic History* 30.1 (Mar. 1970): 33-50.

Inglis, Fred. *Culture*. Cambridge: Polity, 2004.

Isiugo-Abanihe, Uche C. "Child Fostering in West Africa." *Population and Development Review* 11.1 (Mar. 1985): 53-73.

Jung, Carl Gustav. *Psychology and Religion*. New Haven: Yale UP, 1938.

Kamara, Gibreel M. "Regaining Our African Aesthetics and Essence through Our African Traditional Religion." *Journal of Black Studies* 30.4 (Mar. 2000): 502-14.

Kanaganayakam, Chelva. "Religious Myth and Subversion in *The God of Small Things.*" *Literary Canons and Religious Identity.* Ed. Erik Borgman, et al. Aldershot: Ashgate, 2000. 141-50.

Kandiyoti, Deniz. "Identity and Its Discontents: Women and the Nation." *Colonial Discourse and Post-Colonial Theory: A Reader.* Ed. Patrick Williams and Laura Chrisman. New York: Columbia UP, 1994. 376-91.

Khot, Mohini. "The Feminist Voice in Arundhati Roy's *The God of Small Things.*" *Indian Feminisms.* Ed. Jasbir Jain and Avadhesh Singh. New Delhi: Creative, 2001. 213-22.

Killam, G.D. *An Introduction to the Writings of Ngugi.* London: Heinemann, 1980.

Kincaid, Jamaica. *A Small Place.* New York: Farrar, 1998.

King, Jane. "A Small Place Writes Back." *Callaloo* 25.3 (Summer 2002): 885-909.

Lane, Richard J. "The Optical Unconscious: Arundhati Roy's *The God of Small Things.*" *The Postcolonial Novel.* Cambridge: Polity, 2006. 97-108.

Lang-Peralta, Linda, ed. *Jamaica Kincaid and Caribbean Double Crossings.* Newark: U of Delaware, 2006.

Laremont, Ricardo Rene. *Islam and the Politics of Resistance in Algeria: 1783-1992.* Trenton: World, 2000.

Lewis, Barbara. "An Interview with Maryse Condé." *Callaloo* 18.3 (Summer 1995): 543-50.

Lima, Maria Helena. "Imaginary Homelands in Jamaica Kincaid's Narratives of Development." *Callaloo: A Journal of African-American and African Arts and Letters* 25.3 (2002): 857-67.

Lovesey, Oliver. *Ngugi wa Thiong'o.* New York: Twayne, 2000.

Madsen, Deborah L. "Beyond the Commonwealth: Post-Colonialism and American Literature." *Post-Colonial Literatures: Expanding the Canon.* Ed. Deborah L. Madsen. London: Pluto, 1999. 1-13.

Masih, Archana. "Independence Has Failed." *Rediff on the Net.* 8 March 2009 <http://www.rediff.com/news/dec/24devi.htm>

Mazrui, Ali A. *The Africans: A Triple Heritage.* Boston: Brown, 1986.

Mazrui, Ali A. and Michael Tidy. *Nationalism and New States in Africa.* Portsmouth: Heinemann, 1984.

Mbiti, John S. *African Religions and Philosophy.* Garden City: Anchor, 1970.

McEwan, Cheryl. "Building a Postcolonial Archive? Gender, Collective Memory and Citizenship in Post-apartheid South Africa." *Journal of South Africa Studies* 29.3 (Sept. 2003): 739-57.

McGillis, Roderick. Introduction. *Voices of the Other: Children's Literature and the Postcolonial Context.* New York: Garland, 2000. xix-xxiv.

Mda, Zakes. *Ways of Dying.* New York: Picador, 1995.

Mervis, Margaret "Fiction for Development: Zakes Mda's *Ways of Dying.*" *Current Writing: Text and Reception in Southern Africa* 10.1 (Apr. 1998): 39-56.

Mezu, Rose Ure. "Theorizing the Feminist Novel, Women and the State of African Literature Today." *A History of Africana Women's Literature.* Ed. Rose Ure Mezu. Baltimore: Black Academy, 2004. 24-47.

Murray, David A. B. "The Cultural Citizen: Negations of Race and Language in the Making of Martiniquais." *Anthropological Quarterly* 70.2 (Apr. 1997): 79-90.

Needham, Anuradha Dingwaney. "'The Small Voice of History' in Arundhati Roy's *The God of Small Things.*" *Interventions* 7.3 (2005): 369-91.

N'gom, M'bare. "The Recovered Voice: Nafissatou Niang Diallo's The *Princess of Tiali.*" *A History of Africana Women's Literature.* Ed. Rose Ure Mezu. Baltimore: Black Academy, 2004. 265-81.

Nuttal, Sarah. "City Forms and Writing 'Now' in South Africa." *Journal of Southern African Studies* 30.4 (Dec. 2004): 731-48.

Offiong, Daniel A. "Traditional Healers in the Nigerian Health Care Delivery System and the Debate over Integrating Traditional and Scientific Medicine." *Anthropological Quarterly* 72.3 (July 1999): 118-30.

Ogude, James A. "Ngugi's Concept of History and the Post-colonial Discourses in Kenya." *Canadian Journal of African Studies* 31.1 (1997): 86-112.

---. *Ngugi's Novels as African History: Narrating the Nation.* London: Pluto, 1999.

O'Regan, Derek. *Postcolonial Echoes and Evocations: The Intertextual*

Appeal of Maryse Condé. New York: Lang, 2006.

Page, Kezia. "'What if He Did Not Have a Sister [Who Lived in the United States]?' Jamaica Kincaid's *My Brother* as Remittance Text." *Small Axe: A Caribbean Journal of Criticism* 21 (Oct. 2006): 37-53.

Paravisini-Gebert, Lizabeth. *Jamaica Kincaid: A Critical Companion.* Westport: Greenwood, 1999.

Patel, Sandhya. "The Difficulty of Being: Reading and Speaking in Arundhati Roy's *The God of Small Things.*" *Embracing the Other: Addressing Xenophobia in the New Literature in English.* Ed. Dunja M. Mohr. Amsterdam: Rodopi, 2008. 227-43.

Pati, Mitali R. "Mahasweta Devi's Rhetoric of Subversion in 'Draupadi.'" *South Asian Review* 20.17 (Dec. 1996): 86-91.

Pelton, Theodore. "Ngugi wa Thiong'o and the Politics of Language." *Humanist* 53.2 (Mar./Apr. 1993): 15-20.

Perret, Delphine, and Steve Arkin. "Dialogue with the Ancestors." *Callaloo* 18.3 (Summer 1995): 652-67.

Pfohl, Stephen, and Aimee Van Wagenen. "Culture, Power, and History: An Introduction." *Culture, Power, and History: Studies in Critical Sociology.* Eds. Stephen Pfohl, et al. Leiden: Brill, 2006.

Pobee, John. "Aspects of African Traditional Religion." *Sociological Analysis* 37.1 (Spring 1976): 1-18.

---. "Social Change and African Traditional Religion." *Sociological Analysis* 38.1 (Spring 1977): 1-12.

Podis, Leonard A., and Yakubu Saaka. "*Anthills of the Savannah* and *Petals of Blood*: The Creation of a Usable Past." *Journal of Black Studies* 22.1 (Sept. 1991): 104-22.

Prasad, Anshuman. Introduction. *Postcolonial Theory and Organizational Analysis: A Critical Engagement.* Ed. Anshuman Prasad. New York: Palgrave, 2003. 3-46.

Ramchand, Kenneth. *The West Indian Novel and Its Background.* New York: Barnes & Noble, 1970.

Radhakrishnan, R. *Diasporic Mediations: Between Home and Location.* Minneapolis: U. of Minnesota P., 1996.

Roberts, Andrew. "The Imperial Mind" *Colonial Moment in Africa: Essays on the Movement of Minds and Materials 1900-1940.* Ed. Andrew Roberts. Cambridge: Cambridge UP, 1986. 24-76.

Robison, David. "An Approach to Islam in West African History." *Faces of Islam inAfrican Literature*. Ed. Kenneth W. Harrow. Portsmouth: Heinemann, 1991. 107-130.

Rodrigues, Angela Lamas. "Beyond Nativism: An Interview with Ngugi Wa Thiong'o." *Research in African Literature* 35.3 (Fall 2004): 161-67.

Rose, Arnold M. "Hindu Values and Indian Social Problems." *The Sociological Quarterly* 8.4 (Summer 1967): 329-39.

Roy, Arundhati. *The God of Small Things*. New York: Random, 1997.

Rushdie, Salman. *In Good Faith*. New York: Granta, 1990.

---.*The Satanic Verses*. New York: Penguin, 1989.

Said, Dibinga wa. "An African Theology of Decolonization." *The Harvard Theological Review* 64.4 (Oct. 1971): 501-24.

Said, Edward. *Culture and Imperialism*. New York: Knopf, 1993.

---. *Orientalism*. New York: Vintage, 1979.

Salgado, Minoli. "Tribal Stories, Scribal Worlds: Mahasweta Devi and the Unreliable Translator." *Journal of Commonwealth Literature* 35.1 (2000): 131-45.

Samin, Richard. "Marginality and History in Zakes Mda's *Ways of Dying*." *Anglophonia: French Journal of English Studies* 7 (2000): 189-200.

Sanga, Jaina C. *Salman Rushdie's Postcolonial Metaphors: Migration, Translation Hybridity, Blasphemy and Globalization*. Wesport: Greenwood, 2001.

Sardesai, K. S., et al., ed. *Unique Quintessence of Modern India: 1757-1947*. New Delhi: Unique, 1993.

Schwerdtner, Karin. "Wandering, Women and Writing: Maryse Condé's Desirada." *Dalhousie French Studies* 73 (Winter 2005): 129-37.

Scutter, Heather. "Hunting for History: Children's Literature Outside, Over There, and Down Under." *A Review of International English Literature* 28.1 (Jan. 1997): 21-38.

Sharma, Anand. "History of Youth Movement in India" 8 March 2009 <http://www.indianyouthcongress.in/aboutiyc-2.htm>

Sicherman, Carol, ed., *Ngugi Wa Thiong'o: The Making of a Rebel: A Source Book in Kenyan Literature and Resistance*. London: Zell, 1990.

---. "Ngugi's Colonial Education: "The Subversion …of the African Mind"." *African Studies Review* 38.3 (Dec. 1995): 11-41.

Simmons, Diane. "Jamaica Kincaid and the Canon: In Dialogue with *Paradise Lost* and *Jane Eyre*." *MELUS* 23.2 (Summer 1998): 65-85.

Skelcher, Bradley. "Apartheid and the Removal of Black Spots from Lake Bhanghazi in Kwazulu-Natal, South Africa." *Journal of Black Studies* 33.6 (July 2003): 761-83.

Smith, Arlette M. "The Semiotics of Exile in Maryse Condé's Fictional Works." *Callaloo* 14.2 (Spring 1991): 381-388.

Spivak, Gayatri Chakravorty. "Can the Subaltern Speak?" *Colonial Discourse and Post-Colonial Theory: A Reader*. Ed. Patrick Williams and Laura Chrisman. New York: Columbia UP, 1994. 66-111.

---. "Poststructuralism, Marginality, Postcoloniality and Value." *Contemporary Postcolonial Theory: A Reader*. Ed. Padmini Mongia. New York: Arnold, 1996.

---. "'Telling History': Gayatri Chakravorty Spivak Interviews Mahasweta Devi." *Chotti Munda and His Arrow*. By Mahasweta Devi. 1980. Trans.
Gayatri Chakravorty Spivak. Calcutta: Seagull, 2002.

---. "Translator's Foreword." *Chotti Munda and His Arrow*. By Mahasweta Devi. 1980. Trans. Gayatri Chakravorty Spivak. Calcutta: Seagull, 2002.

Steinmeyer, Elke. "Chanting the Song of Sorrow: Threnody in Homer and Zakes Mda." *Current Writing: Text and Reception in Southern Africa* 15.2 (Oct. 2003): 156-72.

Suleri, Sara. "Woman Skin Deep: Feminism and Postcolonial Condition." *Contemporary Postcolonial Theory: A Reader*. Ed. Padmini Mongia. New York: Arnold, 1996.

Suzman, Susan M. "Names as Pointers: Zulu Personal Naming Practices." *Language in Society* 23.2 (June 1994): 253-72.

Thiong'o, Ngugi wa. *Barrel of a Pen: Resistance to Repression in Neocolonial Kenya*. Trenton: World, 1983.

---. *Decolonising the Mind: The Politics of Language in African Literature*. London: Heinemann, 1981.

---. *Devil on the Cross*. Johannesburg: Heinemann, 1982.

---. *Petals of Blood*. New York: Penguin, 1977.

Vandermeersch, Celine, and O. Chimere-Dan. "Child Fostering Under Six in Senegal in 1992-1993." *Population* 57.4/5 (July-Oct. 2002): 659-85.

Walker, Alice. *In Search of Our Mothers' Gardens*. New York: Brace, 1983.

Walker, Wyatt Tee. "Roots—Musically Speaking" *Religion and Society: Black Creativity & the State of the Race*. Ed. Rose Ure Mezu. Randallstown: Black Academy, 1999. 17-42.

Wenzel, Jennifer. "Epic Struggles over India's Forests in Mahasweta Devi's Short Fiction." *Alif: Journal of Comparative Poetics* 18 (1998): 127-58.

Wenzel, Marita. "Appropriating space and transcending boundaries in *The Africa House* by Christina Lamb and *Ways of Dying* by Zakes Mda." *Journal of Literary Studies* 19.3/4 (Dec. 2003): 316-30.

Williams, Patrick. *Ngugi wa Thiong'o*. Manchester: Manchester U P, 1999.

Williams, Piper Kendrix. "Journeys of Détour in Maryse Condé's *A Season in Rihata*." *Canadian Woman Studies/Les Cahiers de la Femme* 23.2 (Winter 2004): 76-81.

Woodward, Wendy. "Laughing Back at the Kingfisher: Zakes Mda's *The Heart of Redness* and Postcolonial Humour." *Cheeky Fictions: Laughter and the Postcolonial*. Ed. Susanne Reichl and Mark Stein. Amsterdam: Rodopi, 2005.

Zungu, Yeyedwa. "The Education for Africans in South Africa." *The Journal of Negro Education* 46.3 (Summer 1977): 202-18.

PERMISSIONS

Citations from the following copyrighted works have been used with permission.

- ❑ *Barrel of a Pen: Resistance to Repression in Neocolonial Kenya*, by Ngugi wa Thiong'o. Copyright © 1983 by Ngugi wa Thiong'o.
- ❑ *Decolonising the Mind: The Politics of Language in African Literature*, by Ngugi wa Thiong'o. Copyright © 1981 by Ngugi wa Thiong'o.
- ❑ *Petals of Blood*, by Ngugi wa Thiong'o. Copyright © 1977 by Ngugi wa Thiong'o.
- ❑ *Morning Yet on Creation Day*, by Chinua Achebe. Copyright © 1975 by The Wylie Agency (UK) Ltd

Index

Breinigsville, PA USA
27 April 2010
236858BV00003B/1/P